AAT

CENTRAL ASSESSMENT
KIT

Technician Units 8 & 9

Managing Costs and Allocating Resources

In this August 2000 edition

- Additional central assessment questions

- The December 1999 Central Assessments to attempt as 'mocks' under 'exam conditions'

FOR DECEMBER 2000 AND JUNE 2001 CENTRAL ASSESSMENTS

BPP Publishing
August 2000

First edition 1998
Third edition August 2000

ISBN 0 7517 6241 5 (Previous edition 0 7517 6174 5)

British Library Cataloguing-in-Publication Data
A catalogue record for this book
is available from the British Library

Published by

BPP Publishing Limited
Aldine House, Aldine Place
London W12 8AW

www.bpp.com

Printed in Great Britain by Ashford Colour Press

We are grateful to the Lead Body for Accounting for permission to reproduce
extracts from the Standards of Competence for Accounting.

Page

INTRODUCTION

(vii)

How to use this Central Assessment Kit – Central Assessment
technique – Unit 8 and Unit 9 Standards of Competence – Assessment strategy

The headings indicate the units to which the questions refer and the main topics, but questions often
cover several different topics. We have indicated below at the end of each section of questions other
questions which cover the topic.

U11 or U12 (U11, 6/96, say) after the question title refers to a central assessment set under the
previous version of the standards.

Contents

> Forecasting is also covered in questions 16, 18, 21, 41, 50, 51 and 52.

PART E: REDUCING COSTS AND ENHANCING VALUE (Unit 9)

Cost reduction techniques

Quality

Quality is also covered in question 19.

Performance measurement

Contents

ORDER FORM

REVIEW FORM & FREE PRIZE DRAW

HOW TO USE THIS CENTRAL ASSESSMENT KIT

Aims of this Central Assessment Kit

> To provide the knowledge and practice to help you succeed in the central assessments for Technician Unit 8 *Contributing to the Management of Costs and the Enhancement of Value* and Unit 9 *Contributing to the Planning and Allocation of Resources*.

To pass the central assessments you need a thorough understanding in all areas covered by the standards of competence.

> To tie in with the other components of the BPP Effective Study Package to ensure you have the best possible chance of success.

Interactive Text

This covers all you need to know for central assessment for Unit 8 *Contributing to the Management of Costs and the Enhancement of Value* and Unit 9 *Contributing to the Planning and Allocation of Resources*. Icons clearly mark key areas of the text. Numerous activities throughout the text help you practise what you have just learnt.

Central Assessment Kit

When you have understood and practised the material in the Interactive Text, you will have the knowledge and experience to tackle the Central Assessment Kit for Units 8 and 9. It contains the AAT's December 1998, June and December 1999 and Sample Central Assessments for Unit 8 and Unit 9 plus relevant questions from central assessments set under the previous version of the Standards.

Recommended approach to this Central Assessment Kit

- To achieve competence in all units, you need to be able to do **everything** specified by the standards. Study the text very carefully and do not skip any of it.

- Learning is an **active** process. Do **all** the activities as you work through the text so you can be sure you really understand what you have read.

- After you have covered the material in the Interactive Text, work through the **Central Assessment Kit**.

  The Kit is made up of three different types of question:

  ○ **Practice questions** are designed to help you practise techniques in particular areas of the Standards at a lower level than you will experience in the central assessments themselves. They are 'warm-ups' which you may find particularly useful to do if it is some time since you studied the Interactive Text and the activities it contains.

  ○ **Full central assessment standard questions** give you plenty of practice in the type of question that comes up in the central assessment. Most are taken from central assessments set by the AAT under the previous version or the revised version of the Standards. All have full answers with tutorial notes.

  ○ The AAT's **December 1999 Central Assessments** for these Units with full answers provided by BPP.

- The structure of the main body of this Kit follows that of its companion Interactive Text, with banks of both practice and full central assessment standard questions for each area of the Standards. You may opt to do all the practice questions from across the range of the Standards first, or you may prefer to do questions of both levels in a particular area of the Standards before moving on. In either case, it is probably best to leave the December 1999 Central Assessments until the last stage of your revision, and then attempt them as a 'mock' under 'exam conditions'. This will help you develop some key techniques in attempting questions and allocating time correctly. For guidance on this, please see **Central Assessment Technique** on page (ix).

- This approach is only a suggestion. You college may well adapt it to suit your needs.

Remember this is a **practical** course.

- Try to relate the material to your experience in the workplace or any other work experience you may have had.

- Try to make as many links as you can to your study of the other Units at this level.

CENTRAL ASSESSMENT TECHNIQUE

Passing central assessments at this level is half about having the knowledge, and half about doing yourself full justice on the day. You must have the right **technique**.

The day of the central assessment

1   Set at least one **alarm** (or get an alarm call) for a morning central assessment

2   Have **something to eat** but beware of eating too much; you may feel sleepy if your system is digesting a large meal

3   Allow plenty of **time to get to where you are sitting the central assessment**; have your route worked out in advance and listen to news bulletins to check for potential travel problems

4   **Don't forget** pens, pencils, rulers, erasers

5   Put **new batteries** into your calculator and take a spare set (or a spare calculator)

6   **Avoid discussion** about the central assessment with other candidates outside the venue

Technique in the central assessment

1   *Read the instructions (the 'rubric') on the front of the paper carefully*

    Check that the format of the paper hasn't changed. It is surprising how often assessors' reports remark on the number of students who attempt too few questions. Make sure that you are planning to answer the **right number of questions**.

2   *Select questions carefully*

    Read through the paper once - don't forget that you are given 15 minutes' reading time - then quickly jot down key points against each question in a second read through. Select those questions where you could latch on to 'what the question is about' - but remember to check carefully that you have got the right end of the stick before putting pen to paper. Use your 15 minutes' reading time wisely.

3   *Plan your attack carefully*

    Consider the **order** in which you are going to tackle questions. It is a good idea to start with your best question to boost your morale and get some easy marks 'in the bag'.

4   *Check the time allocation for each section of the paper*

    Time allocations are given for each section of the paper. When the time for a section is up, you must go on to the next section. Going even one minute over the time allowed brings you a lot closer to failure.

5   *Read the question carefully and plan your answer*

    Read through the question again very carefully when you come to answer it. Plan your answer to ensure that you **keep to the point**. Two minutes of planning plus eight minutes of writing is virtually certain to earn you more marks than ten minutes of writing.

6   *Produce relevant answers*

Particularly with written answers, make sure you **answer the question set,** and not the question you would have preferred to have been set.

7   *Gain the easy marks*

Include the obvious if it answers the question, and don't try to produce the perfect answer.

Don't get bogged down in small parts of questions. If you find a part of a question difficult, get on with the rest of the question. If you are having problems with something, the chances are that everyone else is too.

8   *Produce an answer in the correct format*

The assessor will state *in the requirements* the format in which the question should be answered, for example in a report or memorandum.

9   *Follow the assessor's instructions*

You will annoy the assessor if you ignore him or her. The **assessor will state** whether he or she wishes you to 'discuss', 'comment', 'evaluate' or 'recommend'.

10   *Lay out your numerical computations and use workings correctly*

Make sure the layout fits the **type of question** and is in a style the assessor likes.

Show all your **workings** clearly and explain what they mean. Cross reference them to your answer. This will help the assessor to follow your method (this is of particular importance where there may be several possible answers).

11   *Present a tidy paper*

You are a professional, and it should show in the **presentation of your work.** Students are penalised for poor presentation and so you should make sure that you write legibly, label diagrams clearly and lay out your work neatly. Markers of scripts each have hundreds of papers to mark; a badly written scrawl is unlikely to receive the same attention as a neat and well laid out paper.

12   *Stay until the end of the central assessment*

Use any spare time **checking and rechecking** your script.

13   *Don't worry if you feel you have performed badly in the central assessment*

It is more than likely that the other candidates will have found the assessment difficult too. Don't forget that there is a competitive element in these assessments. As soon as you get up to leave the venue, **forget** that central assessment and think about the next - or, if it is the last one, celebrate!

14   *Don't discuss a central assessment with other candidates*

This is particularly the case if you **still have other central assessments to sit.** Even if you have finished, you should put it out of your mind until the day of the results. Forget about assessments and relax!

UNIT 8 AND UNIT 9 STANDARDS OF COMPETENCE

The structure of the Standards for Unit 8 and Unit 9

The Unit commences with a statement of the **knowledge and understanding** which underpin competence in the Unit's elements.

The Unit of Competence is then divided into **elements of competence** describing activities which the individual should be able to perform.

Each element includes the following.

(a) A set of **performance criteria** which define what constitutes competent performance

(b) A **range statement** which defines the situations, contexts, methods etc in which competence should be displayed

(c) **Evidence requirements**, which state that competence must be demonstrated consistently, over an appropriate time scale with evidence of performance being provided from the appropriate sources

(d) **Sources of evidence**, being suggestions of ways in which you can find evidence to demonstrate that competence. These fall under the headings: 'observed performance; work produced by the candidate; authenticated testimonies from relevant witnesses; personal account of competence; other sources of evidence.'

The elements of competence for Unit 8 *Contributing to the Management of Costs and the Enhancement of Value* and Unit 9 *Contributing to the Planning and Allocation of Resources* are set out below. Knowledge and understanding required for the units as a whole are listed first, followed by the performance criteria and range statements for each element. Performance criteria are cross-referenced below to chapters in the Units 8 & 9 *Managing Costs and Allocating Resources* Interactive Text.

Unit 8: Contributing to the Management of Costs and the Enhancement of Value

What is the unit about?

This unit is concerned with **collecting and analysing cost information to assist in highlighting trends in costs** and **making suggestions for the reduction of costs and adding value**. The unit requires you to obtain information from a variety of internal and external sources and monitor performance indicators and movements in prices over an appropriate timescale. The unit also requires you to use the information to prepare and present management reports.

Knowledge and understanding

The business environment

- External sources of information on costs and prices: government statistics, trade associations, financial press, quotations, price lists (Element 8.1)

- General economic environment (Element 8.1)

Accounting techniques

- Basic time series analysis, moving averages, seasonal trends (Element 8.1)

- Methods of presenting information in graphical, diagrammatic and tabular form (Element 8.1)

- The use of index numbers (Element 8.1)

- Interpretation of performance indicators: productivity, unit costs; resource utilisation; profitability; quality of service (Element 8.2)

- Standard costing and budgetary control systems (Element 8.2)

- Control ratios: efficiency, capacity and activity (Element 8.2)

Accounting principles and theory

- The use and limitation of published statistics (Element 8.1)

- Quality control methods, quality circles (Element 8.2)

- Value analysis (Element 8.2)

- Principles of Total Quality Management (Element 8.2)

The organisation

- Understanding that the accounting systems of an organisation are affected by its organisational structure, its administrative systems and procedures and the nature of its business transactions (Elements 8.1 & 8.2)

- Knowledge and understanding of the organisation's external environment and specific external costs is required (Element 8.1)

- Background knowledge of the contribution of functional specialists in an organisation (eg marketing, design, engineering, quality control etc) to cost reduction and value enhancement (Element 8.2)

Element 8.1 Collect, analyse and disseminate information about costs

Performance criteria	Chapters in the Text
1 Valid, relevant information is identified from internal and external sources	4
2 Trends in prices are monitored for movements and analysed on a regular basis and potential implications are identified	5
3 Standard costs are compared with actual costs and any variances are analysed	7
4 Forecasts of trends and changes in factor prices and marketing conditions are consistent with previous experience of factor prices and market conditions	10
5 Relevant staff in the organisation are consulted about the analysis of trends	10
6 Reports highlighting significant trends are presented to management in an appropriate form	6, 10, 13
Range statement	
1 Information: movements in prices charged by suppliers; movements in prices charged by competitors; movements in prices charged by providers of services; general price changes	4, 6, 10, 13
2 Methods of presenting information: report; table; diagram	6
3 Variance analysis: materials variances: usage, price; labour variances: rate, efficiency; fixed overhead variances: expenditure, volume, capacity, efficiency	7

Element 8.2 Make recommendations to reduce costs and enhance value

Performance criteria	Chapters in the Text
1 Routine cost reports are analysed, compared with other sources of information and the implications of findings are identified	7, 8, 13-15
2 Relevant performance indicators are monitored and the results are assessed to identify potential improvements	15
3 Relevant specialists are consulted to assist in the identification of ways to reduce costs and enhance value	13, 14
4 Exception reports to follow up matters which require further investigation are prepared	7, 8, 13-15
5 Specific recommendations are made to management and are explained in a clear and appropriate form	13
Range statement	
1 Performance indicators to measure: productivity; unit costs; resource utilisation; profitability; quality of service	15
2 Recommendations: efficiencies; modifications to work processes	14, 15

BPP PUBLISHING

Unit 9: Contributing to the Planning and Allocation of Resources

What is the unit about?

This unit is concerned with **producing forecasts of income and expenditure, producing budget proposals and monitoring performance against budgets.** The unit requires that you are responsible for ensuring the budget has taken all relevant data into account and that the appropriate people have been consulted.

Knowledge and understanding

Accounting techniques

- Basic statistical methods: index numbers, time series, sampling techniques; linear regression (Element 9.1)

- Use of relevant computer packages (Element 9.1)

- Co-ordination of the budget system (Elements 9.2 & 9.3)

- Budget factor (Elements 9.2 & 9.3)

- The effect of capacity levels on budgets, flexible budgets (Limiting factor) (Elements 9.2 & 9.3)

- Understanding of the effect of budgetary control systems on the motivation of managers (Element 9.2)

- The significance of budget variances and the type of action which may be required of managers in response to variances (Element 9.3)

Accounting principles and theory

- The principles and purposes of budgetary control: planning and co-ordinating activities, cost control (Elements 9.1, 9.2 & 9.3)

- Relationship between budgets, forecasts and planning cycles (Elements 9.1, 9.2 & 9.3)

- Different types of budgets: budget for current expenditure; resource budget; capital budget (Elements 9.2 & 9.3)

The organisation

- Understanding that the accounting systems of an organisation are affected by its organisational structure, its administrative systems and procedures and the nature of its business transactions (Elements 9.1, 9.2 & 9.3)

- A knowledge of the structure of the organisation and its responsibility centres and an understanding of the inter-relationships between departments and functions is required (Elements 9.1, 9.2 & 9.3)

- Responsibility centres: expense centres; profit centres; investment centres (Element 9.3)

Element 9.1 Prepare forecasts of income and expenditure

Performance criteria	Chapters in the Text
1 Relevant data for projecting forecasts is identified	4, 10
2 Relevant individuals are given the opportunity to raise queries and to clarify forecasts	10
3 Forecasts are produced in a clear format with explanations of assumptions, projections and adjustments	10
4 The validity of forecasts is reviewed in the light of any significant anticipated changes	10

Range statement

1 Forecasts: income; expenditure	4, 10
2 Data: accounting information; wage and salary information; market information; general economic information	4, 10

Element 9.2 Product draft budget proposals

Performance criteria	Chapters in the Text
1 Draft budget proposals are presented to management in a clear and appropriate format and on schedule	11
2 Draft budget proposals are consistent with organisational objectives, have taken all relevant data into account and are agreed with budget holders	11
3 Annual budgets are broken down into periods in accordance with anticipated seasonal trends	10
4 Discussions with budget holders are conducted in a manner which maintains goodwill	12

Range statement

1 Types of budgets: budget for current expenditure; resource budget; capital budget	11
2 Data: accounting information; wage and salary information; market information; general economic information; strategic plans	4, 11

BPP PUBLISHING

Element 9.3 Monitor the performance of responsibility centres against budgets

Performance criteria	Chapters in the Text
1 Budget figures are checked and reconciled on an ongoing basis	12
2 Actual cost and revenue data are correctly coded and allocated to responsibility centres	9
3 Variances are clearly identified and reported to management in routine reports	12
4 Significant variances are discussed with managers and assistance is given to managers to take remedial action	12
Range statement	
1 Types of budgets: budget for current expenditure; resource budget	12
2 Variances: actual; potential	12
3 Responsibility centres: expense centres; profit centres	9

ASSESSMENT STRATEGY

Unit 8 and Unit 9 are assessed by **central assessment** only.

A central assessment is a means of collecting evidence that you have the **essential knowledge and understanding** which underpins competence. It is also a means of collecting evidence across the **range of contexts** for the standards, and of your ability to transfer skills, knowledge and understanding to different situations. Thus, although central assessments contain practical tests linked to the performance criteria, they also focus on the underpinning knowledge and understanding. You should in addition expect each central assessment to contain tasks taken from across a broad range of the standards.

Unit 8 Contributing to the Management of Costs and the Enhancement of Value

Central assessment tasks will be divided into two sections and will be based on mini case studies set within the context of an organisation. The first section of the central assessment will be concerned with the management of costs, the second with the measurement and enhancement of value, and the two elements of the unit will be assessed across the two sections. This approach is demonstrated in the following table, where the major generic concepts and techniques are identified. The table is indicative only, and should not be considered as exhaustive.

	Section 1 Managing costs	Section 2 Enhancing value
Element 8.1	• Index numbers • Trends • Forecasting • Valid, relevant information from internal and external sources	• Index numbers • Trends • Valid, relevant information from internal and external sources
Element 8.2	• Standard costing • Activity based costing	• Performance indicators • Total Quality Management

Both sections will require knowledge and understanding of the organisation detailed in the task data. In addition, analysis, interpretation and presentation of information to management will be assessed in both sections.

Where possible, there will be two tasks per section, but there may be occasions when it will be necessary to exceed this number in order either to make task requirements clearer or to reduce the amount of data that candidates have to consider when answering a task. Only in rare circumstances will the number of tasks exceed three per section.

The central assessment will last for three hours plus 15 minutes reading time.

Unit 9 Contributing to the Planning and Allocation of Resources

The theme throughout this unit is budgetary planning and control in all its facets, from forecasting income and expenditure through preparing budget proposals to comparing those proposals with actual figures and identifying and reporting variances. Tasks will be assessed within mini-case studies or scenarios.

The central assessment will be focused within the context of the organisation and there will be two sections. All three elements will be assessed across the two sections.

Although there is not a natural division between planning and control and between the three elements, this subdivision has been taken as the basis for the table below. The table is indicative only, and the contents should not be considered as exhaustive.

	Section 1 Planning	Section 2 Control
Element 9.1	• Data gathering • Forecasting • Index numbers • Time series • Sampling techniques • Linear regression • Key factors	
Element 9.2	• Fixed and flexible budgeting • Functional budgeting • Key factors / budget factors • Limiting factors • Motivation of managers	• Fixed and flexible budgeting • Functional budgeting • Trends, seasonal variations • Motivation of managers
Element 9.3		• Responsibility centres • Variance analysis • Significance of variances • Remedial action • Motivation of managers

All three elements will require knowledge and understanding of the organisation detailed in the task data. There is significant overlap in terms of the knowledge and understanding required of accounting techniques, accounting principles and theory and the organisation, which will impact on the tasks set within each section.

Generally there will be two tasks per section but there may be occasions when it will be necessary to increase this in order to clarify task requirements, to further develop a theme, or to reduce the amount of data that candidates have to consider when performing a task. It is not anticipated that the number of tasks per section will exceed three.

The central assessment will last for three hours plus 15 minutes reading time.

Questions

1 PRACTICE QUESTION: COST BEHAVIOUR

You are the assistant management accountant in a medium-sized manufacturing organisation.

Task

Prepare a report for the managing director of your company explaining how costs may be classified by their behaviour, with particular reference to the effects both on total and on unit costs.

Your report should do the following.

(a) Say why it is necessary to classify costs by their behaviour

(b) Be illustrated by sketch graphs within the body of the report

2 PRACTICE QUESTION: ABSORPTION COSTING

Your organisation has three production departments - A, B and C - and a service department which works for the production departments in the ratio of 3 : 2 : 1.

The following costs and relevant data, which represent normal activity levels, have been budgeted for the period ending 31 December 20X6.

Costs	A £'000	B £'000	C £'000	Service dept £'000	Total £'000
Direct wages	58	72	90	-	220
Direct materials	40	29	15	-	84
Indirect wages	15	21	8	58	102
Depreciation					84
Rates					22
Power					180
Personnel					60
Insurance					48

Other data					
Direct labour hours	7,250	9,000	15,000		31,250
Machine hours	15,500	20,000	2,500	2,000	40,000
Floor area (m²)	800	1,200	1,000	1,400	4,400
Fixed assets	£160,000	£140,000	£30,000	£70,000	£400,000
Employees	40	56	94	50	240

As accounts assistant, you have been asked to assist with completing the overhead budget for the period ending 31 December 20X6.

Tasks

(a) Prepare an overhead analysis sheet for your organisation for the period ending 31 December 20X6.

(b) Calculate appropriate overhead absorption rates for the production departments.

(c) The following data are available for the actual results of department A for the period ending 31 December 20X6.

Actual overheads	£211,820
Actual labour hours	7,380
Actual machine hours	16,250

Calculate the under/over recovery of overheads for department A.

3   PRACTICE QUESTION: ABSORPTION COSTING AND MARGINAL COSTING

To help decision making during budget preparation, your supervisor has prepared the following estimates of sales revenue and cost behaviour for a one-year period, relating to one of your organisation's products.

Activity	60%	100%
Sales and production (thousands of units)	36	60
	£'000	£'000
Sales	432	720
Production costs		
Variable and fixed	366	510
Sales, distribution and administration costs		
Variable and fixed	126	150

The normal level of activity for the current year is 60,000 units, and fixed costs are incurred evenly throughout the year.

There were no stocks of the product at the start of the quarter, in which 16,500 units were made and 13,500 units were sold. Actual fixed costs were the same as budgeted.

Task

(a)   Calculate the following using absorption costing.

    (i)   The amount of fixed production costs absorbed by the product

    (ii)   The over/under absorption of fixed product costs

    (iii)   The profit for the quarter

(b)   Calculate the net profit or loss for the quarter using marginal costing.

You may assume that sales revenue and variable costs per unit are as budgeted.

4   PRACTICE QUESTION: ABC

You are the assistant management accountant for a company which assembles and programs electronic equipment to suit individual customers' requirements.

Two jobs are currently in progress, order JM3 and order AM5.

Estimated direct costs

	Order JM3 £	Order AM5 £
Purchased equipment	9,750	8,490
Purchased software	3,500	3,510
Assembly labour	2,300	1,600
Additional programming	1,850	2,900
	17,400	16,500

Additional information

	Order JM3	Order AM5
Distance to customer (miles)	3	100
Sales visits needed	2	8
Extra design time (hours)	10	100
Sourcing required (items)	3	16
Testing (hours)	5	80
Customer training (hours)	10	150
Special packaging	None	£200
Delivery cost	£50	£800
Overtime needed	None	for all programming

Activity	Annual cost	Cost driver	Cost driver units pa
Sales	£50,000	Miles travelled	20,000
Design	£40,000	Design hours worked	2,000
Sourcing	£30,000	Items bought in	1,000
Testing	£30,000	Testing hours	2,000
Training	£30,000	Training hours	2,000

Overtime will add 50% to estimated programming cost.

Task

Calculate the estimated costs of each order.

5   PRACTICE QUESTION: BENEFITS OF ABC

You have recently been employed by the legal firm of Thomson, Simons and Barfleet as their management accountant. The senior partner, Lucy Thomson, has doubts about the usefulness of the figures produced by the previous management accountant. She has heard that activity based costing (ABC) may be an appropriate system for the firm to adopt.

Task

In response to a request from Ms Thomson, prepare a brief paper setting out the way in which ABC works and what benefits the firm may expect from introducing the system.

Include a simple illustration.

6   PRACTICE QUESTION: DATA COLLECTION

The adult population of your organisation's Northern sales territory is 500,000. The territory is divided into a number of regions as follows.

Region	Adult population '000
Northia	90
Wester	10
Southam	140
Eastis	40
Midshire	120
Centrasia	100

In order to provide sales forecasting information, it has been decided to carry out a survey based on a 2% sample of the Northern sales territory's population.

Tasks

(a)   Describe how the sampling should be organised if the following methods are to be employed.

    (i)   Simple random
    (ii)   Cluster
    (iii)   Stratified
    (iv)   Systematic

(b)   Discuss which of these methods would be likely to give the most representative sample and why. Your answer should include discussion of the disadvantages of the other methods.

7 PRACTICE QUESTION: INDEX NUMBERS

You have been asked by your Managing Director to analyse the following data on the wages of your organisation's employees before the annual pay review process begins. You have already calculated an average earnings index for June 20X5 to May 20X6 and have obtained the RPI for the same period as shown below.

		Index	
		Average earnings (Jan 20X0 = 100)	*Retail prices* (Jan 20X3 = 100)
20X5	June	243.2	151.8
	July	248.4	154.1
	August	252.8	165.3
	September	257.2	173.4
	October	265.1	178.2
	November	270.4	184.6
	December	274.7	188.3

		Index	
		Average earnings (Jan 20X0 = 100)	*Retail prices* (Jan 20X3 = 100)
20X6	January	280.6	193.2
	February	296.5	196.3
	March	302.4	200.2
	April	308.6	205.1
	May	315.3	210.4

Tasks

(a) Rebase both indices to a base of June 20X5 = 100.

(b) Determine an index of real earnings over the given period and comment on your results.

8 PRACTICE QUESTION: Z CHARTS

The manufacturing costs of Prodco Ltd (the company where you work) for the period from January 20X6 to December 20X7 are displayed in the table below.

Month *20X6*	*Manufacturing* *costs* £'000	*Month* *20X7*	*Manufacturing* *costs* £'000
January	35.8	January	43.9
February	33.6	February	40.1
March	35.5	March	46.0
April	37.5	April	48.7
May	37.2	May	48.9
June	34.6	June	46.0
July	36.3	July	48.3
August	36.0	August	47.9
September	35.4	September	48.2
October	30.4	October	47.0
November	36.1	November	49.4
December	37.5	December	51.6

Tasks

(a) Draw a Z chart using the above data.

(b) Describe the purpose of such a chart. Use the diagram that you have just drawn to illustrate your answer.

9 PRACTICE QUESTION: STANDARD COSTING

You are assistant management accountant at PQ Limited, an organisation which has two production departments - machining and assembly. Two of its main products are the Major and the Minor, the standard data for which are as follows.

	Per unit	
	Major	*Minor*
Direct materials:		
Material @ £15 per kg	2.2 kgs	1.4 kgs
Direct labour:		
Machining department @ £6 per hour	4.8 hrs	2.9 hrs
Assembly department @ £5 per hour	3.6 hrs	3.1 hrs
Machining time	3.5 hrs	0.9 hrs

The overhead rates for the period are as follows.

Machining department	*Assembly department*
£16.00 per machine hour	£9.50 per labour hour

Tasks

(a) Calculate the standard production cost for each product.

(b) During the period, actual results for labour were as follows.

		Major	*Minor*
Production		650 units	842 units
Direct labour:			
Machining department		2,990 hrs	2,480 hrs
	costing	£18,239	£15,132
Assembly department		2,310 hrs	2,595 hrs
	costing	£11,700	£12,975

Calculate the direct labour total variance and the rate and efficiency variances for each product and each department.

(c) Explain briefly what information the above variances provide for management.

10 PRACTICE QUESTION: MORE STANDARD COSTING

You have collected the following data for the month of April for your company, which operates a standard absorption costing system.

Actual production of product EM		600 units

Actual costs incurred		£
Direct material E	660 metres	6,270
Direct material M	200 metres	650
Direct wages	3,200 hours	23,200
Fixed production overhead		27,000

Variances		
	£	
Direct material price		
material E	330	Favourable
material M	50	Adverse
Direct material usage		
material E	600	Adverse
material M	nil	
Direct labour rate	800	Adverse
Direct labour efficiency	1,400	Adverse
Fixed production overhead		
Expenditure	500	Favourable
Volume	2,500	Favourable

Opening and closing work in progress figures were identical, so can be ignored.

Tasks

(a) Prepare for the month of April a statement of total standard costs for product EM.

(b) Present a standard product cost sheet for one unit of product EM.

(c) Calculate the number of units of product EM which were budgeted for April.

(d) State how the material and labour cost standards for product EM would originally have been determined.

11 PRACTICE QUESTION: CALCULATING COST VARIANCES

Your organisation manufactures two types of tennis racket, the Henman and the Lendl. The budget for October was as follows.

	Henman	Lendl
Production (units)	4,000	1,500
Direct materials: wood (£0.30 per metre)	7 metres	5 metres
gut (£1.50 per metre)	6 metres	4 metres
Other materials	£0.20	£0.15
Direct labour (£3 per hour)	30 mins	20 mins

	£
Fixed overheads:	
supervision	8,000
heating and lighting	1,200
rent	4,800
depreciation	7,000
	21,000

Actual results for October were as follows.

Production:	Henman	3,700 units
	Lendl	1,890 units

Direct materials, bought and used:			£
	wood	37,100 metres	11,000
	gut	29,200 metres	44,100
	other materials		1,000
Direct labour		2,200 hours	6,850
Supervision			7,940
Heating and lighting			1,320
Rent			4,800
Depreciation			7,000

Task

Calculate cost variances for the month of October. Assume that a standard absorption costing system is in operation.

12 PRACTICE QUESTION: RECONCILIATION STATEMENT

You work for an organisation which manufactures a standard leather shoe, model number TS3, for which the standard unit cost price is as follows.

		£	£
Direct materials			
Leather	3 units at £5 per unit	15	
Other materials		3	
			18
Direct labour	1^1/2 hours at £4 per hour		6
Fixed production overheads	1^1/2 hours at £6 per hour		9
Standard cost			33

Budgeted production and sales for period 7 were 3,000 units.

During period 7 of 20X8, actual results were as follows.

Production of TS3	3,200 units
Costs	
Leather purchased and used: quantity	9,200 units
cost	£45,400
Other materials purchased and used	£9,500
Direct labour: production time	5,100 hours
labour cost	£24,100
Fixed production overheads	£31,500

Task

Prepare a statement for period 7 reconciling standard cost of actual production and actual cost of production and specifying all the relevant variances.

13   STATELY HOTELS PLC (40 mins)   *U11, 6/95 (amended)*

You work as the assistant to the management accountant for a large conference centre. The finance director is experimenting with the use of standard costing to plan and control the costs of preparing and cleaning the centre's five large conference rooms. (There are also a number of small and medium sized conference rooms available.)

Two of the costs involved in this activity are cleaning labour and the supply of presentation pen and notepaper sets.

Cleaning labour

Part-time staff are employed to clean and prepare the conference rooms. The employees are paid for the number of hours that they work, which fluctuates on a daily basis depending on how many conference rooms need to be prepared each day.

The employees are paid a standard hourly rate for weekday work and a higher hourly rate at the weekend. The standard cost control system is based on an average of these two rates at £5 per hour.

The standard time allowed for cleaning and preparing a conference room is fifteen hours.

Presentation pen and notepaper set

A presentation pen and notepaper set is provided for each conference delegate every day. Most delegates use the pen and notepaper or take them home with them, but many do not. The standard usage of sets used for planning and control purposes is one set per delegate per day.

The pens and notepaper are purchased from a number of different suppliers and the standard price is £2.50 per set. Stocks of the pens and notepaper are valued in the accounts at standard price.

Actual results for May

During May, the large conference rooms were cleaned and prepared seventy times and there were 4,100 conference delegates. The following data was recorded for cleaning labour and pen and notepaper sets.

Cleaning labour paid for:

Weekday labour	900	hours @ £4.20 per hour
Weekend labour	340	hours @ £5.60 per hour
	1,240	

Presentation pen and newspaper sets purchased and used:

2,800	sets at £2.50
1,060	sets at £2.80
420	sets at £2.95
4,280	

Tasks

(a) Using the data above, calculate the following cost variances for May.
- (i) Pen and notepaper set price
- (ii) Pen and notepaper set usage
- (iii) Cleaning labour rate
- (iv) Cleaning labour utilisation or efficiency

(b) Suggest one possible cause for each of the variances which you have calculated, and outline any management action which may be necessary.

14 OMEGA (70 mins)   *U11, 12/95 (amended)*

You are employed as part of the management accounting team in a large industrial company which operates a four-weekly system of management reporting. Your division makes a single product, the Omega, and, because of the nature of the production process, there is no work in progress at any time.

The group management accountant has completed the calculation of the material and labour standard costing variances for the current period to 1 April but has not had the time to complete any other variances. Details of the variances already calculated are reproduced in the working papers below, along with other standard costing data.

Standard costing and budget data – four weeks ended 1 April			
	Quantity	*Unit price*	*Cost per unit*
Material (kgs)	7	£25.00	£175
Labour (hours)	40	£7.50	£300
Fixed overheads (hours)	40	£12.50	£500
			£975
	Units	*Standard unit cost*	*Standard cost of production*
Budgeted production for the four weeks	4,100	£975	£3,997,500

Working papers:

Actual production and expenditure for the four weeks ended 1 April

Units produced	3,850
Cost of 30,000 kgs of materials consumed	£795,000
Cost of 159,000 labour hours worked	£1,225,000
Expenditure on fixed overheads	£2,195,000

Material and labour variances	
Material price variance	£45,000 (A)
Material usage variance	£76,250 (A)
Labour rate variance	£32,500 (A)
Labour efficiency variance	£37,500 (A)

Tasks

You have been requested to do the following.

(a) Calculate the following expenses.

  (i)   The fixed overhead expenditure variance
  (ii)   The fixed overhead volume variance
  (iii) The fixed overhead capacity variance
  (iv)   The fixed overhead efficiency variance

(b) Prepare a report for presentation to the production director reconciling the standard cost of production for the period with the actual cost of production.

(c) The production director, who has only recently been appointed, is unfamiliar with fixed overhead variances. Because of this, the group management accountant has asked you to prepare a *brief* memo to the production director.

Your memo should do the following.

  (i)   Outline the similarities and differences between fixed overhead variances and other cost variances such as the material and labour variances.

  (ii)   Explain what is meant by the fixed overhead expenditure, volume, capacity and efficiency variances, and show, by way of examples, how these can be of help to the production director in the planning and controlling of the division.

15   GRANSDEN LTD (35 mins)   *U11, 6/96*

Gransden Ltd makes and retails a variety of furniture products. One year ago, the directors realised that their traditional financial accounting system was not providing sufficient information for the managers. As a result, they established a management accounting department headed by William Jones. He quickly established standard costing throughout the organisation as well as introducing performance reports for each division in the company. Both techniques have been effective and, as a result, you were recently appointed as the Assistant Management Accountant to the company.

Some managers, however, are still having difficulty understanding the meaning of the standard costing reports prepared each month. One manager, Helen Dale, particularly feels that the report for May was misleading. Her department manufactures high quality wooden display cabinets. She wrote to William Jones about the report, and an extract from the letter is reproduced below.

'In May, my department produced 5,000 cabinets, 500 more than required in my budget. According to your own figures, each cabinet requires five metres of wood at a standard price of £100 per metre, a total cost of £2,500,000 metres. For some reason, you show the result of this as being an overall adverse variance of £200,000, which you then break down into price and usage, despite my department only using 22,500 metres of wood in May.

Also, only yesterday, I read that the Retail Prices Index stood at 168 compared with an index of 160 when the standards were agreed. This shows inflation at 8% and so the £200,000 overspend on standard cost is entirely due to price inflation, which is out of my control. Your standard costing is not therefore particularly helpful to me as a manager.'

Tasks

William Jones plans to discuss with Helen the issues raised in her letter. Before doing so, however, he has asked you to do the following.

(a) (i) Determine the material price and usage variances within the overall adverse variances.

(ii) Check the accuracy of the index of inflation calculated by Helen Dale.

(b) Prepare the diagram or graph showing the standard cost, the variances and the extent of inflation within the price variance which may help Helen understand the overall variance.

(c) Identify THREE difficulties which might be experienced in interpreting the price variance, including the inflation element.

16 PRIORY LTD (80 mins)   *U11, 12/96 (amended)*

(a) You are employed as the assistant management accountant to Priory Ltd. Priory Ltd manufactures a single product, the Addid, an ingredient used in food processing. The basic raw material in Addid production is material A. The average unit prices for material A in each control period last year, and the seasonal variations based on several years' observations, are reproduced below.

	Control period 1	Control period 2	Control period 3	Control period 4
Average unit price of A	£90	£105	£80	£75
Seasonal variations	+£10	+£20	−£10	−£20

Tasks

(i) Calculate the seasonally adjusted unit price of material A for each of the four control periods of last year.

(ii) Assuming a similar pattern of price movements in the future, forecast the likely purchase price for the four control periods of the current year.

(b) Priory Ltd operates a standard absorption costing system. Standards are established at the beginning of each year. Each week the management accounting section prepares a statement for the production director reconciling the actual cost of production with its standard cost. Standard costing data for week 7 of control period 2 in the current year is given below.

Standard costing and budget data for week 7 of control period 2			
	Quantity	*Unit price*	*Cost per unit*
Material (litres)	21	£110	£2,310
Labour (hours)	7	£7.00	£49
Fixed overheads (hours)	7	£42.00	£294
Standard unit cost			£2,653
	Budgeted units	*Standard cost per unit*	*Standard cost of production*
Budgeted production for week 7	1,150	£2,653	£3,050,950

During week 7, production of Addid totalled 950 units and the actual costs for that week were:

Inputs	*Units*	*Total cost*
Materials (litres)	18,200	£2,003,100
Labour (hours)	7,100	£41,200
Fixed overheads (hours)	7,100	£420,000

Using this data, a colleague has already calculated the fixed overhead variances. These were as follows.

Fixed overhead expenditure variance	£81,900 adverse
Efficiency variance	£18,900 adverse
Capacity variance	£39,900 adverse

Tasks

Your colleague asks you to do the following.

(i) Calculate the following variances.

  (1) Material price
  (2) Material usage
  (3) Labour rate
  (4) Labour efficiency

(ii) Prepare a statement reconciling the actual cost of production with the standard cost of actual production.

(c) The production director of Priory Ltd is concerned that the material price variance may not accurately reflect the efficiency of the company's purchasing department.

Tasks

You have been asked by your finance director to write a *brief* memorandum to the production director. Your note should:

(i) explain what variances are attempting to measure★;

(ii) list THREE general ways production variances arise other than through errors★;

(iii) identify THREE general reasons why there might be errors in reporting variances★;

(iv) use your solution to the task in (a) to suggest why the production director's concern might be justified.

★*Note.* In parts (i), (ii) and (iii) of this task, you should restrict your comments to variances in general and not address issues arising from particular types of variances.

17   MALTON LTD (70 mins)   *U11, 6/97*

(a)   Malton Ltd operates a standard marginal costing system. As the recently appointed management accountant to Malton's Eastern division, you have responsibility for the preparation of that division's monthly cost reports. The standard cost report uses variances to reconcile the actual marginal cost of production to its standard cost.

The Eastern division is managed by Richard Hill. The division only makes one product, the Beta. Budgeted Beta production for May 20X8 was 8,000 units although actual production was 9,500 units.

In order to prepare the standard cost report for May, you have asked a member of your staff to obtain standard and actual cost details for the month of May. This information is reproduced below.

	Unit standard cost				*Actual details for May*	
	Quantity	*Unit price*	*Cost per Beta*		*Quantity*	*Total cost*
			£			£
Material	8 litres	£20	160	Material	78,000 litres	1,599,000
Labour	4 hours	£6	24	Labour	39,000 hours	249,600
Standard marginal cost			184	Total cost		1,848,600

Tasks

(i)   Calculate the following.

(1)   The material price variance
(2)   The material usage variance
(3)   The labour rate variance
(4)   The labour efficiency variance

(ii)   Prepare a standard costing statement reconciling the actual marginal cost of production with the standard marginal cost of production.

(b)   After Richard Hill has received your standard costing statement, you visit him to discuss the variances and their implications. Richard, however, raises a number of queries with you. He makes the following points.

(i)   An index measuring material prices stood at 247.2 for May but at 240.0 when the standard for the material price was set.

(ii)   The Eastern division is budgeted to run at its normal capacity of 8,000 units of production per month but during May it had to manufacture an additional 1,500 Betas to meet a special order agreed at short notice by Malton's sales director.

(iii)   Because of the short notice, the normal supplier of the raw material was unable to meet the extra demand and so additional materials had to be acquired from another supplier at a price per litre of £22.

(iv)   This extra material was not up to the normal specification, resulting in 20% of the special purchase being scrapped *prior* to being issued to production.

(v)   The work force could only produce the special order on time by working overtime on the 1,500 Betas at 50% premium.

Tasks

(i)   Calculate the amounts within the material price variance, the material usage variance and the labour rate variance which arise from producing the special order.

(ii) (1) Estimate the revised standard price for materials based on the change in the material price index.

(2) For the 8,000 units of normal production, use your answer in (ii)(1) to estimate how much of the price variance calculated in task (a) is caused by the general change in prices.

(iii) Using your answers to parts (i) and (ii) of this task, prepare a revised standard costing statement. The revised statement should subdivide the variances prepared in task (a) into those elements controllable by Richard Hill and those elements caused by factors outside his divisional control.

(iv) Write a *brief* note to Richard Hill justifying your treatment of the elements you believe are outside his control and suggesting what action should be taken by the company.

18 DEBUSSY LTD (70 mins) *U11, 12/97*

You have recently accepted an appointment as the accountant to Debussy Limited, a small family firm manufacturing a specialised fertiliser. The fertiliser is produced using expensive ovens which need to be kept at a constant temperature at all times, even when not being used. Because of this, the power which provides the heating does not vary with changes in production output and so its costs are viewed as being fixed.

The managing director, Claude Debussy, is concerned that the existing accounting system is not providing adequate information for him to run the business. By way of example, he shows you the accounts for the year ended 30 November 20X8. An extract from those accounts showing budgeted and actual results is reproduced below.

Extract from the Profit and Loss Account of Debussy Ltd for the year ended 30 November 20X8								
	Annual Budget		*Annual Results*		*Quarter 4 Budget*		*Quarter 4 Results*	
Units produced (tonnes)	12,000		13,000		3,000		2,400	
	£	£	£	£	£	£	£	£
Material		144,000		188,500		36,000		35,280
Labour		192,000		227,500		48,000		42,240
Fixed overheads:								
Lease of machinery	60,000		60,000		15,000		15,000	
Rent	40,000		40,000		10,000		10,000	
Rates	56,000		64,000		14,000		16,000	
Insurance	48,000		52,000		12,000		13,000	
Power	120,00		140,000		30,000		36,000	
		324,000		356,000		81,000		90,000
Total expenses		660,000		72,000		165,000		167,520

Claude Debussy draws your attention to the high level of fixed overheads and how these are absorbed using labour hours.

'I do not fully understand the fixed overhead figures for the fourth quarter' he explained. 'The way they are presented in the accounts does not help me to plan and control the business. It is no good blaming the production workers for the increase in fixed overheads as we have been paying them £8 per hour – the same amount as agreed in the budget – and they have never worked any overtime.'

15 **BPP**
PUBLISHING

Claude Debussy turns to you for advice. He is particularly interested in understanding why the fixed overheads have increased in the fourth quarter despite production falling. He is also interested in knowing how many labour hours were planned to be worked and how many hours were actually worked in that quarter.

Tasks

(a) For the fourth quarter, calculate the following information for Claude Debussy.

   (i)   The labour hours budgeted to be worked
   (ii)   The labour hours actually worked
   (iii) The budgeted hours per tonne of fertiliser
   (iv)   The actual hours per tonne of fertiliser

(b) Calculate the following variances for the fourth quarter.

   (*Note*. You should base your calculations on the TOTAL amount of fixed overheads and NOT the individual elements.)

   (i)   The fixed overhead expenditure variance (sometimes known as the price variance)
   (ii)   The fixed overhead volume variance
   (iii) The fixed overhead capacity variance
   (iv)   The fixed overhead efficiency variance (sometimes known as the usage variance)

(c) Claude Debussy is unfamiliar with standard costing, although he believes the actual fixed overheads for the year are higher than budgeted because more tonnes of fertiliser have been produced. He would like to use standard costing to control fixed overheads, but is uncertain what is meant by the fixed overhead variances you have prepared.

   Write a memo to Claude Debussy. Your memo should:

   (i)   *briefly* comment on his explanation for the increase in fixed overheads for the year;

   (ii)   for each of the following three variances, give ONE possible reason why they might have occurred:

       (1) the fixed overhead expenditure (or price) variance;
       (2) the fixed overhead capacity variance;
       (3) the fixed overhead efficiency (or usage) variance.

(d) On receiving your memo, Claude Debussy tells you that the annual budgeted fixed overheads have, in the past, simply been apportioned equally over the four quarters. However, the expenditure on power varies between quarters in a regular way depending on the outside temperature. The seasonal variations, based on many years' experience, are as follows:

	1st Quarter	2nd Quarter	3rd Quarter	4th Quarter
Seasonal variations for power costs	+5%	−10%	−20%	+25%

   Claude Debussy believes that it would be more meaningful if the budgeted expenditure on power reflected these seasonal variations, but he is uncertain how this would affect the variances calculated in task (b).

   Prepare notes for Claude Debussy. Your notes should:

   (i)   use the seasonal variations to calculate the revised power budget for the four quarters of the year to 30 November 20X8;

(ii)   *briefly* discuss whether or not the revised power budget for the fourth quarter should be used for calculating the fixed overhead expenditure (or price) and volume variances for that quarter.

19   HAMPSTEAD PLC (70 mins)   *U11,6/98*

(a)   You are employed as the assistant management accountant in the group accountant's office of Hampstead plc. Hampstead recently acquired Finchley Ltd, a small company making a specialist product called the Alpha. Standard marginal costing is used by all the companies within the group and, from 1 August 20X8, Finchley Ltd will also be required to use standard marginal costing in its management reports. Part of your job is to manage the implementation of standard marginal costing at Finchley Ltd.

John Wade, the managing director of Finchley, is not clear how the change will help him as a manager. He has always found Finchley's existing absorption costing system sufficient. By way of example, he shows you a summary of his management accounts for the three months to 31 May 20X8. These are reproduced below.

Statement of budgeted and actual cost of Alpha production - 3 months ended 31 May 20X8					
	Actual		**Budget**		**Variance**
Alpha production (units)		10,000		12,000	
	Inputs	£	*Inputs*	£	£
Materials	32,000 metres	377,600	36,000 metres	432,000	54,400
Labour	70,000 hours	422,800	72,000 hours	450,000	27,200
Fixed overhead absorbed		330,000		396,000	66,000
Fixed overhead unabsorbed		75,000		0	(75,000)
		1,205,400		1,278,000	72,600

John Wade is not convinced that standard marginal costing will help him to manage Finchley. 'My current system tells me all I need to know,' he said. 'As you can see, we are £72,600 below budget which is really excellent given that we lost production as a result of a serious machine breakdown.'

To help John Wade understand the benefits of standard marginal costing, you agree to prepare a statement for the three months ended 31 May 20X8 reconciling the standard cost of production to the actual cost of production.

Tasks

(i)   Use the budget data to determine the following.

   (1)   The standard marginal cost per Alpha

   (2)   The standard cost of actual Alpha production for the three months to 31 May 20X8

(ii)   Calculate the following variances.

   (1)   Material price variance
   (2)   Material usage variance
   (3)   Labour rate variance
   (4)   Labour efficiency variance
   (5)   Fixed overhead expenditure variance

(iii) Write a *short* memo to John Wade. You memo should:

   (1)   include a statement reconciling the actual cost of production to the standard cost of production;

        (2) give TWO reasons why your variances might differ from those in his original management accounting statement despite using the same basic data;

        (3) *briefly* discuss ONE further reason why your reconciliation statement provides improved management information.

(b) On receiving your memo, John Wade informs you that the machine breakdown resulted in the workforce having to be paid for 12,000 hours even though no production took place, and that an index of material prices stood at 466.70 when the budget was prepared but at 420.03 when the material was purchased.

Task

Using this new information, prepare a revised statement reconciling the standard cost of production to the actual cost of production. Your statement should subdivide both the labour variances into those parts arising from the machine breakdown and those parts arising from normal production, and the material price variance into that part due to the change in the index and that part arising for other reasons.

(c) Barnet Ltd is another small company owned by Hampstead plc. Barnet operates a job costing system making a specialist, expensive piece of hospital equipment.

Existing system

Currently, employees are assigned to individual jobs and materials are requisitioned from stores as needed. The standard and actual costs of labour and materials are recorded for each job. These job costs are totalled to produce the marginal cost of production. Fixed production costs - including the cost of storekeeping and inspection of deliveries and finished equipment - are then added to determine the standard and actual cost of production. Any costs of remedial work are included in the materials and labour for each job.

Proposed system

Carol Johnson, the chief executive of Barnet, has recently been to a seminar on modern manufacturing techniques. As a result, she is considering introducing Just-in-Time stock deliveries and Total Quality Management. Barnet would offer suppliers a long-term contract at a fixed price but suppliers would have to guarantee the quality of their materials.

In addition, she proposes that the workforce is organised as a single team with flexible work practices. This would mean employees helping each other as necessary, with no employee being allocated a particular job. If a job was delayed, the workforce would work overtime without payment in order for the job to be completed on time. In exchange, employees would be guaranteed a fixed weekly wage and time off when production was slack to make up for any overtime incurred.

Cost of quality

Carol has asked to meet you to discuss the implications of her proposals on the existing accounting system. She is particularly concerned to monitor the *cost of quality*. This is defined as the total of all costs incurred in preventing defects plus those costs involved in remedying defects once they have occurred. It is a single figure measuring all the explicit costs of quality - that is, those costs collected within the accounting system.

Task

In preparation for the meeting, produce *brief* notes. Your notes should:

(i) identify FOUR general headings (or classifications) which make up the *cost of quality*;

(ii) give ONE example of a type of cost likely to be found within each category;

(iii) assuming Carol Johnson's proposals are accepted, state, with reasons, whether or not:

    (1) a standard marginal costing system would still be of help to the managers;

    (2) it would still be meaningful to collect costs by each individual job;

(iv) identify one cost saving in Carol Johnson's proposals which would not be recorded in the existing costing system.

20 COUNTRYSIDE COMMUNICATIONS PLC (100 mins)   *U11,12/98*

(a) The Eastern Division of Countryside Communications plc assembles a single product, the Beta. The Eastern Division has a fixed price contract with the supplier of the materials used in the Beta. The contract also specifies that the materials should be free of any faults. Because of these clauses in the contract, the Eastern Division has no material variances when reporting any differences between standard and actual production.

You have recently accepted the position of assistant management accountant in the Eastern Division. One of your tasks is to report variances in production costs on a four-weekly basis. Fixed overheads are absorbed on the basis of standard labour hours. A colleague provides you with the following data.

Standard costs and budgeted production - four weeks ended 27 November 20X8			
	Quantity	*Unit price* £	*Standard cost per Beta* £
Material	30 metres	12.00	360.00
Labour	10 hours	5.25	52.50
Fixed overhead	10 hours	15.75	157.50
Standard cost per Beta			570.00
Budgeted production	1,200 Betas	£570.00	£684,000

Actual production - four weeks ended 27 November 20X8		
	Quantity	*Total cost* £
Actual cost of material	31,200 metres	374,400
Actual cost of labour	11,440 hours	59,488
Actual fixed overheads		207,000
		640,888
Actual production	1,040 Betas	

Tasks

(i) Calculate the following variances.

    (1) The labour rate variance

    (2) The labour efficiency variance (sometimes called the utilisation variance)

    (3) The fixed overhead expenditure variance (sometimes known as the price variance)

    (4) The fixed overhead volume variance

(5)   The fixed overhead capacity variance

(6)   The fixed overhead efficiency variance (sometimes known as the usage variance)

(ii)   Prepare a statement reconciling the standard cost of actual production with the actual cost of actual production.

(b)   When the Eastern Division's budget for the four weeks ended 27 November 20X8 was originally prepared, a national index of labour rates stood at 102.00. In preparing the budget, Eastern Division had allowed for a 5% increase in labour rates. For the actual four weeks ended 27 November 20X8, the index stood at 104.04.

Because of this, Ann Green, Eastern Division's production director, is having difficulty understanding the meaning of the labour rate variance calculated in task (a)(i)(1).

Task

Write a memo to Ann Green. Your memo should do the following.

(i)   Identify the original labour rate before allowing for the 5% increase.

(ii)   Calculate the revised standard hourly rate using the index of 104.04.

(iii)   Subdivide the labour rate variance calculated in task (a)(i)(1) into that part due to the change in the index and that part arising for other reasons.

(iv)   *Briefly* interpret the possible meaning of these two subdivisions of the labour rate variance.

(v)   Give TWO reasons why the index of labour rates might not be valid in explaining part of the labour rate variance.

(vi)   *Briefly* explain the meaning of the following variances calculated in task (a) and for each variance suggest ONE reason why it may have occurred.

(1)   The fixed overhead expenditure (or price) variance
(2)   The fixed overhead capacity variance
(3)   The fixed overhead efficiency (or usage) variance

21   ORIGINAL HOLIDAYS LTD (70 mins)   *Specimen central assessment*

(a)   You are employed as an Accounting Technician by Original Holidays Limited. Original Holidays commenced business one year ago as a tour operator specialising in arranging holidays to the small island of Zed. Recent newspaper reports have stated that the cost of hotel bedrooms per night in Zed has been increasing over the last twelve moths due to its government refusing to allow further hotels to be built despite increasing demand from tourists.

The managing director of Original Holidays, Jane Armstrong, is concerned that this will affect the profitability of the company's operations to the island. She asked Colin Ware, the financial accountant, to provide data showing the nightly cost of a bedroom charged to Original Holidays over the last four quarters. Colin's response is reproduced below.

MEMO

To: **Jane Armstrong**   Date: 5 January 20X8

From: **Colin Ware**

Subject: **Nightly cost per bedroom**

Thank you for your recent enquiry concerning the cost per night of a bedroom in Zed. I have analysed the amounts paid per quarter over the last twelve months and divided that amount by the number of bedrooms hired per night. The nightly cost per bedroom is as follows:

	Quarter 1	*Quarter 2*	*Quarter 3*	*Quarter 4*
Cost per night	£102.400	£137.760	£134.480	£68.921

(Note: all figures in pounds to 3 decimal places.)

On receiving the memo, Jane notices that the cost to Original Holidays per bedroom per night has actually been falling over the last three quarters and has asked for your help in reconciling this with the newspaper reports. You obtain the following information.

Over several years, there has been a consistent seasonal variation in the cost of bedrooms per night. According to the marketing manager, these are:

	Quarter 1	*Quarter 2*	*Quarter 3*	*Quarter 4*
Seasonal variation *as percentage of trend*	−20%	+5%	+40%	−25%

A financial newspaper provides you with the following exchange rates between the UK pound and the Zed franc:

Quarter 1	*Quarter 2*	*Quarter 3*	*Quarter 4*
2,000 francs	2,000 francs	2,800 francs	3,000 francs

Tasks

(i)   Using the quarterly exchange rates given, identify the actual nightly cost per bedroom in Zed francs for each quarter.

(ii)   Using the information provided by the marketing manager, identify the trend in costs in Zed francs for each quarter.

(iii)   Identify the quarterly percentage increase in the cost of a bedroom per night in Zed francs and express this as an annual percentage to 2 decimal places.

(iv)   Forecast the cost in British pounds of a bedroom per night for the first quarter of next year using the exchange rate for the fourth quarter.

(b)   On receiving your analysis of the cost per bedroom per night, Jane Armstrong expresses concern that the company's existing reporting system does not provide sufficient information to monitor operations. She shows you a copy of the operating statement for the third quarter prepared using the existing system. The statement excludes marketing, administrative and other head-office overheads and is reproduced below.

Original Holidays Operating Statement for the 3rd Quarter - 20X7		
	Budget	*Actual*
Number of holidays	6,000	7,800
	£	£
Turnover	1,800,000	2,262,000
Accommodation	840,000	1,048,944
Air transport	720,000	792,000
Operating profit	240,000	421,056

Jane has shared her concerns with Colin Ware, the financial accountant. He has suggested that a standard costing report, reconciling standard cost to actual cost, would provide more meaningful information for management. To demonstrate to Jane Armstrong the improved quality of a standard costing system of reporting, Colin asks you to reanalyse the operating statement for the third quarter. To help you, he provides you with the following information:

- The accommodation is a variable cost. Its usage variance is nil.

- Air transport is a fixed cost and relates to the company's own 105-seat aircraft.

- The budget provided for 80 return flights in the quarter with each flight carrying 75 tourists. This volume was used to calculate the fixed overhead absorption rate when costing individual holidays.

- Due to operational difficulties, the aircraft only undertook 78 return flights, carrying a total of 7,800 passengers in quarter 3.

Tasks

(i)   Using the budgeted data, calculate the standard absorption cost per holiday.

(ii)   Using your answer to part (i), calculate the standard absorption cost of 7,800 holidays.

(iii)   Calculate the following variances.

   (1)   Material price variance for the accommodation
   (2)   Fixed overhead expenditure variance for the air transport
   (3)   Fixed overhead capacity variance for the air transport
   (4)   Fixed overhead efficiency variance for the air transport

(iv)   Prepare a statement reconciling the budgeted (or standard) absorption cost to the actual cost.

(v)   Identify the single most important reason for the difference between budgeted and actual cost.

(c) Write a memo to Jane Armstrong *briefly* explaining what the following variances attempt to measure and giving ONE possible reason why each variance might have occurred.

(i)   The fixed overhead expenditure variance
(ii)   The fixed overhead capacity variance
(iii)   The fixed overhead efficiency variance

22 PRONTO LTD (95 mins)

(a) Pronto Ltd was recently established in the UK to assemble cars. All parts are sent directly to the UK in the form of a kit by Pronto's owner from its headquarters in a country called Erehwon.

The contract between Pronto and its owner is a fixed price contract per kit and the contract specifies zero faults in all of the parts. This fixed price was used to establish the standard cost per kit. Despite this, the managing director of Pronto, Richard Jones, is concerned to receive the following statement from the management accounting department where you are employed as an accounting technician.

	September 20X8	October 20X8	November 20X8
Kits delivered	2,000	2,100	2,050
Actual cost invoiced	£12,059,535	£11,385,495	£10,848,600
Unit cost per kit to nearest £	£6,030	£5,422	£5,292

Richard Jones cannot understand why, with a fixed price contract and guaranteed quality, the unit cost should vary over the three months. He provides you with the following information.

- The contract's cost was fixed in Erehwon dollars of $54,243 per kit.

- There has been no change in the agreed cost of the parts and no other costs incurred.

On further investigation you discover that the exchange rate between the UK pound and the Erehwon dollar was as follows.

At time of contract	September 20X8	October 20X8	November 20X8
$9.80	$9.00	$10.00	$10.25

Task

Prepare a memo to Richard Jones. Your memo should include the following.

(i) A calculation of:

    (1) the UK cost per kit at the time the contract was agreed;

    (2) the UK cost of the kits delivered using the exchange rates given for each of the three months;

    (3) the price variance due to exchange rate differences for each of the three months;

    (4) any usage variance in each of the three months, assuming no other reason for the price variance;

(ii) A *brief* discussion about whether price variances due to exchange rate differences should be excluded from any standard costing report prepared for the production manager of Pronto Ltd.

(b) Pronto uses a highly mechanised and computerised moving assembly line known as a track to build the cars. Although individual employees are assigned to particular parts of the track, they work in teams. If the production of cars slows below the speed of the track, teams help each other to maintain the speed of the track and the production of cars. Because of this approach, labour is viewed as a fixed cost and machine hours (the hours that the track is in use) are used to charge overheads to production.

For the week ended 28 November 20X8, the management accounting department has prepared a statement of budgeted and actual fixed overhead for Richard Jones. This is reproduced below.

Pronto Ltd: Budgeted and actual fixed overheads - week ended 28 November 20X8		
	Budget	*Actual*
Car production	560	500
Machine (or track) hours of production	140	126
Fixed overheads:	£	£
Rent and rates	16,000	16,000
Maintenance and depreciation	10,000	13,000
Power	75,000	71,000
Labour	739,000	742,000
Total	840,000	842,000

Richard Jones finds that the statement is not particularly helpful as it does not give him sufficient information to manage the company. He asks for your help.

Tasks

In preparation for a meeting with Richard Jones, do the following.

(i)   Calculate the following.

   (1)   Budgeted overheads per machine (or track) hour

   (2)   Budgeted number of cars produced per machine (or track) hour

   (3)   Standard hours of actual production

(ii)   Calculate the following variances using the information identified in (i).

   (1)   Fixed overhead expenditure variance

   (2)   Fixed overhead volume variance

   (3)   Fixed overhead efficiency variance

   (4)   Fixed overhead capacity variance

(iii)   Prepare a statement for the week ended 28 November 20X8 reconciling the fixed overheads incurred to the fixed overheads absorbed in production

23   BRIGHTER CHEMICALS LTD (85 mins)   6/99

(a)   You are the management accountant at Brighter Chemicals Ltd. Brighter Chemicals makes a single product, Zed, which is sold in 5 litre tins.

One of your responsibilities is to prepare a report each month for the management team comparing the actual cost of Zed production with its standard cost of production. This involves taking data from a computer printout, preparing standard cost variances and reconciling the standard cost of actual production to the actual cost of actual production. After the data is analysed, you attend a management meeting where the performance of the company is discussed. The printout for May 20X2 is reproduced below.

Brighter Chemicals Ltd – Production report for May 20X2					
Number of tins of Zed			*Budgeted production* 1,750		*Actual production* 1,700
Inputs	*Units of input*	*Standard cost per unit of input* £	*Standard cost per tin of Zed* £	*Standard cost of budgeted production* £	*Actual cost per unit of input* £	*Actual cost of actual production* £
Material	5 litres	40.00	200.00	350,000	40.20	338,283
Labour	10 hours	6.00	60.00	105,000	5.90	110,330
Fixed overheads	10 hours	24.00	240.00	420,000		410,000
			500.00	875,000		858,613

Tasks

In preparation for the management meeting, do the following.

(i)   Calculate the following.

   (1) Actual litres of material used in producing the 1,700 tins of Zed

   (2) Actual hours worked in May

   (3) Standard litres of material which should have been used to produce 1,700 tins of Zed

   (4) Standard number of labour hours that should have been incurred in producing 1,700 tins of Zed

   (5) Standard hours of fixed overheads charged to the *budgeted* production of 1,750 tins

   (6) Standard hours of fixed overheads charged to the *actual* production of 1,700 tins

(ii) Calculate the following variances, making use of the answers in task (i).

   (1) Material price variance
   (2) Material usage variance
   (3) Labour rate variance
   (4) Labour efficiency variance
   (5) Fixed overhead expenditure variance
   (6) Fixed overhead volume variance
   (7) Fixed overhead capacity variance
   (8) Fixed overhead efficiency variance

(iii) Prepare a report reconciling the standard cost of *actual* production to the actual cost of *actual* production.

(b) On receiving your report, the production director makes the following comments.

   •   The material used in Zed production is purchased in drums. A notice on each drum states that the *minimum* content per drum is 50 litres.

   •   Finished production of Zed is automatically poured into tins by a machine which also measures the contents. An error of 0.5% either way in the accuracy of measurement is acceptable.

- The reported material price variance does not truly reflect the efficiency of the purchasing department. An index of raw material prices stood at 124.00 when the standard price was set. It stood at 125.86 in May.

- It seems unnecessary to investigate favourable variances. Favourable variances improve profitability and should be encouraged. Only adverse variances should be investigated.

Task

Write a *short* memo to the production director. Your memo should do the following.

(i)   Subdivide the material price variance calculated in task (a) into that part caused by the change in the standard cost as measured by the material price index and that part caused by efficiency or inefficiency of the purchasing department.

(ii) Give THREE separate reasons why Zed production might result in a favourable material usage variance.

(ii) *Briefly* discuss whether or not a favourable material usage variance should be investigated.

24   PRACTICE QUESTION RESPONSIBILITY CENTRES

Your organisation is implementing a system of responsibility accounting and you have been asked to provide some information about responsibility centres to be included in a report about the system which will be circulated to key staff.

Task

Identify three types of responsibility centre and describe the essential features of each.

25   PRACTICE QUESTION: FORECASTING

The following data show the sales of the product sold by your company in the period 20X6-X8.

Year	Quarter 1 £'000	Quarter 2 £'000	Quarter 3 £'000	Quarter 4 £'000
20X6	86	42	57	112
20X7	81	39	55	107
20X8	77	35	52	99

Tasks

(a) Plot the data and comment on them.

(b) By means of a moving average find the trend.

(c) The seasonal adjustments are as follows.

Quarter 1	Quarter 2	Quarter 3	Quarter 4
+9	−32	−16	+39

Give the sales for 20X8 seasonally adjusted.

(d) Forecast sales for each quarter of 20X9 using a 'rule-of-thumb' approach and comment on the likely accuracy of your forecasts.

26   PRACTICE QUESTION: FORECASTING AGAIN

You are the assistant management accountant for a company which is preparing revenue plans for the last quarter of 20X8/X9, and for the first three quarters of 20X9/Y0. The data below refer to one of the main products.

Revenue	April - June Quarter 1 £'000	July - September Quarter 2 £'000	October - December Quarter 3 £'000	January - March Quarter 4 £'000
20X5/X6	49	37	58	67
20X6/X7	50	38	59	68
20X7/X8	51	40	60	70
20X8/X9	50	42	61	-

Tasks

(a) Calculate the four-quarterly moving average trend for this set of data.

(b) Calculate the seasonal factors using either the additive model or the multiplicative model, but not both.

(c) Explain, but do not calculate, how you would use the results in part (a) and (b) of this question to forecast the revenue for the last quarter of 20X8/X9 and for the first three quarters of 20X9/Y0.

27 PRACTICE QUESTION: TIME SERIES ANALYSIS

You have collected the following data on your company's quarterly sales in recent years.

	Quarter			
	1 Units	2 Units	3 Units	4 Units
20X2	200	110	320	240
20X3	214	118	334	260
20X4	220	124	340	278

As part of the sales budget preparation you have been asked to analyse these data.

Tasks

(a) Calculate a moving average of quarterly sales.
(b) Calculate the average seasonal variations.

28 HENRY LTD (35 mins)   *U12, 6/95*

You work as the assistant to the management accountant for Henry Limited, a medium-sized manufacturing company. One of their products, product P, has been very successful in recent years, showing a steadily increasing trend in sales volumes.

Sales volumes for the four quarters of last year were as follows.

	Quarter 1	Quarter 2	Quarter 3	Quarter 4
Actual sales volume (units)	420,000	450,000	475,000	475,000

A new assistant has recently joined the marketing department and she has asked you for help in understanding the terminology which is used in preparing sales forecasts and analysing sales trends.

She has said: 'My main problem is that I do not see why my boss is so enthusiastic about the growth in product P's sales volume. It looks to me as though the rate of growth is really slowing down and has actually stopped in Quarter 4. I am told that I should be looking at the deseasonalised or seasonally adjusted sales data but I do not understand what is meant by this.'

You have found that product P's sales are subject to the following seasonal variations.

	Quarter 1	Quarter 2	Quarter 3	Quarter 4
Seasonal variation (units)	+ 25,000	+ 15,000	0	- 40,000

Tasks

(a)   Adjust for the seasonal variations to calculate deseasonalised or seasonally adjusted sales volumes (ie the trend figures) for each quarter of last year.

(b)   Assuming that the trend and seasonal variations will continue, forecast the sales volumes for each of the four quarters of next year.

(c)   Prepare a memorandum to the marketing assistant which explains

   (i)   what is meant by seasonal variations and deseasonalised or seasonally adjusted data; and

   (ii)   how they can be useful in analysing a time series and preparing forecasts.

   Use the figures for product P's sales to illustrate your explanations.

29   ALAN DUNN (35 mins)   *U12, 12/96*

The managing director of Edge Ltd, Alan Dunn, has also only recently been appointed. He is keen to develop the company and has already agreed to two new products being developed. These will be launched in eighteen months' time. While talking to you about the budget he mentions that the quality of sales forecasting will need to improve if the company is to grow rapidly. Currently, the budgeted sales figure is found by initially adding 5% to the previous year's sales volume and then revising the figure following discussions with the marketing director. He believes this approach is increasingly inadequate and now requires a more systematic approach.

A few days later Alan Dunn sends you a memo. In that memo, he identifies three possible strategies for increasing sales volume. They are:

•   more sales to existing customers;

•   the development of new markets;

•   the development of new products.

He asks for your help in forecasting likely sales volume from these sources.

Task

Write a brief memo to Alan Dunn. Your memo should:

(a)   identify FOUR ways of forecasting future sales volume;

(b)   show how each of your four ways of forecasting can be applied to ONE of the sales strategies identified by Alan Dunn and justify your choice;

(c)   give TWO reasons why forecasting methods might not prove to be accurate.

30   ESKAFELD INDUSTRIAL MUSEUM (40 mins)   *U12, 12/97*

Eskafeld Industrial Museum opened ten years ago and soon became a market leader with many working exhibits. In the early years there was a rapid growth in the number of visitors. However, with no further investment in new exhibits, this growth has not been maintained in recent years.

Two years ago, John Derbyshire was appointed as the museum's chief executive. His initial task was to increase the number of visitors to the museum and, following his appointment, he has made several improvements to make the museum more successful.

Another of John's tasks is to provide effective financial management. This year, the museum's Board of Management has asked him to take full responsibility for producing the 20X9 budget. One of his first tasks is to prepare estimates of the number of visitors next year. John had previously played only a limited role in budget preparation and so he turns to you, an accounting technician, for advice.

He provides you with the following information.

*   Previous budgets had assumed a 10% growth in attendance but this has been inaccurate.

*   Very little is known about the visitors to the museum.

*   The museum keeps details of the number of visitors by quarter but this has never been analysed.

*   The number of visitors per quarter for the last two years is as follows.

Year	Quarter	Number of visitors
20X7	1	5,800
	2	9,000
	3	6,000
	4	14,400
20X8	1	6,600
	2	9,800
	3	6,800
	4 (Estimate)	15,200

Tasks

(a) Calculate the *Centred Four-Point Moving Average Trend* figures and the seasonal variations.

(b) Construct a graph showing the trend line and actual number of visitors, by quarter, for presentation to the Board of Management.

(c) Estimate the forecast number of visitors for each quarter of 20X9, assuming that there is the same trend and seasonal variations for 20X8.

(d) Prepare notes on forecasting for John Derbyshire. Your notes should:

    (i) identify two ways to improve the forecasting of visitor numbers and highlight any limitations to your proposals;

    (ii) explain why telephone sampling might be preferable to using postal questionnaires;

    (iii) explain how the concept of the product life cycle could be applied to the museum.

31 STAR FUELS (50 mins)   *Specimen central assessment*

Star Fuels is a multinational oil company selling oil for industrial and domestic purposes through a network of distributors. Distributors purchase fuel oil from Star Fuels and then sell it on to their own customers.

A regular complaint of the distributors is that they either have to pay for the fuel on delivery to their storage tanks or be charged interest on a daily basis on the amount owed. This problem could be reduced if the distributors were able to forecast their demands more accurately.

You are employed as the Assistant Management Accountant to Northern Fuel Distributors Ltd, a major distributor of Star Fuels's fuel oils. You recently attended a meeting with Mary Lamberton, a member of Star Fuels's central staff. At the meeting, she demonstrated a statistical software package used for estimating demand for fuel oil. The user enters sales volumes per period and the package then calculates the least-squares regression equation for the data. This is in the form $y = a + bx$ where x is the time period, y is the forecast and a and b are terms derived from the original data. Following further inputs by the user, the package can also estimate seasonal variations. Two forms of seasonal variation are calculated: the first calculates the seasonal variance as an absolute amount, the second as a percentage.

One week after the meeting, your copy of the software arrives at the head office of Northern Fuel Distributors Ltd and you immediately set about testing its capability. Purely for the purpose of testing, you assume seasonal variations occur quarterly. You enter this assumption along with the sales turnover figures for fuel oil for the last 20 quarters. Within moments, the software outputs the following information.

Regression line $y = £2,000,000 + £40,000x$

Seasonal variations

Quarter	A	B	C	D
Amount	+£350,000	+£250,000	−£400,000	−£200,000
Percentage	+15%	+10%	−15%	−10%

Quarter A refers to the first quarter of annual data, B to the second quarter, C to the third and D to the fourth. The pattern then repeats itself. In terms of the specific data you input, seasonal variation A refers to quarter 17, B to quarter 18, C to quarter 19 and D to quarter 20.

Actual sales turnover for quarters 17 to 20 was as follows.

Quarter	17	18	19	20
Sales turnover	£3,079,500	£3,002,400	£2,346,500	£2,490,200

Tasks

(a) Making use of the formula derived by the software package, calculate the forecast sales turnover for quarters 17 to 20 using:

   (i)   the absolute seasonal variations;
   (ii) the percentage seasonal variations.

(b) (i)   From your answers to Task (a), determine which method of calculating seasonal variations gives the best estimate of actual sales turnover.

   (ii) Having identified the preferred method, use that method to forecast the sales turnover for quarters 21 to 24.

(c) Write a memorandum to your Managing Director. The memorandum should do the following.

   (i)   Explain what is meant by seasonal variations and seasonally adjusted data. Illustrate your explanation with examples relevant to Northern Fuel Distributors.

   (ii) Suggest why your chosen method of seasonal adjustment might be more accurate.

   (iii) Show how an understanding of seasonal variations and seasonally adjusted data can help Northern Fuel Distributors be more efficient.

   (iv) Identify TWO weaknesses within your approach to forecasting undertaken in Tasks (a) and (b).

32   PRACTICE QUESTION: BUDGETS

The company for which you work makes two products, the Tork and the Larf, and is preparing an annual budget for 20X3.

Task

Using the information given below, prepare the following.

(a) Production budget
(b) Direct materials cost budget
(c) Purchases budget
(d) Direct wages budget
(e) Budgeted profit and loss account (an analysis by divisions is not required)

STANDARD DATA PER UNIT OF PRODUCT

Direct material	*Standard price per kg*	*Tork*	*Larf*
	£	kg	kg
Cri	1.50	8	4
Showt	4.00	5	10

Direct wages	*Standard rate per hour*	*Tork*	*Larf*
	£	Hours	Hours
Sobbers	3.50	6	12
Screamers	1.00	10	6

Fixed production overhead is absorbed on a direct labour hour basis. There is no variable overhead. Administration, selling and distribution costs are absorbed on a budgeted basis of $16^2/_3\%$ of factory cost.

Gross profit on factory cost is budgeted at 25% of selling price.

BUDGETED DATA: SALES FOR THE YEAR

	Tork	*Larf*
	£'000	£'000
Division:		
1	1,808	1,280
2	600	1,600
3	900	2,600
4	500	800
Finished goods stock, valued at standard factory cost:		
1 January 20X3	238	628
31 December 20X3	595	1,413
Direct material stocks, valued at standard prices:		
1 January 20X3	120	160
31 December 20X3	40	180

Fixed production overhead, per annum = £3,717,000
Direct labour hours, per annum = 1,062,000 hours

It is expected that there will be no work in progress at the beginning or end of the year.

33 PRACTICE QUESTION: BUDGET PREPARATION

You are assistant management accountant for an ice cream manufacturer and you are in the process of preparing budgets for the next few months. The following draft figures are available.

Sales forecast

June	6,000 cases
July	7,500 cases
August	8,500 cases
September	7,000 cases
October	6,500 cases

A case has a standard cost of £15 and a standard selling price of £25.

Each case uses 2½ kgs of ingredients and it is policy to have stocks of ingredients at the end of each month to cover 50% of next month's production. There are 5,800 kgs in stock on 1 June.

There are 750 cases of finished ice cream in stock on 1 June and it is policy to have stocks at the end of each month to cover 10% of the next month's sales.

Tasks

(a) Prepare a production budget (in cases) for the months of June, July, August and September.

(b) Prepare an ingredients purchase budget (in kgs) for the months of June, July and August.

(c) Calculate the budgeted gross profit for the quarter June to August.

(d) Describe briefly what advantages there would be for the firm if it adopted a system of flexible budgeting.

34 PRODUCT Q (60 mins)

U12, 6/95

Product Q is a product which is manufactured and sold by Alfred Limited. In the process of preparing budgetary plans for next year the following information has been made available to you.

- Forecast sales units of product Q for the year = 18,135 units

- Closing stocks of finished units of product Q at the end of next year will be increased by 15% from their opening level of 1,200 units.

- All units are subject to a quality control check. The budget plans are to allow for 1% of all units checked to be rejected and scrapped at the end of the process. All closing stocks will have passed this quality control check.

- Five direct labour hours are to be worked for each unit of product Q processed, including those which are scrapped after the quality control check. Of the total hours to be paid for, 7.5% are budgeted to be idle time.

- The standard hourly rate of pay for direct employees is £6 per hour.

- Material M is used in the manufacture of product Q. One finished unit of product Q contains 9 kg of M but there is a wastage of 10% of input of material M due to evaporation and spillage during the process.

- By the end of next year stocks of material M are to be increased by 12% from their opening level of 8,000 kg. During the year a loss of 1,000 kg is expected due to deterioration of the material in store.

Tasks

(a) Prepare the following budgets for the forthcoming year.

    (i)   Production budget for product Q, in units

(ii)   Direct labour budget for product Q, in hours and in £

(iii) Material usage budget for material M, in kg

(iv)   Material purchases budget for material M, in kg

(b) The supplier of material M has warned that available supplies will be below the amount indicated in your budget for task (a) part (iv) above.

Explain the implications of this shortage and suggest four possible actions which could be taken to overcome the problem. For each suggestion identify any problems which may arise.

35   ARDEN ENGINEERING LTD (60 mins) {#35-arden-engineering-ltd-60-mins}

U12, 12/95

(a) Arden Engineering Ltd makes a single product and, for planning purposes, the company breaks its annual budget into 13 four-weekly periods. From information provided by the marketing director, total sales for the year will be 3,296,500 units. This is broken down as follows.

Period	1	2	3	4	Each subsequent period
Units sales	190,000	228,000	266,000	304,000	256,500

A similar pattern and volume of sales is expected next year. Because of the technical nature of the product, manufacturing has to take place one period prior to sale. In addition, there is a five per cent wastage which is only discovered on completion. This wastage has no monetary value.

Manufacturing labour is employed by the week and the wages cost per four-week period totals £270,000. The production director believes it is possible to manufacture up to 290,000 gross units per period although, because of wastage, good production will be below this figure. Any increase beyond the gross production of 290,000 units will involve paying overtime at a rate equivalent to £1.50 per extra unit produced. The material component of each unit costs £3.50. The only other production cost relates to fixed overheads. For the forthcoming year these are estimated at £6,940,000. Fixed overheads are charged to production on the basis of the gross number of units produced.

Task

For the first three periods of the forthcoming year, prepare the production budget, in a form suitable for consideration by the production director, on the assumption that all production takes place one period before it is sold. Your budget should show the total units to be produced per period, the production cost per period and the unit cost per period.

(b) The production director is concerned that the budget involves overtime payments and suggests this is not necessary.

Two proposals are put forward: that part of the production is sourced from outside suppliers at a unit cost of £5.95 or that production is brought forward to periods when there is surplus capacity.

If production is brought forward, this will involve financing and other costs equivalent to 50p per unit per four-week period.

Task

Evaluate the two proposals given above and show, with supporting workings, the revised production schedule in units and the savings possible from your preferred proposal.

36   ALDERLEY LTD (40 mins)   *U12, 12/96*

You have recently been appointed as the management accountant to Alderley Ltd a small company manufacturing two products, the Elgar and the Holst. Both products use the same type of material and labour but in different proportions. In the past, the company has had poor control over its working capital. To remedy this, you have recommended to the directors that a budgetary control system be introduced. This proposal has now been agreed.

Because Alderley Ltd's production and sales are spread evenly over the year, it was agreed that the annual budget should be broken down into four periods, each of 13 weeks, and commencing with the 13 weeks ending 4 April 20X8. To help you in this task, the sales and production directors have provided you with the following information.

Marketing and production data

	Elgar	Holst
Budgeted sales for 13 weeks (units)	845	1,235
Material content per unit (kilograms)	7	8
Labour per unit (standard hours)	8	5

Production labour

The 24 production employees work a 37-hour, five-day week and are paid £8 per hour. Any hours in excess of this involve Alderley in paying an overtime premium of 25%. Because of technical problems, which will continue over the next 13 weeks, employees are only able to work at 95% efficiency compared to standard.

Purchasing and opening stocks

The production director believes that raw material will cost £12 per kilogram over the budget period. He also plans to revise the amount of stock being kept. He estimates that the stock levels at the commencement of the budget period will be as follows.

Raw materials	Elgar	Holst
2,328 kilograms	163 units	361 units

Closing stocks

At the end of the 13-week period, closing stocks are planned to change. On the assumption that production and sales volumes for the second budget period will be similar to those in the first period:

- raw material stocks should be sufficient for 13 days' production;
- finished stocks of the Elgar should be equivalent to 6 day's sales volume;
- finished stocks of the Holst should be equivalent to 14 days' sales volume.

Tasks

Prepare in the form of a statement the following information for the 13-week period to 4 April 20X8.

(a) The production budget in units for the Elgar and the Holst
(b) The purchasing budget for Alderley Ltd in units
(c) The cost of purchases for the period
(d) The production labour budget for Alderley Ltd in hours
(e) The cost of production labour for the period

Note. Assume a five-day week for both sales and production.

37   PICKERINGS CANNING COMPANY (50 mins)

The Pickerings Canning Company produces a range of canned savoury and sweet products. The company prepares its budgets annually. The cost accountant has recently left and you, as the assistant cost accountant, have been requested to take over the responsibility of budget preparation. The managers of the company need the information quickly but they realise that the full budget will take too long to prepare. Because of this, a short-term budget for the month of September is requested. Before leaving, the cost accountant provided you with the following information.

- The only product which will be produced during the month is Apple Pie Filling and 80,000 cans per month are required by customers.

- The apples are purchased whole and there is approximately 50% waste in production.

- The net amount of apple in 1,000 cans is 100 kg.

- At the final stage of the production process 5% of the cans are damaged and they are sold to employees.

- The labour required to produce 1,000 cans is 6 hours.

- Each employee works 38 hours per week.

- The employees are currently in dispute with the company and there is 10% absenteeism. This problem is likely to continue for the foreseeable future.

- The employees are paid £4 per hour.

- The buyer at the company has provided prices for the apples but these are estimates mainly based on the actual figures for last year.

    ° The basic price of apples is budgeted at £200 per tonne for August.

    ° An internal index of apple prices for last year for the same period was:

    20X7
    August   120
    September   125

Tasks

(a) For the month of September 20X8:

   (i)   prepare a materials purchases budget (at basic price);

   (ii)   prepare a labour budget in terms of numbers of employees;

   (iii) assuming the rate of price increase is the same this year as last year, recalculate the cost of materials purchased.

(b) The budget has been discussed with the production manager and he is concerned about two issues, namely:

   (i)   how useful are the materials price indices supplied by the buyer for budgeting the costs of materials?

   (ii)   given that the wages costs are significant, what information should be supplied daily, weekly and monthly to control this area?

   Prepare a memo for the production manager. Your memo should:

   (i)   address the issues of concern;
   (ii)   suggest and justify an alternative method for predicting materials prices.

38   GEORGE PHILLIPS (50 mins)   *U12, 12/97*

(a)   George Phillips makes and sells two types of garden ornament, the Alpha and the Beta. George prepared his 20X8 budget several months ago but since then he has discovered that there is a shortage of raw material used for making the ornaments. As a result, he will only be able to acquire 20,000 kilograms of the raw material for the first 13 weeks of 20X8

An extract from his original budget is reproduced below.

Sales budget

	Units	Selling price £	Turnover £
Alpha	6,500	36.00	234,000
Beta	7,800	39.00	£304,200

Extract from the production budget

	Units produced	Material per unit kg	Total material kg
Alpha	6,900	2.0	13,800
Beta	9,000	1.5	13,500
Materials issued to production			27,300

Purchases budget

	Kilograms	Price per kilogram £	Total cost £
Materials issued to production	27,300	5.00	136,500
Opening stock	(6,000)	5.00	(30,000)
Closing stock	6,600	5.00	33,000
Purchases	27,900		139,500

Labour budget

	Units produced	Labour hours per unit	Total hours
Alpha	6,900	2.500	17,250
Beta	9,000	2.785	25,065
Labour hours			42,315
Labour cost			169,260

George also provides you with the following additional information.

- The budget is based on a 13-week period.

- Employees work a 35-hour week.

- The closing stocks of materials and finished products must be kept to the figures in the original budget.

- The original sales budget represents the maximum demand for the Alpha and the Beta in a 13-week period.

Task

You are the recently appointed accounting trainee at the company. George Phillips asks you to revise his budget for the first 13 weeks of 20X8 to take account of the shortage of the raw materials. You should prepare the budgets for:

(i)   materials purchases;
(ii)   materials issued to production;
(iii)   sales volume and turnover;

(iv)   labour hours and cost;

(v)   the number of employees required.

(b)   On reviewing the revised figures George realises that there are too many employees and he calls a meeting of the managers of the business. During the meeting the following issues are raised.

   (i)   The production manager does not wish to reduce the number of employees as he will lose key trained staff who may not wish to be re-employed later. He argues that the labour costs are fixed as the employees are not employed on a piece work basis.

   (ii)   In preparing the original budget George had been advised by one of the partners at the firm's auditors that the key factor should be identified before the budget was prepared. He had assumed that sales would be a key factor and therefore the budget had been based on sales; this was invalid since materials are now the limiting factor.

   (iii)   George complains that the original budget took many hours to prepare and he seeks your advice on the benefits of using a relevant spreadsheet package.

Task

You have been requested to prepare a report covering the issues raised by George Phillips and his managers at the meeting.

39   GARDEN EQUIPMENT LTD (90 mins)   *U12, 12/98*

(a)   You have recently accepted the position of management accountant in the Agricultural Division of Garden Equipment Ltd. The Agricultural Division was established six months ago to make two products, Exe and Wye. The budget for the five weeks ending 5 February 20X9 is reproduced below.

Budgeted profit and loss statement for the Agricultural Division				
5 weeks ending 5 February 20X9				
Product	*Exe*	*Exe*	*Wye*	*Wye*
	Quantities	£	Quantities	£
Raw material	8,740 litres	26,220	13,300 litres	39,900
Labour	4,370 hours	21,850	21,280 hours	106,400
Marginal cost of production	2,185 Exe	48,070	2,660 Wye	146,300
Add opening finished stock	350 Exe	7,700	400 Wye	22,000
Less closing finished stock	480 Exe	10,560	520 Wye	28,600
Marginal cost of sales	2,055 Exe	45,210	2,540 Wye	139,700
Turnover		152,070		248,920
Factory contribution		106,860		109,220

Exe is sold under a long-term contract to a large retail company. The contract specifies the volume of deliveries per week. Because of this, the budgeted sales equal the actual sales for each week of the financial year. Wye is sold to individual shops. Since its launch six months ago, the demand for Wye has consistently been well above the budgeted figures.

You were recently called to a meeting with the production and finance directors to discuss the budgeted and likely actual performance of the division for the five weeks ending 5 February 20X9. At the meeting, you were given the following information.

   •   Both products use the same grade of raw materials and labour but in different proportions.

- The budgeted opening stock of raw materials was 3,040 litres and the budgeted closing stock 6,200 litres.

- Because of current transport problems, ALL budgeted stocks must also be the actual stocks.

- Only 80% of budgeted purchases of raw materials will be available for the five weeks ending 5 February 20X9.

- After the budget was prepared, it was found that there was a 5% loss of raw materials due to evaporation. This only occurs when raw materials are issued to production.

- Apart from this evaporation, there has been no change in costs or required inputs of either raw material or labour.

- Because of penalty clauses in the contract, it is not possible to reduce Exe's sales volume.

- Marginal costing is used in the preparation of the management accounts.

Tasks

(i) Using the data in the ORIGINAL budget and IGNORING EVAPORATION, calculate the following.

  (1) Litres of material required to produce one unit of Exe and one unit of Wye

  (2) Labour hours required to produce one unit of Exe and one unit of Wye

  (3) Cost of raw material per litre

  (4) Labour rate per hour

  (5) Unit selling price of Exe and Wye

  (6) Budgeted raw material purchases in litres before allowing for the shortage of raw materials

(ii) Prepare a statement identifying the number of units of Exe and Wye to be produced in the five weeks ending 5 February 20X9 after allowing for evaporation and the shortage of raw materials, using the information calculated in (i).

(iii) Prepare a revised *production* budget in units and value for the five weeks ending 5 February 20X9 using the information calculated in (i) and (ii).

(b) On receiving your revised budget, the production director is concerned about the performance of the Agricultural Division and asks for your advice.

Task

Write a *short* memo to the production director. Your memo should identify the following.

(i) TWO possible ways of overcoming the shortage of raw material in the future

(ii) ONE possible consequence for the division if the raw material shortages continue

40   AMBER LTD (75 mins)   *12/98*

(a) Amber Ltd is a subsidiary of Colour plc and makes a single product, the Delta. Budgets are prepared by dividing the accounting year into 13 periods, each of four weeks. Amber's policy is to avoid overtime payments wherever possible and this was one of the assumptions built into the preparation of Amber's budget for this year. However, some overtime payments have been necessary.

Helen Roy, Amber's finance director, has recently carried out an investigation and discovered why overtime has been paid. She found that the labour hours available over each four-week period were more than sufficient to meet the four-weekly production targets. However, *within* any four-week period, production levels could vary considerably. As a result, in some weeks, overtime had to be paid.

You are employed in the management accounting section of Colour plc as an assistant to Helen Roy. Although Helen did not have the next period's *production* volumes analysed by individual week, she was able to explain the problem by showing you the forecast *sales* of Deltas over each of the next four weeks. These are reproduced below.

Week	1	2	3	4
Forecast *sales* of Deltas (units)	23,520	27,440	28,420	32,340

Helen Roy also gives the following information.

- Amber's maximum production capacity per week before overtime and rejections is 30,400 Deltas.

- For technical reasons, production has to take place at least one week before it is sold.

- At present, all production takes place exactly one week before it is sold.

- Sales cannot be delayed to a subsequent week.

- The weekly fixed costs of wages before overtime is £21,280.

- Overtime is equivalent to £2 per unit produced in excess of 30,400 Deltas.

- The cost of material per Delta is £5.

- There is a 2% rejection rate in the manufacture of Deltas. Rejected Deltas are only discovered on completion and have no monetary value.

- Budgeted fixed production overheads for the year are estimated to be £3,792,825. These are absorbed on the basis of an estimated annual production before rejections of 1,685,700 Deltas.

Task

Helen Roy asks you to prepare Amber's WEEKLY production budgets for weeks 1 to 3 on the current basis that all production takes place exactly one week before it is sold. The budget should identify the following.

(i)   The number of Deltas to be produced in each of the three weeks

(ii) The cost of any overtime paid

(iii) The cost of production for each of the three weeks, including fixed production overheads

(b) You give Helen Roy Amber's production budget for the next three weeks. She now tells you that it may be possible to save at least some of the overtime payments by manufacturing some Deltas in advance of the normal production schedule. However, any Deltas made earlier than one week before being sold will incur financing costs of 20p per Delta per week.

Task

Helen Roy asks you to calculate the following.

(i)   The number of Deltas to be produced in each of the three weeks if the overall costs are to be minimised

(ii)   The net savings if your revised production plan in (i) is accepted

41   WILMSLOW LTD (85 mins)   *6/99*

(a)   Wimlslow Ltd makes two products, the Alpha and the Beta. Both products use the same material and labour but in different amounts. The company divides its year into four quarters, each of 12 weeks. Each week consists of five days and each day comprises seven hours.

You are employed as the management accountant to Wilmslow Ltd and you originally prepared a budget for quarter 3, the 12 weeks to 17 September 20X5. The basic data for that budget is reproduced below.

Original budgetary data: quarter 3 12 weeks to 17 September 20X5		
Product	**Alpha**	**Beta**
Estimated demand	1,800 units	2,100 units
Material per unit	8 kilograms	12 kilograms
Labour per unit	3 hours	6 hours

Since the budget was prepared, three developments have taken place.

•   The company has begun to use linear regression and seasonal variations to forecast sales demand. Because of this, the estimated demand for quarter 3 has been revised to 2,000 Alphas and 2,400 Betas.

•   As a result of the revised sales forecasting, you have developed more precise estimates of sales and closing stock levels.

The sales volume of both the Alpha and Beta in quarter 4 (the 12 weeks ending 10 December 20X5) will be 20% more than in the revised budget for quarter 3 as a result of seasonal variations.

The closing stock of finished Alphas at the end of quarter 3 should represent five days sales for quarter 4.

The closing stock of finished Betas at the end of quarter 3 should represent ten days sales for quarter 4.

Production in quarter 4 of both Alpha and Beta is planned to be 20% more than in the revised budget for quarter 3. The closing stock of materials at the end of quarter 3 should be sufficient for **20 days production** in quarter 4.

•   New equipment has been installed. The workforce is not familiar with the equipment. Because of this, for quarter 3, they will only be working at 80% of the efficiency assumed in the original budgetary data.

Other data from your original budget which has not changed is reproduced below.

•   50 production employees work a 35 hour week and are each paid £210 per week.

•   Overtime is paid for at £9 per hour.

•   The cost of material is £10 per kilogram.

- Opening stocks at the beginning of quarter 3 are as follows.

Finished Alphas	500 units
Finished Betas	600 units
Material	12,000 kilograms

- There will not be any work in progress at any time.

Task

The production director of Wilmslow Ltd wants to schedule production for quarter 3 (the 12 weeks ending 17 September 20X5) and asks you to use the revised information to prepare the following.

(i)   The revised production budget for Alphas and Betas
(ii) The material purchases budget in kilograms
(iii) A statement showing the cost of material purchases
(iv) The labour budget in hours
(v)   A statement showing cost of labour

(b) Margaret Brown is the financial director of Wilmslow Ltd. She is not convinced that the use of linear regression, even when adjusted for seasonal variation, is the best way of forecasting sales volumes for Wilmslow Ltd.

The quality of sales forecasting is an agenda item for the next meeting of the Board of Directors and she asks for your advice.

Task

Write a *brief* memo to Margaret Brown. Your memo should do the following.

(i)   Identify TWO limitations of the use of linear regression as a forecasting technique

(ii) Suggest TWO other ways of sales forecasting

42   PRACTICE QUESTION: FLEXED BUDGETS

Extracts from the budgets of Dexter Ltd, the company where you work as accounts assistant, are given below.

	Period 1	Period 2	Period 3	Period 4	Period 5
		Sales and stock budgets (units)			
Opening stock	4,000	2,500	3,300	2,500	3,000
Sales	15,000	20,000	16,500	21,000	18,000

	Cost budgets		
	Period 1	Period 2	Period 3
	£'000	£'000	£'000
Direct labour	270.0	444.0	314.0
Direct materials	108.0	166.4	125.6
Production overhead (excluding depreciation)	117.5	154.0	128.5
Depreciation	40.0	40.0	40.0
Administration overhead	92.0	106.6	96.4
Selling overhead	60.0	65.0	61.5

The following information is also available.

(a) Production above 18,000 units incurs a bonus in addition to normal wage rates.

(b) Any variable costs contained in selling overhead are assumed to vary with sales. All other variable costs are assumed to vary with production.

41

Tasks

(a) Calculate the budgeted production for periods 1 to 4.

(b) Prepare a suitable cost budget for period 4.

(c) In period 4 the stock and sales budgets were achieved and the following actual costs recorded.

	£'000
Direct labour	458
Direct material	176
Production overhead	181
Depreciation	40
Administration overhead	128
Selling overhead	62
	1,045

Show the budget variances from actual.

43 PRACTICE QUESTION: FLEXIBLE BUDGETING

You are the assistant management accountant at the Arcadian Hotel which operates a budgeting system and budgets expenditure over eight budget centres as shown below. Analysis of past expenditure patterns indicates that variable costs are some budget centres vary according to Occupied Room Nights (ORN) whilst in others the variable proportion of costs varies according to the number of visitors (V).

The budgeted expenditures for a period with 2,000 ORN and 4,300 V were as follows.

Budget centre	Variable costs vary with:	Budgeted expenditure £	Partial cost analysis Budget expenditure includes:
Cleaning	ORN	13,250	£2.50 per ORN
Laundry	V	15,025	£1.75 per V
Reception	ORN	13,100	£12,100 fixed
Maintenance	ORN	11,100	£0.80 per ORN
Housekeeping	V	19,600	£11,000 fixed
Administration	ORN	7,700	£0.20 per ORN
Catering	V	21,460	£2.20 per V
General overheads		11,250	all fixed

In period 9, with 1,850 ORN and 4,575 V, actual expenditures were as follows.

Budget centre	Actual expenditure £
Cleaning	13,292
Laundry	14,574
Reception	13,855
Maintenance	10,462
Housekeeping	19,580
Administration	7,930
Catering	23,053
General overheads	11,325

Tasks

(a) Prepare a flexible budget for period 9.

(b) Show the individual expenditure variance for each budget centre.

(c) Discuss briefly the advantages that a budgeting system brings to the Arcadian Hotel.

44   PRACTICE QUESTION: FLEXIBLE BUDGETS AND VARIANCES

Aware of the uncertain nature of the market facing your organisation (Clooney Ltd) in the coming year, your supervisor has prepared budgeted cost forecasts based on 90%, 100% and 105% activity as follows.

	90%	100%	105%
	£	£	£
Material costs	337,500	375,000	393,750
Labour costs	440,000	485,000	507,500
Production overhead costs	217,500	235,000	243,750
Administration costs	120,000	130,000	135,000
Selling and distribution costs	70,000	75,000	77,500
	1,185,000	1,300,000	1,357,500

100% activity represents production of 50,000 units.

In fact, actual activity has turned out far worse than expected and only 37,500 units were produced, with the following results.

	£
Material costs	311,750
Labour costs	351,500
Production overhead costs	171,250
Administration costs	117,500
Selling and distribution costs	66,500
	1,018,500

Tasks

As assistant finance officer you have been asked to do the following.

(a)   Given that the fixed element of the budgeted costs will remain unchanged at all levels of production, prepare a statement for the year showing the flexed budget at the actual level of activity, the actual results and the variance for each item of cost.

(b)   Examine the variances of £20,000 or greater, analysing the possible reasons for such variances and suggesting the follow up action management can take.

45   GEORGE LTD (25 mins)   *U12, 6/95*

You work as the assistant to the management accountant for George Limited, a medium-sized manufacturing company.

The company's marketing assistant has approached you for help in understanding the company's planning and control systems. She has been talking with the distribution manager who has tried to explain how flexible budgets are used to control distribution costs within George Limited. She makes the following comment:

'I thought that budgets were supposed to provide a target to plan our activities and against which to monitor our costs. How can we possibly plan and control our costs if we simply change the budgets when activity levels alter?'

Task

Prepare a memorandum to the marketing assistant which explains the following.

(a)   Why fixed budgets are useful for planning but flexible budgets may be more useful to enable management to exercise effective control over distribution costs.

(b)   Two possible activity indicators which could be used as a basis for flexing the budget for distribution costs.

(c) How a flexible budget cost allowance is calculated and used for control purposes. Use your own examples and figures where appropriate to illustrate your explanations.

46 PARMOD PLC (70 mins) *U12, 6/96*

(a) Six months ago, Parmod plc established a new subsidiary, Trygon Ltd. Trygon was formed to assemble and sell computers direct to the public. Its annual budget was drawn up by Mike Barratt, Parmod's Finance Director. Trygon's plant was capable of producing 150,000 computers per year although the budget for the first year was only 80% of this amount. Factory overheads - defined as all factory fixed costs other than labour - were to be charged to finished stocks *at all times* on the basis of this 80% activity, irrespective of actual activity.

Trygon had entered into an agreement with the employees whereby their wages were guaranteed, provided the employees made themselves available to produce 120,000 computers per year. Because of this agreement, the labour element in finished stocks was always to be based on a production level of 120,000 computers. If output exceeded the 120,000 units, additional overtime equivalent to £70 per computer would be paid. Managers were also to be given a bonus of £15 per computer produced in excess of 120,000 units in the year.

At the beginning of the year, Mike had given all the managers a financial statement showing the annual budget (based on 80% activity) and the effect of operation at only half the planned activity. This is reproduced below.

Trygon Ltd budgeted profit for the year to 31 December 20X8

Activity	Annual budget £	40% £
Direct materials	24,000,000	12,000,000
Direct labour	7,200,000	7,200,000
Light, heat and power	4,000,000	2,200,000
Production management salaries	1,500,000	1,500,000
Factory rent, rates and insurance	9,400,000	9,400,000
Depreciation of factory machinery	5,500,000	5,500,000
National advertising	20,000,000	20,000,000
Marketing and administration	2,300,000	2,300,000
Delivery costs	2,400,000	1,200,000
Total costs	76,300,000	61,300,000
Sales revenue	84,000,000	42,000,000
Operating profit/(loss)	7,700,000	(19,300,000)

In preparing the financial statement, Mike Barratt had made the following assumptions.

- Unit selling prices were the same over the different activity levels.

- No quantity discounts or other similar efficiencies had been assumed for purchases.

- Production fixed overheads comprised the depreciation of the machinery, the rent, rates and insurance, the production management salaries (other than any possible bonus) and part of the cost of light, heat and power.

Six months after Mike Barratt had issued the statement, you are called to a meeting of the directors of Trygon Ltd. Anne Darcy, the managing director, tells you that production and sales for the year are likely to be 112,500 computers.

Task

You are the Management Accountant to Trygon. Anne Darcy asks you to prepare a flexible budget for the year using the data given by Mike Barratt and assuming 112,500 computers are produced and sold. She also asks you to identify the budgeted profit.

(b) On receiving your flexible budget, Anne Darcy reminds her fellow directors that Trygon plans a major marketing campaign at the beginning of the next financial year and this will require a building up of stocks in preparation for the campaign. The production director, Alan Williams, believes it is feasible to increase production close to capacity without increasing any of the fixed costs. As a result, the Board agrees to budget for sales of 112,500 units by the year end but to produce at 95% capacity.

A discussion then followed about the role of budgeting in Trygon Ltd. 'I do not know why we should take up all this time discussing budgets' said Anne Darcy. 'They are not my figures. I had no say in their preparation. Let Mike Barratt take responsibility for them - after all, it was his budget - and let us get on with the job of building up a business.'

'I agree,' Alan Williams said. 'I wish Mike would make up his mind what we are supposed to be doing. Are we just concerned with making short-term profits or are we supposed to be building up a quality product? Just what are our objectives when budgeting? Besides, you can prove anything with figures. Just look at the budget prepared by the Management Accountant compared with the annual budget prepared by Mike Barratt.'

Anne Darcy then turns to you. 'We need to resolve these issues. Will you please write a short report to the Board members giving us your advice.'

Task

In response to Anne Darcy's request, you are asked to write a short report drawing on the information given above. The report should do the following.

(i) Recalculate the flexible budget based on production at 95% capacity assuming fixed overheads in finished stock are based on 80% activity.

(ii) Explain why the revised flexible budget may differ from the one prepared in task (a).

(iii) Answer the issues raised by Alan Williams regarding the two different budget statements, the uncertainty about budgetary objectives and the manipulation of budget data.

(iv) Briefly discuss whether or not Anne Darcy should have been responsible for preparing the original budget.

47 **CLUB ATLANTIC (45 mins)** *U12, 12/96*

(a) Club Atlantic is an all-weather holiday complex providing holidays throughout the year. The fee charged to guests is fully inclusive of accommodation and all meals. However, because the holiday industry is so competitive, Club Atlantic is only able to generate profits by maintaining strict financial control of all activities.

The club's restaurant is one area where there is a constant need to monitor costs. Susan Green is the manager of the restaurant. At the beginning of each year, she is given an annual budget which is then broken down into months. Each month, she receives a statement monitoring actual costs against the actual budget and highlighting any variances. The statement for the month ended 31 October 20X8 is reproduced below along with a list of assumptions.

Club Atlantic Restaurant Performance Statement - Month to 31 October 20X8

	Actual	Budget	Variance (Over)/under
Number of guest days	11,160	9,600	(1,560)
	£	£	£
Food	20,500	20,160	(340)
Cleaning materials	2,232	1,920	(312)
Heat, light and power	2,050	2,400	350
Catering wages	8,400	7,200	(1,200)
Rent, rates, insurance and depreciation	1,860	1,800	(60)
	35,042	33,480	(1,562)

Assumptions

- The budget has been calculated on the basis of a 30-day calendar month with the cost of rents, rates, insurance and depreciation being an apportionment of the fixed annual charge.

- The budgeted catering wages assume there is one member of the catering staff for every forty guests staying at the complex and the daily cost of a member of the catering staff is £30.

- All other budgeted costs are variable costs based on the number of guest days.

Task

Using the data above, prepare a revised performance statement using flexible budgeting. Your statement should show both the revised budget and the revised variances.

(b) Club Atlantic uses the existing budgets and performance statements to motivate its managers as well as for financial control. If managers keep expenses below budget, they receive a bonus in addition to their salaries. A colleague of Susan's is Brian Hilton. Brian is in charge of the swimming pool and golf course, both of which have high levels of fixed costs. Each month, he manages to keep expenses below budget and, in return, enjoys regular bonuses. Under the current reporting system, Susan Green only rarely receives a bonus.

At a recent meeting with Club Atlantic's directors, Susan Green expressed concern that the performance statement was not a valid reflection of her management of the restaurant. You are currently employed by Hall and Co, the club's auditors, and the directors of Club Atlantic have asked you to advise them whether there is any justification for Susan Green's concern.

At the meeting with the Club's directors, you were asked the following questions.

(i) Do budgets motivate managers to achieve objectives?

(ii) Does motivating managers lead to improved performance?

(iii) Does the current method of reporting performance motivate Susan Green and Brian Hilton to be more efficient?

Task

Write a *brief* letter to the directors of Club Atlantic addressing their questions and justifying your answers.

Note. You should make use of the data given in this task plus your findings from task (a).

48   VIKING SMELTING COMPANY (70 mins)

(a)   The Viking Smelting Company established a division, called the reclamation division, in April 1995, to extract silver from jewellers' waste materials. The waste materials are processed in a furnace, enabling silver to be recovered. The silver is then further processed into finished products by three other divisions within the company.

A performance report is prepared each month for the reclamation division which is then discussed by the management team. Sharon Houghton, the newly appointed financial controller of the reclamation division, has recently prepared her first report for the four weeks to 31 May 20X8. This is shown below.

Performance Report - Reclamation Division - 4 weeks to 31 May 20X8

	Actual	Budget	Variance	Comments
Production (tonnes)	200	250	50 (A)	
	£	£	£	
Wages and social security costs	46,133	45,586	547 (A)	Overspend
Fuel	15,500	18,750	3,250 (F)	
Consumables	2,100	2,500	400 (F)	
Power	1,590	1,750	160 (F)	
Divisional overheads	21,000	20,000	1,000 (A)	Overspend
Plant maintenance	6,900	5,950	950 (A)	Overspend
Central services	7,300	6,850	450 (A)	Overspend
Total	100,523	101,386	863 (F)	

(A) = adverse, (F) = favourable

In preparing the budgeted figures, the following assumptions were made for May.

(i)   The reclamation division was to employ four teams of six production employees.

(ii)   Each employee was to work a basic 42 hour week and be paid £7.50 per hour for the four weeks of May.

(iii)   Social security and other employment costs were estimated at 40% of basic wages.

(iv)   A bonus, shared amongst the production employees, was payable if production exceeded 150 tonnes. This varied depending on the output achieved.

     (1)   If output was between 150 and 199 tonnes, the bonus was £3 per tonne produced.

     (2)   If output was between 200 and 249 tonnes, the bonus was £8 per tonne produced.

     (3)   If output exceeded 249 tonnes the bonus was £13 per tonne produced.

(v)   The cost of fuel was £75 per tonne.

(vi)   Consumables were £10 per tonne.

(vii)   Power comprised a fixed charge of £500 per four weeks plus £5 per tonne for every tonne produced.

(viii) Overheads directly attributable to the division were £20,000.

(ix)   Plant maintenance was to be apportioned to divisions on the basis of the capital values of each division.

(x)   The cost of Viking's central services was to be shared equally by all four divisions.

You are the deputy financial controller of the reclamation division. After attending her first monthly meeting with the board of the reclamation division, Sharon Houghton arranges a meeting with you. She is concerned about a number of issues, one of them being that the current report does not clearly identify those expenses and variances which are the direct responsibility of the reclamation division.

Task

Sharon Houghton asks you to prepare a flexible budget report for the reclamation division for May 20X8 in a form consistent with responsibility accounting.

(b) On receiving your revised report, Sharon tells you about the other questions raised at the management meeting when the original report was presented. These are summarised below.

(i) Why are the budgeted figures based on two year old data taken from the proposal recommending the establishment of the reclamation division?

(ii) Should the budget data be based on what we are proposing to do or what we actually did do?

(iii) Is it true that the less we produce the more favourable our variances will be?

(iv) Why is there so much maintenance in a new division with modern equipment and why should we be charged with the actual costs of the maintenance department even when they overspend?

(v) Could the comments explaining variances be improved?

(vi) Should all the variances be investigated?

(vii) Does showing the cost of central services on the divisional performance report help control these costs and motivate the divisional managers?

Task

Prepare a memo for the management of the reclamation division. Your memo should:

(i) answer their queries and justify your comments;

(ii) highlight the main objective of your revised performance report developed in task (a) and give two advantages of it over the original report.

49 VECSTAR LTD (70 mins)

U12, 6/98

(a) Vecstar Ltd produces and sells a single product, the Alpha. The company uses an accounting software package which calculates variances by comparing the fixed budget for the year against actual expenditure. For accounting purposes, the company divides its year into 13, four-weekly periods. The report for the four weeks ended 29 May 20X8 is reproduced below.

Vecstar Ltd Performance Report for four weeks ended 29 May 20X8				
		Actual	*Budget*	*Variance*
Units produced:		60,000	48,000	12,000 F
		£	£	£
Variable costs:	Material	18,546	12,480	6,066 A
	Labour	7,200	5,760	1,440 A
Semi-variable costs:	Power	900	1,060	160 F
	Maintenance	1,600	1,680	80 F
Fixed costs:	Supervision	3,400	3,440	40 F
	Rent and insurance	2,050	1,820	230 A
	Depreciation	4,000	4,000	
Total		37,696	30,240	7,456 A
Key: A = adverse; F = favourable				

You are employed as an accounting technician by Green and Co, the auditors to Vecstar Ltd. On a recent visit to Vecstar, you suggested to James Close, the company's managing director, that the variances calculated by the software package are likely to be misleading and that a system of flexible budgeting would produce more meaningful management information.

James tells you that the following assumptions were made when preparing the budget.

- The four-weekly cost of power was estimated at £100 and the additional cost of power per Alpha produced was estimated at 2p.

- The fixed cost of maintenance was estimated at £1,200 per four weeks and 1p per Alpha produced.

- The annual fixed overhead absorption rate is 20p per Alpha. This was derived by adding the budgeted fixed costs to the fixed element of the budgeted semi-variable costs and dividing by the normal annual production.

Tasks

(i)   Prepare a flexible budget statement for the four weeks to 29 May 20X8.

(ii)   Estimate the normal ANNUAL production of Alphas used to determine the fixed overhead absorption rate.

(b) When you present James Close with the revised budget, he writes to tell you that he cannot understand why some budgeted costs have changed but others have remained the same as in the original fixed budget. In addition, he is concerned that the budgeted cost data becomes increasingly inaccurate, the closer the accounting period is to the year end. By way of example, he gives you the following general indices of production costs.

- Index when budget prepared   160.00
- Index at commencement of accounting year   162.40
- Average index for four weeks ended 26 June 20X8 (estimated) 165.12

Finally James is disappointed that the revised report no longer highlights the variations in the units produced between original budget and actual. For May 20X8, production increased by 25% from 48,000 to 60,000 units but this has been largely ignored.

Tasks

Prepare a letter to James Close. Your letter should:

(i)   *briefly* explain why in the flexible budget, some budgeted costs have remained the same while others have altered;

(ii)   estimate the *total cost* of producing 62,000 Alphas in the four weeks to 26 June using your answer in task (a) and the indices given above;

(iii) give ONE possible reason why the index used may not be an appropriate one for Vecstar Ltd;

(iv)   suggest ONE way of expressing in a meaningful form for management the variation between original budgeted units and actual units produced.

50   MAYFIELD SCHOOL (50 mins)   *U12, 6/98*

(a) Jim Smith has recently been appointed as the Head Teacher of Mayfield School in Midshire. The age of the pupils ranges from 11 yeas to 18 years. For many years, Midshire County Council was responsible for preparing and reporting on the school budget. From June 20X8, however, these responsibilities passed to the Head Teacher of Mayfield School.

You have recently accepted a part-time appointment as the accountant to Mayfield School, although your previous accounting experience has been gained in commercial organisations. Jim Smith is hoping that you will be able to apply that experience to improving the financial reporting procedures at Mayfield School.

The last budget statement prepared by Midshire County Council is reproduced below. It covers the ten months to the end of May 20X8 and all figures refer to cash *payments* made.

Midshire County Council				Mayfield School
Statement of school expenditure against budget: 10 months August 20X7-May 20X8				
	Expenditure to date	*Budget to date*	*Under/ overspend*	*Total budget for year*
Teachers - full time	1,680,250	1,682,500	2,250 Cr	2,019,000
Teachers - part time	35,238	34,600	638	41,520
Other employee expenses	5,792	15,000	9,208 Cr	18,000
Administrative staff	69,137	68,450	687	82,140
Caretaker and cleaning	49,267	57,205	7,938 Cr	68,646
Resources (books etc)	120,673	100,000	20,673	120,000
Repairs and maintenance	458	0	458	0
Lighting and hearing	59,720	66,720	7,000 Cr	80,064
Rates	23,826	19,855	3,971	23,826
Fixed assets: furniture and equipment	84,721	100,000	15,279 Cr	120,000
Stationery, postage and phone	1,945	0	1,945	0
Miscellaneous expenses	9,450	6,750	2,700	8,100
Total	2,140,477	2,151,080	10,603 Cr	2,581,296

Tasks

Write a memo to Jim Smith. Your memo should:

(i)   identify FOUR weaknesses of the existing statement as a management report;

(ii) include an improved OUTLINE statement format showing revised column headings and a more meaningful classification of costs which will help Jim Smith to manage his school effectively (FIGURES ARE NOT REQUIRED);

(iii) give TWO advantages of your proposed format over the existing format.

(b) The income of Mayfield School is based on the number of pupils at the school. Jim Smith provides you with the following breakdown of student numbers.

Mayfield School: Student numbers as at 31 May 20X8		
School year	*Age range*	*Current number of pupils*
1	11-12	300
2	12-13	350
3	13-14	325
4	14-15	360
5	15-16	380
6	16-17	240
7	17-18	220
Total number of students		2,175

Jim also provides you with the following information relating to existing pupils.

•   Pupils move up one school year at the end of July.

- For those pupils entering year 6, there is an option to leave the school. As a result only 80% of the current school-year 5 pupils go on to enter school-year 6.

- Of those currently in school-year 6 only 95% continue into school-year 7.

- Pupils currently in school-year 7 leave to go on to higher education or employment.

- The annual income per pupil is £1,200 in years 1 to 5 and £1,500 in years 6 to 7.

The new year 1 pupils come from the final year at four junior schools. Not all pupils, however, elect to go to Mayfield School. Jim has investigated this matter and derived accurate estimates of the proportion of final year pupils at each of the four junior schools who go on to attend Mayfield School.

The number of pupils in the final year at each of the four junior schools is given below along with Jim's estimate of the proportion likely to choose Mayfield School.

Junior school	*Number in final year at 31 May 20X8*	*Proportion choosing Mayfield School*
Ranmoor	60	0.9
Hallamshire	120	0.8
Broomhill	140	0.9
Endcliffe	80	0.5

Tasks

(i)   Forecast the number of pupils and the income of Mayfield School for the year August 20X8 to July 20X9.

(ii) Assuming expenditure next year is 5% more than the current annual budgeted expenditure, calculate the budgeted surplus or deficit of Mayfield School for next year.

51   HAPPY HOLIDAYS LTD (90 mins)   *U12, 12/98*

(a) Happy Holidays Ltd sells holidays to Xanadu through newspaper advertisements. Tourists are flown each week of the holiday season to Xanadu, where they take a 10 day touring holiday. In 20X8, Happy Holidays began to use the least-squares regression formula to help forecast the demand for its holidays.

You are employed by Happy Holidays as an accounting technician in the financial controller's department. A colleague of yours has recently used the least-squares regression formula on a spreadsheet to estimate the demand for holidays per year. The resulting formula was y = 640 + 40x, where y is the annual demand and x is the year. The data started with the number of holidays sold in 20X1 and was identified in the formula as year 1. In each subsequent year the value of x increases by 1 so, for example, 20X6 was year 6. To obtain the *weekly* demand the result is divided by 25, the number of weeks Happy Holidays operates in Xanadu.

Tasks

(i)   Use the least-squares regression formula developed by your colleague to estimate the weekly demand for holidays in Xanadu for 20X9.

(ii) In preparation for a budget meeting with the financial controller, draft a *brief* note. Your note should identify THREE weaknesses of the least-squares regression formula in forecasting the weekly demand of holidays in Xanadu.

(b) The budget and actual costs for holidays to Xanadu for the 10 days ended 27 November 20X8 is reproduced below.

<table>
<tr><td colspan="4">Happy Holidays Ltd Cost Statement
10 days ended 27 November 20X8</td></tr>
</table>

	Fixed budget	Actual	Variances
	£	£	£
Aircraft seats	18,000	18,600	600 A
Coach hire	5,000	4,700	300 F
Hotel rooms	14,000	14,200	200 A
Meals	4,800	4,600	200 F
Tour guide	1,800	1,700	100 F
Advertising	2,000	1,800	200 F
Total costs	45,600	45,600	0

Key: A = adverse, F = favourable

The financial controller gives you the following additional information.

Cost and volume information

- Each holiday lasts 10 days.

- Meals and hotel rooms are provided for each of the 10 days.

- The airline charges £450 per return flight per passenger for each holiday but the airline will only sell seats at this reduced price if Happy Holidays purchases seats in blocks of 20.

- The costs of coach hire, the tour guide and advertising are fixed costs.

- The cost of meals was budgeted at £12 per tourist per day.

- The cost of a single room was budgeted at £60 per day.

- The cost of a double room was budgeted at £70 per day.

- 38 tourists travelled on the holiday requiring 17 double rooms and 4 single rooms.

Sales information

- The price of a holiday is £250 more if using a single room.

Task

Write a memo to the financial controller. Your memo should:

(i)   take account of the cost and volume information to prepare a revised cost statement using flexible budgeting and identifying any variances;

(ii)   state and justify which of the two cost statements is more useful for management control of costs;

(iii) identify THREE factors to be taken into account in deciding whether or not to investigate individual variances.

---

52   PROFESSOR PAULINE HEATH (70 mins)   *Specimen central assessment*

It is 1 March and Professor Pauline Heath has just taken up her new appointment as the head of the postgraduate business department in a new university. Due to unfilled vacancies throughout the current academic year, the department has had to rely on part-time academic staff. The cost of part-time staff who are self-employed is coded to account number 321, while those who are taxed under the pay-as-you-earn system are charged to account code 002. Both types of staff enter their claims within ten days of each month-end and these then appear in the management reports of the subsequent month. There are also unfilled clerical and administrative staff vacancies.

The university has a residential conference centre which the department makes use of from time to time. Sometimes this is because the department's allocated rooms are all in use and sometimes because the department teaches at weekends. The charge for the use of the centre is coded to account 673. An alternative to using the conference centre is to hire outside facilities at local hotels in which case the expenditure is coded to account 341.

The main forms of income are tuition fees and higher education grant from the government. The extent of this grant is known before the commencement of the academic year and is payable in two parts, one third at the end of December and the balance at the end of April.

One of Professor Heath's first tasks was to check the enrolments for the current year. The financial and academic year commenced 1 September and is subdivided into three terms, each lasting four months. The Autumn term commenced 1 September and the Spring term 1 January. All courses commence at the beginning of the Autumn term, the MBA and MSc courses lasting three terms and the diploma course two terms.

The departmental administrator has presented Professor Heath with the enrolment data for the current academic year. Whilst absorbing this information, she also receives the latest management accounts for the department. Both sets of information are reproduced below.

Professor Heath is experiencing difficulties in understanding the latest management report. She has written a memo to the university's finance director expressing her anxieties about the presentation of the report and its detailed contents.

Enrolment data - current academic year	*Fee* £	*Enrolments*	*Income* £
MBA - three terms	3,500	160	560,000
MSc - three terms	3,200	80	256,000
Diploma Course - two terms	1,200	100	120,000
			936,000

DEPARTMENT OF POSTGRADUATE BUSINESS STUDIES
MONTHLY MANAGEMENT REPORT - FEBRUARY

Code	Account heading	*Annual budget*	*Actual*	*Budget*	*Variance*	*Budget remaining*
			\multicolumn 6 months to 28 February			
	Expenses					
001	Full-time academic	600,000	230,000	300,000	70,000	370,000
002	Part-time academic	84,000	48,000	42,000	–6,000	36,000
003	Clerical and administrative	84,000	36,000	42,000	6,000	48,000
218	Teaching and learning material	30,000	0	15,000	15,000	30,000
321	Teaching and research fees	20,000	19,000	10,000	–9,000	1,000
331	Agency staff (clerical and administrative)	300	2,400	150	–2,250	–2,100
341	External room hire	1,000	400	500	100	600
434	Course advertising (Press)	26,000	600	13,000	12,400	25,400
455	Postage and telephone recharge	8,000	1,200	4,000	2,800	6,800
673	Internal room hire	24,000	14,000	12,000	–2,000	10,000
679	Central services recharge	340,000	170,000	170,000	0	170,000
680	Rental light and heat recharge	260,000	130,000	130,000	0	130,000
		1,477,300	651,600	738,650	87,050	825,700
	Income					
802	Tuition fees	900,000	936,000	900,000	–36,000	–36,000
890	Higher education grant	750,000	250,000	250,000	0	500,000
		1,650,000	1,186,000	1,150,000	–36,000	464,000
	Net surplus/deficit	172,700	534,400	411,350	–123,050	–361,700

Tasks

(a) (i) Rearrange the account headings in a more meaningful form for managers. This should include columnar headings for any financial data you feel is appropriate but you DO NOT need to include any figures.

(ii) Briefly justify your proposals.

(b) In her memo, Professor Heath states that the current form of report does not help her manage her department. Identify the strengths and weaknesses apparent in the current system, other than the presentational ones covered in Task (a), and make and justify outline proposals which will help her manage the department.

(c) Referring to the detailed financial data under the heading of INCOME above, reproduce the actual income to date in a form consistent with accounting principles.

All working should be shown.

53 COLOUR PLC (105 mins)   *12/98*

(a) Colour plc has two more subsidiaries, Red Ltd and Green Ltd. Red Ltd makes only one product, a part only used by Green Ltd. Because Green is the only customer and there is no market price for the part, the part is sold to Green at cost.

Last year, Red prepared two provisional budgets because Green was not certain how many parts it would buy from Red in the current year. These two budgets are reproduced below.

Red Ltd provisional budgets - 12 months to 30 November 20X8		
Volume (units)	18,000	20,000
	£	£
Material	180,000	200,000
Labour	308,000	340,000
Power and maintenance	33,000	35,000
Rent, insurance and depreciation	98,000	98,000
Total cost	619,000	673,000

Shortly afterwards, Green told Red that it needed 20,000 parts over the year to 30 November 20X8. Red's budget for the year was then based on that level of production.

During the financial year, Green Ltd only bought 19,500 parts. Red's performance statement for the year to 30 November 20X8 is reproduced below.

Red Ltd performance statement - year to 30 November 20X8			
	Budget	*Actual*	*Variances*
Volume (units)	20,000	19,500	
	£	£	£
Material	200,000	197,000	3,000 (F)
Labour	340,000	331,000	9,000 (F)
Power and maintenance	35,000	35,000	-
Rent, insurance and depreciation	98,000	97,500	500 (F)
Total cost	673,000	660,500	12,500 (F)
Key: (F) = favourable, (A) = adverse			

Tasks

(i)   Using the data in the provisional budgets, calculate the fixed and variable cost elements within each of the expenditure headings.

(ii)   Using the data in the performance statement and your solution to part (i), prepare a revised performance statement using flexible budgeting. Your statement should show both the revised budget and the variances.

(b)   Colour plc is about to introduce performance-related payments for senior managers in the three subsidiaries. The purpose is to motivate senior managers to improve performance.

For Red Ltd, the additional payments will be based on two factors.

*   Achieving or exceeding annual budgeted volumes of production set by the Board of Directors of Colour plc at the beginning of the year

*   Keeping unit costs below budget

Tony Brown, the managing director of Red Ltd, is about to call a meeting of his senior managers to discuss the implications of the proposals. He is not certain that performance-related pay will automatically lead to improved performance in the subsidiaries. Even if it does, he is not certain that performance-related pay will help *his* subsidiary improve performance.

Task

Write a memo to Tony Brown. Your memo should identify the following.

(i)   THREE general conditions necessary for performance-related pay to lead to improved performance

(ii)   TWO reasons why the particular performance scheme might not be appropriate for the senior management of Red Ltd

(iii)   ONE example where it would be possible for the managers of Red Ltd to misuse the proposed system by achieving performance-related pay without extra effort on their part

54   RIVERMEDE LTD (95 mins)   6/99

(a)   Rivermede Ltd makes a single product called the Fasta. Last year, Steven Jones, the managing director of Rivermede Ltd, attended a course on budgetary control. As a result, he agreed to revise the way budgets were prepared in the company. Rather than imposing targets for managers, he encouraged participation by senior managers in the preparation of budgets.

An initial budget was prepared but Mike Fisher, the sales director, felt that the budgeted sales volume was set too high. He explained that setting too high a budgeted sales volume would mean that his sales staff would be de-motivated because they would not be able to achieve the sales volume. Steven Jones agreed to use the revised sales volume suggested by Mike Fisher.

Both the initial and revised budgets are reproduced below complete with the actual results for the year ended 31 May 20X5.

Rivermede Ltd – budgeted and actual costs for the year ended 31 May 20X5

	Original budget	Revised budget	Actual results	Variances from revised budget
Fasta production and sales (units)	24,000	20,000	22,000	2,000 (F)
	£	£	£	£
Variable costs				
Material	216,000	180,000	206,800	26,800 (A)
Labour	288,000	240,000	255,200	15,200 (A)
Semi-variable costs				
Heat, light and power	31,000	27,000	33,400	6,400 (A)
Fixed costs				
Rent, rates and depreciation	40,000	40,000	38,000	2,000 (F)
	575,000	487,000	533,400	46,400 (A)

Assumptions in the two budgets

1 No change in input prices
2 No change in the quantity of variable inputs per Fasta

As the management accountant at Rivermede Ltd, one of your tasks is to check that invoices have been properly coded. On checking the actual invoices for heat, light and power for the year to 31 May 20X5, you find that one invoice for £7,520 had been incorrectly coded. The invoice should have been coded to materials.

Tasks

(i) Using the information in the original and revised budgets, identify the following.

    (1) The variable cost of material and labour per Fasta
    (2) The fixed and unit variable cost within heat, light and power

(ii) Prepare a flexible budget, including variances, for Rivermede Ltd after correcting for the miscoding of the invoice.

(b) On receiving your flexible budget statement, Steven Jones states that the total adverse variance is much less than the £46,400 shown in the original statement. He also draws your attention to the actual sales volume being greater than in the revised budget. He believes these results show that a participative approach to budgeting is better for the company and wants to discuss this belief at the next board meeting. Before doing so, Steven Jones asks for your comments.

Task

Write a memo to Steven Jones. Your memo should do the following.

(i) *Briefly* explain why the flexible budgeting variances differ from those in the original statement given in the data to task (a).

(ii) Give TWO reasons why a favourable cost variance may have arisen other than through the introduction of participative budgeting.

(iii) Give TWO reasons why the actual sales volume compared with the revised budget's sales volume may not be a measure of improved motivation following the introduction of participative budgeting.

55   **BOARD OF MANAGEMENT (30 mins)**

Eskafield Industrial Museum opened ten years ago and soon became a market leader with many working exhibits. In the early years there was a rapid growth in the number of visitors but with no further investment in new exhibits, this growth has not been maintained in recent years.

Two years ago, John Derbyshire was appointed as the museum's chief executive. His initial task was to increase the number of visitors to the museum and, following his appointment, he had made several improvements to make the museum more successful.

Another of John's tasks is to provide effective financial management. This year the museum's Board of Management has asked him to take full responsibility for producing the 20X9 budget. He has asked you to prepare estimates of the number of visitors next year.

Shortly after receiving your notes, John Derbyshire contacts you. He explains that he had prepared a draft budget for the Board of Management based on the estimated numbers for 20X9. This had been prepared on the basis that:

- most of the museum's expenses such as salaries and rates are fixed costs;

- the museum has always budgeted for a deficit;

- the 20X9 deficit will be £35,000.

At the meeting with the Board of Management, John was congratulated on bringing the deficit down from £41,000 in 20X7 to £37,000 (latest estimate) in 20X8. However, the Board of Management raised two issues.

- They felt that the planned deficit of £35,000 should be reduced to £29,000 as this would represent a greater commitment.

- They also queried why the budget had been prepared without any consultation with the museum staff, ie a top down approach.

Task

Draft a memo to John Derbyshire. Your memo should:

(a)   discuss the motivational implications of imposing the budget reduction from £35,000 to £29,000;

(b)   consider the arguments for and against using a top-down budgeting approach for the museum.

56   **GOVERNMENT DEPARTMENT (35 mins)**

You work as a finance officer in a small organisation which has very recently changed its status from that of a government department to an autonomous agency responsible to government but given considerable new powers of self direction and management with a duty to finance future operations by charging for its services. The budgetary planning and control system in your organisation has been centrally managed and controlled by the chief executive and was typically set by using the previous year's expenditure adjusted for any change in inflation and any change to the government grant which was used to finance operations.

Your chief executive has just come back from a management seminar at which suggestions of moving away from a purely incremental development of budgets and also the use of delegating budget responsibility was seen as necessary to support the new culture of self management which the change in organisational status implied.

Your chief executive does not have a financial background and is unsure of the implications of such changes.

Task

Provide a briefing paper to your chief executive which explains the role the budget should have in the newly constituted organisation, the management development implications of a move from centrally held to delegated budget responsibility and how the use of a zero base budget review might be used to improve the process of budget development.

57 ACCOUNTANCY COLLEGE (35 mins)

You have been approached by a principal of an accountancy college that is going to teach the AAT, to advise them on the financial implications of their plans for their first year of operation.

You ascertain that the college staff will consist of the principal, an administration department under the control of a deputy principal and two departments, accounting and business studies, each of these under a head of department. The teaching will be provided by staff within the departments.

The principal gives you the following projected information for the first year. He is rather proud of his estimates, having referred to nobody else in the college.

Level	Number of students	Fee per student £
Foundation	400	2,000
Intermediate	300	3,000
Technician	250	4,000

For the foundation and intermediate stages you are told that there are to be 20 students in each class and for the technician level there are to be ten students in each class. The college year will consist of 30 weeks tuition and each class will have the following.

Level	Hours tuition per week	Tuition cost per class hour £
Foundation	16	20
Intermediate	20	22
Technician	22	24

Tasks

(a) Prepare budgets showing the following information for the college's first year of operation.

   (i) College revenue by level and in total
   (ii) Number of classes required at each level
   (iii) Tuition costs for each level and in total
   (iv) Total student hours and the tuition cost per student hour at each level

(b) Acting upon the information given, evaluate the principal's method of budgeting and advise him of any alternative course of action for year 2 so that he maximises the benefit that a system of budgeting and budgetary control can bring.

58 WORLD HISTORY MUSEUM (60 mins) *U12, 6/94*

The World History Museum has an education department which specialises in running courses in various subjects. The courses are run on premises which the museum rents for the purpose and they are presented by freelance expert speakers. Each course is of standard type and format and can therefore be treated alike for budgetary control purposes.

The museum currently uses fixed budgets to control expenditure. The following data show the actual costs of the education department for the month of April compared with the budgeted figures.

EDUCATION DEPARTMENT - APRIL

	Actual	Budget	Variance
Number of courses run	5	6	(1)
	£	£	£
Expenditure			
Speakers' fees	2,500	3,180	680
Hire of premises	1,500	1,500	-
Depreciation of equipment	200	180	(20)
Stationery	530	600	70
Catering	1,500	1,750	250
Insurance	700	820	120
Administration	1,650	1,620	(30)
	8,580	9,650	1,070

You have recently started work as the assistant management accountant for the museum. During a discussion with Chris Brooks, the general manager, she expresses to you some doubt about the usefulness of the above statement in providing control information for the education department manager.

Chris is interested in the possibility of using flexible budgets to control the activities of the education department. You therefore spend some time analysing the behaviour patterns of the costs incurred in the education department. Your findings can be summarised as follows.

- Depreciation of equipment is a fixed cost.

- Administration is a fixed cost.

- The budget figures for the catering costs and insurance costs include a fixed element as follows.

    Catering £250
    Insurance £100

    The remaining elements of the catering and insurance costs follow linear variable patterns.

- All other costs follow linear variable patterns.

Tasks

(a) Use the above information to produce a budgetary control statement for April, based on a flexible budget for the actual number of courses run.

(b) Calculate the revised variances based on your flexible budget.

(c) Chris Brooks's interest in the control aspects of budgeting has been sparked by her attendance on a course entitled 'Budgetary control for managers'. She has shown you the following extract from the course notes she was given.

    'A system of participative budgeting involves managers in the process of setting their own budgets. Participative systems are likely to be more successful in planning and controlling the activities of an organisation.'

    Write a brief memo to Chris Brooks which explains the advantages and disadvantages of participative budgeting as part of the budgetary planning and control process.

59

59 PRACTICE QUESTION: COST REDUCTION

You work for a division of a multi-national organisation. Head office have informed you that your division must implement a cost reduction exercise.

Tasks

(a) Distinguish between cost control and cost reduction.

(b) Give TWO examples *each* of the techniques and principles used for (i) cost control and (ii) cost reduction.

60 PRACTICE QUESTION: QUALITY

You work for a small engineering company. Your managing director is keen to implement a total quality management programme and has asked you to provide some information.

Task

List some of the techniques of quality control used within manufacturing industries.

61 LOCAL ENGINEERING LTD (50 mins) *U11, 6/96*

(a) You are employed as the assistant management accountant with Local Engineering Ltd, a company which designs and makes a single product, the X4, used in the telecommunications industry. The company has a goods received store which employs staff who carry out random checks to ensure materials are of the correct specification. In addition to the random checks, a standard allowance is made for failures due to faulty materials at the completion stage and the normal practice is to charge the cost of any remedial work required to the cost of production for the month. Once delivered to the customer, any faults discovered in the X4 during its warranty period become an expense of the customer support department.

At the end of each month, management reports are prepared for the Board of Directors. These identify the cost of running the stores and the number of issues, the cost of production and the number of units manufactured, and the cost of customer support.

Jane Greenwood, Local Engineering's management accountant, has just returned from a board meeting to discuss a letter the company recently received from Universal Telecom, Local Engineering's largest customer. In the letter, Universal Telecom explained that it was determined to maintain its position as a world-class provider of telecommunication services and that there was serious concern about the quality of the units delivered by your company. At the meeting, Local Engineering Ltd's board responded by agreeing to establish a company-wide policy of implementing a Total Quality Management (TQM) programme, commencing with a revised model of the X4. Design work on the new model is scheduled to commence in six month's time.

One aspect of this will involve the management accounting department collecting the *cost of quality*. This is defined as the total of all costs incurred in preventing defects plus those costs involved in remedying defects once they have occurred within the accounting system – attributable to producing output that is not within its specification.

Task

As a first step towards the implementation of TQM, a meeting of the senior staff in the management accounting department has been called to discuss the role the department can play in making TQM a success. Jane Greenwood has asked you to prepare a *brief* background paper for the meeting.

Your paper should do the following.

(i) Explain in outline what is meant by Total Quality Management.

(ii) Briefly discuss why the current accounting system fails to highlight the *cost of quality*.

(iii) Identify FOUR general categories (or classifications) of Local Engineering's activities where expenditure making up the explicit *cost of quality* will be found.

(iv) Give ONE example of a cost found within each category.

(v) Give ONE example of a *cost of quality* not normally identified by the accounting system.

(b) Local Engineering Ltd has capacity to produce no more than 1,000 X4s per month and currently is able to sell all production immediately at a unit selling price of £1,250. A major component of the X4 is a complex circuit board. Spot checks are made on these boards by a team of specialist employees when they are received into stores. In May, 100 units were found to be faulty. Good components are then issued to production along with other material.

Upon completion, each X4 is tested. If there is a fault, this involves further remedial work prior to dispatch to customers. For the month of May, 45 units of the X4 had to be reworked because of subsequent faults discovered in the circuit board. This remedial work cost an additional £13,500 in labour charges.

Should a fault occur after delivery to the customer, Local Engineering is able to call upon a team of self-employed engineers to rectify the fault as part of its customer support function. The cost of the remedial work by the self-employed engineers carried out in May – and the number of times they were used – is shown as contractors under customer support.

Extract from the accounting records of Local Engineering Ltd for the month of May

Stores			Production		
Purchases	*Units*	*£*		*Units*	*£*
Printed circuits	1,000	120,000	Printed circuits	900	108,000
Less returns	(100)	(12,000)	Other material		121,500
Net costs	900	108,000	Labour		193,500
Other material		121,500	Direct production		
Total purchases issued to			overhead		450,000
production		229,500	Cost of production		873,000
Other direct stores costs					
Goods received, labour costs		54,000	Customer support		
and rent					
Inspection costs		10,000	Direct costs		36,000
Costs of returns	100	4,500	Contractors	54	24,300
Costs of stores		68,500			60,300

Task

As part of the continuing development of Total Quality Management, you are asked by Jane Greenwood to calculate the following:

(i) The explicit *cost of quality* for Local Engineering Ltd for the month of May

(ii) A further *cost of quality* not reported in the above accounting records.

62 PRACTICE QUESTION: RATIO ANALYSIS

You work as assistant management accountant for Addison Ltd, which has the following abridged accounts for the past two years.

YEAR ENDED 30 NOVEMBER

	20X8 £	20X7 £
Sales	1,380,000	1,250,000
Direct materials	440,000	375,000
Direct wages	372,000	312,500
Production overheads	201,000	187,500
Selling and distribution overheads	101,000	91,000
Administration overheads	90,000	80,000
	1,204,000	1,046,000
Net profit	176,000	204,000

The following additional data are available.

Production staff	40	39
Selling and distribution staff	8	8
Administration staff	5	5
Capital employed	£2.2 m	£2 m

An analysis of costs gives the following breakdown between variable and fixed elements.

	20X8		20X7	
	Variable %	Fixed %	Variable %	Fixed %
Direct material	100	-	100	-
Direct wages	90	10	90	10
Production overhead	80	20	85	15
Selling and distribution overhead	70	30	65	35
Administration overhead	10	90	10	90

Tasks

(a) Calculate six ratios to compare the performance and profitability of the company in the two years.

(b) Comment on your calculations in (a).

63 PRACTICE QUESTION: PERFORMANCE MEASUREMENT

Your are employed as a management accountant in the head office of a chain of hotels.

Task

List measures of performance that should be used to monitor the performance of the managers in the hotel chain.

64 PRACTICE QUESTION: PERFORMANCE INDICATORS

The following information is available for your company.

	Division A		Division B	
	Year 1 £'000	Year 2 £'000	Year 1 £'000	Year 2 £'000
Stocks				
Value at end of year	300	400.0	440	480
Average stock value	280	336.0	390	390
Value of issues during year	689	695.0	2,000	2,106
Holding costs	40	46.5	108	105
Debtors				
Value at end of year	657	552.0	1,068	1,246
Turnover	4,000	4,200.0	6,000	6,500

Note. All sales are on credit.

The company uses a number of performance indicators.

Indicator	*Method of calculation*
Operating efficiency %	Holding cost/value of issues
Activity efficiency %	Average stock value/turnover
Turnover rate (times)	Value of issues/average stock value

In addition, your company finds that debtors turnover (in days) is useful.

Tasks

(a) Calculate the indicators and debtors turnover for each year to one decimal place.

(b) Comment briefly on your findings.

65   REGENT HOTEL (30 mins)   *U11, 6/95*

The Regent Hotel is experiencing some problems with its full-time employees. They have been complaining for some time that their weekly earnings are beginning to fall behind the amount which they could earn in other hotels in the area. In the past, pay rises have always been based approximately on the annual increase in the Retail Prices Index (RPI).

The new manager is keen to be fair in the rates that he pays and he has asked you as assistant to the management accountant to prepare some information to help him in negotiations with the employees. You have collected the following data.

Regent Hotel: average weekly earnings of full-time employees.

	£ per week
20X4	195
20X7	208

Source: Hotel records

Hotel and Catering Industry: index of average weekly earnings of full-time employees in UK

	Index number
20X4	173.4
20X7	191.2

Source: Trade Association Statistics

Tasks

(a) Calculate what the average weekly earnings of Regent Hotel's full-time employees would have been in 20X7 if, since 20X4, they had increased at the same rate as average earnings in the hotel and catering industry.

(b) Prepare a memorandum for the manager which contains the following.

    (i)   A statement of whether his employees are correct in claiming that their earnings have lagged behind the industry average

    (ii)   Two limitations of a comparison between the hotel's employees' earnings and the average for the hotel and catering industry

    (iii) An explanation of the Retail Prices Index (RPI), describing what the RPI is designed to show and the likely reason why the manager was using it as a basis for calculating wage increases

66   HOMELY LTD (50 mins)   *U11, 6/95*

Stately Hotels plc is considering an offer to buy a small privately owned chain of hotels, Homely Limited. In order to carry out an initial appraisal you have been provided with an abbreviated set of their accounts for 20X8.

Homely Limited - Profit and loss account
for the year ended 31 December 20X8 (extract)

	£'000
Turnover	820
Operating costs	754
Operating profit	66
Interest	4
Profit before tax	62
Taxation	18
Profit after tax	44
Dividends	22
Retained profits	22

Homely Limited - Balance sheet
as at 31 December 20X8 (extract)

	£'000
Fixed assets at net book value	230
Net current assets	70
Total assets	300
Long-term loans	50
	250
Shareholders' funds	250

Number of employees (full-time equivalents)	20
Numbers of rooms, each available for 365 nights	18
Number of room nights achieved in 20X8	5,900

Stately Hotels plc uses a number of key accounting ratios to monitor the performance of the group of hotels and of individual hotels in the chain. An extract from the target ratios for 20X8 is as follows.

Stately Hotels plc
Target ratios for 20X8 (extract)

- Return on capital employed, based on profit before interest and tax   26%

- Operating profit percentage   13%

- Asset turnover   2 times

- Working capital period $= \dfrac{\text{working capital}}{\text{operating costs}} \times 365$ 20 days

- Percentage room occupancy $= \dfrac{\text{number of room nights let}}{\text{number of room nights available}} \times 100\%$ 85%

- Turnover per employee (full-time equivalent)   £30,000

Tasks

(a) Calculate the six target ratios above based on Homely Limited's accounts and present them in a table which enables easy comparison with Stately Hotel's target ratios for 20X8.

(b) Prepare a memorandum for the management accountant of Stately Hotels plc, giving your initial assessment of Homely Limited based on a comparison of these ratios with

Stately Hotel's target ratios. Your memorandum should provide the following information for *each* of the six ratios.

(i) Comments on the performance of Homely Limited and suggestions about the management action which might be necessary to correct any apparent adverse performance

(ii) A discussion of any limitations in the use of the ratio for this performance comparison

67 TRADERS PLC (50 mins)

You are the assistant management accountant to Traders plc, a small retailing chain, and you have just left a meeting with the company's managing director who is concerned about the threat posed by the superior profitability of a major competitor, Sellars plc. Sellars have just published their annual report which shows profits of £1,956,760 generated by shareholders' funds of £5,765,000. A board meeting has been called for two weeks' time to discuss the board's development of a strategy to meet this threat. The summarised profit and loss accounts and balance sheets for both companies are reproduced below.

Trading and profit and loss accounts for the year ended 30 June 20X8

	Traders plc £	Sellars plc £
Turnover	24,000,000	26,800,000
Cost of sales	18,000,000	19,564,000
Gross profit	6,000,000	7,236,000
Administration expenses	4,060,000	4,330,000
Operating profit	1,940,000	2,906,000
Interest		150,000
Profit before taxation	1,940,000	2,756,000
Taxation	640,200	799,240
Profit after taxation	1,299,800	1,956,760
Dividends	800,000	1,200,000
Retained profits	499,800	756,760

Balance sheets as at 30 June 20X8

	Traders plc £	Sellars plc £
Fixed assets (see note 1)	4,320,000	5,270,000
Net current assets	1,500,000	1,995,000
Total assets	5,820,000	7,265,000
Long-term loans		1,500,000
	5,820,000	5,765,000
Financed by:		
Shareholders' funds	5,820,000	5,765,000
	5,820,000	5,765,000
Number of employees	170	200

Note 1

	Traders plc Cost £	Accumulated depreciation £	Net book value £	Sellars plc Cost £	Accumulated depreciation £	Net book value £
Fixed assets						
Land and buildings	5,000,000	1,200,000	3,800,000	12,000,000	7,200,000	4,800,000
Fixtures and fittings	800,000	480,000	320,000	700,000	350,000	350,000
Motor vehicles	400,000	200,000	200,000	600,000	480,000	120,000
Total	6,200,000	1,880,000	4,320,000	13,300,000	8,030,000	5,270,000

	Traders plc			Sellars plc		
	Land and buildings £	Fixtures and fittings £	Motor vehicles £	Land and buildings £	Fixtures and fittings £	Motor vehicles £
Depreciation charge for the year	100,000	160,000	100,000	240,000	70,000	120,000

Tasks

(a) The management accountant of Traders plc has already analysed your company's results, focusing on the following six key ratios.

Return on capital employed (before interest and taxation)	33.33%
Gross profit margin	25%
Net (or sales) margin (before interest and taxation)	8.08%
Asset turnover	4.12 times
Turnover per employee	£141,176
Average age of working capital	30 days

The average age of working capital is defined as $\dfrac{\text{Working capital}}{\text{Cost of sales}} \times 365$

As the assistant management accountant to Traders plc, you are asked to calculate the above ratios for Sellars plc. Present your results in the form of a table alongside the ratios for your own company.

(b) The turnover for Traders plc for the year to 30 June 20X7 was £23,000,000. A trade association index of retail prices stood at 224.50 for June 20X7 and 237.90 for June 20X8.

In anticipation of the board meeting, prepare a briefing paper for circulation to the directors of Traders plc.

Your paper should do the following.

(i)   Explain *in outline* the meaning and limitations of each ratio, making use of the given data where possible.

(ii)   Comment on any strengths and weaknesses found within Traders plc.

(iii) Use the trade association's statistics to show the percentage growth in Traders' sales volume since last year.

(iv)   Suggest two reasons why your estimate of sales volume growth might not be accurate.

68   FURNITURE PRODUCTS (35 mins)   *U11, 6/96*

William Jones heads the management accounting department of Gransden Ltd, a company which makes and retails a variety of furniture products. The company has recently been split into separate divisions. This restructuring had the full agreement of the Board of Directors, who viewed it as a way of giving responsibility to operating managers. Two functions, however, were deliberately retained at the centre: capital investment decisions and cash management.

Gransden's cash management system operates through a central accounting unit within the head office finance department. Divisions inform the unit when a creditor is to be paid. The unit then makes the necessary arrangements for the payment to be made. Similarly, although the divisions retain overall responsibility for credit control, all remittances from debtors are handled directly by the central accounting unit. As a result of this, each division's capital employed is defined as fixed assets plus current assets (other than cash) less current liabilities.

Two divisions, the Northern Division and the Southern Division, are entirely retailing operations. Over the last year, anxieties have been expressed about the Southern Division not adequately contributing to overall company profitability. Details of their results for the year to 31 May 20X8 and the relevant management ratios for the North division are reproduced below.

Operating results for the year ending 31 May 20X8

	North		South	
	£'000	£'000	£'000	£'000
Turnover		135,000		191,000
Opening stocks	25,000		55,000	
Purchases	75,000		105,000	
Closing stocks	20,000		40,000	
		80,000		120,000
Gross profit		55,000		71,000
Wages and salaries	10,000		12,000	
Depreciation	10,000		16,000	
Other costs	9,688		8,620	
		29,688		36,620
Operating profit for the year		25,312		34,380
Net assets				
Fixed assets		100,000		160,000
Depreciation		40,000		48,000
Net book value		60,000		112,000
Finished stocks		20,000		40,000
Debtors		16,875		47,750
Creditors		(12,500)		(8,750)
Capital employed		84,375		191,000

Management ratios for the North Division

Return on capital employed	30.00%	Average age of debtors	1.5 months
Gross profit margin	40.74%	Average age of stock	3 months
Sales margin (operating profit/turnover)	18.75%	Average age of creditors	2 months
Asset turnover	1.6 times		

Tasks

You are the Assistant Management Accountant. You are informed by the Management Accountant that the Board plans to investigate ways of improving the efficiency of the Southern Division and a meeting has been called for this purpose in one week's time.

William Jones has asked you to do the following.

(a) Calculate the relevant management ratios for the Southern Division.

(b) Estimate what the return on capital employed would have been for the Southern Divisions if:

(i)   it had achieved the same asset turnover as the Northern Division;

(ii)   it had the same average age of debtors, stock and creditors as the Northern Division.

Note. For the purpose of task (b)(i) only, you should assume that the wages and salaries, the depreciation and the other costs are all fixed costs and that stock, debtors and creditors remain unaltered.

(c) Identify TWO limitations to your analysis in tasks (a) and (b).

69 MIDDLE PLC (25 mins)

U11, 12/96

Middle plc owns two subsidiaries, East Ltd and West Ltd, producing soft drinks. Both companies rent their premises and both use plant of similar size and technology. Middle plc requires the plant in the subsidiaries to be written off over ten years using straight-line depreciation and assuming zero residual values.

East Ltd was established five years ago but West Ltd has only been established for two years. Goods returned by customers generally arise from quality failures and are destroyed. Financial and other data relating to the two companies are reproduced below.

Profit and loss accounts year to 30 November 20X8	West Ltd £'000	East Ltd £'000	Balance sheets extracts at 30 November 20X8	West Ltd £'000	East Ltd £'000
Turnover	18,000	17,600	Plant	16,000	10,000
less Returns	90	176	Depreciation to date	3,200	5,000
Net turnover	17,910	17,424	Net book value	12,800	5,000
Material	2,000	2,640	Current assets	4,860	3,000
Labour	4,000	4,840	Current liabilities	(2,320)	(1,500)
Production overheads*	3,000	3,080	Net assets	15,340	6,500
Gross profit	8,910	6,864			
Marketing	2,342	1,454			
Research & development	1,650	1,010			
Training	950	450			
Administration	900	1,155			
Operating profit	3,068	2,795			

*Includes plant depreciation of £1,600,000 for West Ltd and £1,000,000 for East Ltd

Other data (000's litres)	West Ltd	East Ltd
Gross sales	20,000	22,000
Returns	100	220
Net sales	19,900	21,780
Orders received in year	20,173	22,854

You are employed by Middle plc as a member of a team monitoring the performance of subsidiaries within the group. Middle plc aims to provide its shareholders with the best possible return for their investment and to meet customers' expectations. It does this by comparing the performance of subsidiaries and using the more efficient ones for benchmarking.

Tasks

Your team leader, Angela Wade, has asked you to prepare a report evaluating the performance of West Ltd and East Ltd. Your report should do the following.

(a) Calculate and explain the meaning of the following financial ratios for each company.

  (i)   The return on capital employed
  (ii) The asset turnover
  (iii) The sales (or operating profit) margin

(b) Calculate the percentage of faulty sales as a measure of the level of customer service for each company.

(c) Identify one other possible measure of the level of customer service which could be derived from the accounting data.

(d) Identify TWO limitations to your analysis in task (a), using the data in the accounts.

70 PETER SMITH (15 mins)
U11, 12/96

Peter Smith has recently been appointed as the chief executive to a charity undertaking scientific research. Previously, he had been a marketing manager for many years in a private sector commercial company.

The legal document establishing the charity states that it should operate in an efficient and effective manner. Peter Smith is unsure what these terms mean and has invited you, as a representative of the charity's auditors, to talk to his staff about efficiency and effectiveness in not-for-profit organisations.

Tasks

In preparing for the talk, you are asked to write a *brief* note. In the note you should do the following.

(a) Define what is meant by efficiency and effectiveness.

(b) Identify and justify ONE major way of measuring efficiency in commercial organisations.

(c) Explain why your chosen measure may not be appropriate in not-for-profit organisations.

(d) Suggest a substitute measure and comment on its limitations.

71 CAM CAR COMPANY (50 mins)
U11, 6/97

The Cam Car Company is a multinational manufacturer of motor vehicles. It operates two divisions, one producing cars and the other producing vans. You are employed as a management accountant in the van division. The labour content for each type of vehicle is very similar although the material content of a car is much greater than that of a van. Both divisions apply straight-line depreciation to fixed assets.

You have been asked to prepare information to be used in the company's annual wage negotiations. Each year, the van employee representatives make comparisons with the car division and one of your tasks is to calculate performance indicators for your division. Financial and other information relating to both divisions is reproduced below along with some of the relevant performance indicators for the car division.

Balance sheet extracts at 31 May 20X8

| | Van division | | | Car division | | |
| | Cost | Dep'n to date | Net | Cost | Dep'n to date | Net |
	£m	£m	£m	£m	£m	£m
Buildings at cost	500	400	100	1,200	240	960
Plant and machinery at cost	400	320	80	800	240	560
	900	720	180	2,000	480	1,520
Stock		60			210	
Trade debtors		210			285	
Cash		(140)			150	
Trade creditors		(30)			(265)	
			100			380
Net assets			280			1,900

Profit and loss accounts for year to 31 May 20X8

	Van division		Car division	
	£m	£m	£m	£m
Turnover		420		1,140
Materials and bought-in				
components	95		790	
Production labour	110		138	
Other production expenses	26		32	
Depreciation - buildings	10		24	
Depreciation - plant and				
machinery	40		80	
Administrative expenses	27		28	
		308		1,092
Profit		112		48

Other information

	Van division	Car division
Vehicles produced	50,000	84,000
Number of production employees	10,000	12,000

Yearly performance indicators for the car division

Return on capital employed	2.53%	Profit margin	4.21%
Asset turnover	0.6 times	Profit per employee	£4,000
Wages per employee	£11,500	Output per employee	7 vehicles
Production labour cost per unit	£1,643	Added value per employee	£29,167

Tasks

(a) You have been asked to calculate the yearly performance indicators for the van division and to present them in a table with the comparable figures for the car division.

(b) Shortly after preparing the performance indicators, you receive a telephone call from Peter Ross, a member of the management team. Peter explains that the employee representatives of the van division wish to negotiate an increase in wages. The representatives are arguing that employees in the van division are paid less than the equivalent staff in the car division despite the van division being more profitable. In addition, the representatives state that their productivity is higher than in the car division. Peter explains that he is not an accountant. He is not clear how productivity is measured nor what is meant by added value.

You are asked to write a memo to Peter Ross. The memo should do the following.

(i) Briefly explain what is meant by the following terms.

(1) Productivity
(2) Added value

(ii) Identify those performance indicators that could be used by the employees of the van division to justify their claims in terms of the following.

(1) Profitability
(2) Productivity

(iii) Give ONE example from the performance indicators that could be used to counter those claims and use the financial data given in task (a) to identify one possible limitation to the indicator.

(iv) Use BOTH the return on capital employed AND the added value per employee to show why the indicators calculated in task (a) might be overstated.

72 GRAND HOTEL (50 mins)

(a) The Grand Hotel is a privately-owned hotel and restaurant located in a major business and tourist centre. Because of this, demand for accommodation is spread evenly throughout the year. However, in order to increase overall demand, the Grand Hotel has recently joined World Rest, an association of similar hotels. World Rest publicises member hotels throughout the world and provides advice and control to ensure common standards amongst its members. In addition, it provides overall performance indicators by location and category of hotel, allowing members to compare their own performance.

You are employed by Green and Co, the Grand Hotel's auditors, and your firm has been asked to calculate the hotel's performance statistics required by World Rest. A colleague informs you that the Grand Hotel:

- operates for 365 days of the year;
- has 80 double or twin bedrooms;
- charges £80 per night for each bedroom;
- charges guests separately for any meals taken.

Your colleague also gives you a copy of World Rest's performance indicators' manual. The manual details the performance indicators required and gives guidance on their calculation. The relevant performance indicators and a summary of Grand Hotel's latest set of accounts are reproduced below.

Extract from World Rest's performance indicators' manual	
Indicator	*Definitions*
Maximum occupancy	Number of days in year × number of bedrooms
Occupancy rate	Annual total of rooms let per night as percentage of maximum occupancy
Gross margin: accommodation	Contribution from accommodation ÷ accommodation turnover
Gross margin: restaurant	Contribution from restaurant ÷ restaurant turnover
Operating profit: hotel	Profit before interest but after all other expenses
Sales margin: hotel	Operating profit ÷ total turnover
Return on capital employed: hotel	Operating profit ÷ net assets
Asset turnover hotel	Standard definition

GRAND HOTEL
PROFIT AND LOSS ACCOUNT
12 MONTHS ENDED 30 NOVEMBER 20X8

	Accommodation	*Restaurant*	*Total*
	£	£	£
Turnover	1,635,200	630,720	2,265,920
Variable costs	1,308,160	473,040	1,781,200
Contribution	327,040	157,680	484,720
Fixed costs			
Depreciation - land and buildings			24,000
Depreciation - fixtures and fitting			29,000
Administration			160,224
Rates and insurance			158,200
Debenture interest			80,000
Profit for the year			33,296

Extract from balance sheet at 30 November 20X8

	Land and buildings £	Fixtures and fitting £	Total £
Fixed assets			
Net book value	1,200,000	145,000	1,345,000
Net current assets			
Debtors		594,325	
Cash		88,125	
Creditors		(611,250)	
			71,200
Net assets			1,416,200

Task

Your colleague asks you to calculate the performance indicators listed above for the Grand Hotel using the definitions laid down by World Rest.

(b) A few days later you receive a letter from Claire Hill, the manager of the Grand Hotel. She enclosed a summary sent to her by the World Rest organisation showing the average performance indicators for hotels in similar categories and locations. This is reproduced below.

World Rest Hotel Association Performance Summary

Location Code B	Category Code 4
Occupancy rate	80%
Gross margin: accommodation	22%
Gross margin: restaurant	20%
Sales margin: hotel	10%
Return on capital employed: hotel	20%
Asset turnover: hotel	2 times

In her letter to you, Claire Hill expresses her concern about the performance of the Grand Hotel and provides you with the following information.

- The restaurant is currently working at maximum capacity. Any volume improvement must, therefore, come from the accommodation side of the hotel's activities.

- It is not possible to change the level of the fixed assets nor the net current assets without adversely affecting the business.

Claire Hill proposes increasing the return on capital employed to 20% by:

- increasing the occupancy rate to 80% of capacity while maintaining current prices; and

- increasing restaurant prices by 5% while decreasing the restaurant's variable costs by 5% without any change in demand.

Task

Write a letter to Claire Hill. Your letter should do the following.

(i) Calculate the operating profit required on the existing capital employed to give a 20% return.

(ii) Show the revised profit of the Grand Hotel if she achieves *both* her proposed occupancy rate and her proposed changes to the restaurant's pricing and costing structure.

(iii) List the following revised performance indicators assuming her proposals are achieved without changing the amount of the capital employed.

       (1)   Return on capital employed

       (2)   Asset turnover

       (3)   Sales margin

(iv)   Use the performance indicators calculated in (iii) to suggest the following.

       (1)   What proportion of the planned increase in profits is due to the increased occupancy rates and what proportion is due to the change in the restaurant's pricing and costing structure

       (2)   ONE possible area of investigation if profits are to be further increased

73   STUDENT HOUSING SOCIETY (50 mins)   *U11,6/98*

(a)   You work as an accounting technician with the Student Housing Society. The Student Housing Society is a registered charity, formed to provide low-cost accommodation for students. The accommodation consists of 100 student bedrooms. The invoiced rent per bedroom is £2,400 per year.

Following the resignation of the previous manager, Helen Brown has recently been appointed as the general manager to the housing society. The society has laid down the following financial objectives for managing the society.

- The affairs of the society must be carried out in an efficient and effective manner.

- The society must attempt to achieve a return on its net assets of between 6% and 8%.

- The annual operating surplus should be at least 15% but no more than 20% of rents receivable.

- The general manager should attempt to achieve a 95% occupancy rate.

- The target average age of rent arrears should be no more than one month.

- In order to avoid liquidity problems, the year-end cash and bank balance should be sufficient to meet the payment of two months' expenses.

In a few days time, the Student Housing Society is due to hold its annual general meeting and an extract from the accounts for the year to 31 May 20X8 is reproduced below.

Opening statement **year ended 31 May 20X8**		**Balance sheet extract** **at 31 May 20X8**			
				Accumltd	*Net book*
		Fixed assets	*Cost*	*amortis'n*	*value*
	£		£	£	£
Rent receivable	192,000	Land	200,000	0	200,000
Expenses		Buildings	700,000	336,000	364,000
Cleaning	16,000		900,000	336,000	564,000
Lighting and heating	4,800				
Maintenance	11,200	*Net current assets*			
Rates payable	76,000	Debtors*		48,000	
Amortisation	14,000	Cash and bank		4,500	
Administration costs	58,000	Creditors		(16,500)	36,000
		Net assets			600,000
Operating surplus	12,000				

* Debtors arise entirely from arrears of rent.

Task

Helen Brown wishes to know whether or not the charity has achieved the financial objectives laid down and asks you to calculate the following performance indicators in preparation for the annual general meeting.

(i)   The return on net assets

(ii)   The operating surplus as a percentage of rents receivable

(iii)   The occupancy rate for the society

(iv)   The average age of rent arrears in months

(v)   The number of months that expenses could be paid from the cash and bank balance

(b)   On receiving your calculations, Helen Brown discovers that the housing society has failed to meet all its objectives. Helen had previously worked in a commercial organisation and was uncertain how an organisation could be both efficient and effective while restricting the return on net assets and operating surplus margins. She also needs to make proposals at the annual general meeting which will ensure that all of the objectives are met next year. Helen believes it is possible to achieve the 95% occupancy rate and reduce the average age of rent arrears to the one month laid down in the objectives.

Helen Brown wants to know the effect on the other performance indicators if these two objectives had been achieved this year. She gives you the following information.

- The only marginal or variable costs relate to cleaning, lighting and heating, and maintenance.

- All other expenses are fixed costs.

- The creditors entirely relate to rates payable and administration costs.

- The figure for creditors would not change with any change in occupancy rates.

Task

Write a memo to Helen Brown. Your memo should do the following.

(i)   Identify the revised operating surplus if a 95% occupancy rate had been achieved.

(ii)   Show the value of debtors and cash as a result of achieving the 95% occupancy rate and the one month average age of rent arrears.

(iii)   Assuming the occupancy rate is 95% and the average age of rent arrears is one month, use your answers to parts (i) and (ii) of this task to calculate the following.

(1)   The revised return on net assets

(2)   The revised operating surplus as a percentage of rents receivable

(3)   The number of months that expenses could be paid from the revised cash and bank balance

(iv)   *Briefly* explain:

(1)   what is meant by efficiency;

(2)   what is meant by effectiveness;

(3)   why the return on net assets might not be an appropriate measure of efficiency for the housing society.

74   ELEXTRIX PLC (80 mins)

(a)   Elextrix plc operates a number of stores selling domestic electrical appliances. You are employed by Elextrix plc as an accounting technician and report to Sarah Barker, the finance director. One of your tasks is to monitor the performance of the stores.

The stores sell two classes of appliances.

- Class 1 goods such as refrigerators, washing machines and cookers
- Class 2 goods such as televisions and hi-fi equipment

Every day, each store banks all cash into a head office bank account. Debtors and creditors are also controlled centrally. Because of this the net assets of each store comprises its fixed assets plus stock.

One of Elextrix plc's stores is based in Midtown. The store's operating profit for the year ended 27 November 20X8, a summary of its net assets and other performance data are reproduced below.

Elextrix plc Midtown store financial statements year ended 27 November 20X8			
Profit summary for the year			
	Class I goods	*Class 2 goods*	*Total*
	£'000	£'000	£'000
Turnover	2,700	2,200	4,900
Cost of sales	1,404	1,540	2,944
Gross profit	1,296	660	1,956
Rates and insurance			700
Wages			327
Commission			98
Depreciation			152
Administration			91
Operating profit			588

Summary of net assets at year end			
Fixed assets		*Depreciation*	*Net book*
	Cost	*to date*	*value*
	£'000	£'000	£'000
Land and buildings	1,600	128	1,472
Fixtures and fittings	600	480	120
	2,200	608	1,592
Current assets			
Stock			368
Net assets			1,960

Number of employees	30
Size of store (square metres)	5,000

Task

Sarah Barker asks you to calculate the following performance indicators for the Midtown store.

(i)   Return on capital employed
(ii)   Asset turnover
(iii)   Gross profit margin of Class 1 goods
(iv)   Gross profit margin of Class 2 goods
(v)   Sales (or operating profit) margin
(vi)   Average age of stocks in months
(vii)   Sales per employee
(viii) Sales per square metre

(b) On receiving your performance indicators, Sarah Barker informs you that a recent Government report is critical of electrical appliance retailing. The report states that the following price reductions would be possible if suppliers allowed greater competition.

- Class 1 goods could be reduced by 12%.
- Class 2 goods could be reduced by 8%.

Sarah Barker also tells you that the sales commission of the Midtown store represents 2% of turnover.

Task

You are asked to prepare a report for Sarah Barker. Your report should do the following.

(i) Include a revised profit summary showing the gross profit of Class 1 and Class 2 goods if the price reductions occurred.

(ii) Forecast the following performance indicators if the price reductions occurred.

    (1) Gross profit margin of Class 1 goods
    (2) Gross profit margin of Class 2 goods
    (3) Return on capital employed

(iii) Identify THREE assumptions used in your analysis in part (i).

(iv) Give TWO limitations to the use of financial data in measuring business performance.

75   DIAMOND LTD (50 mins)   *Specimen central assessment*

(a) Diamond Ltd is a retail jeweller operating 30 branches in similar localities. Common accounting policies operate throughout all branches, including a policy of using straight-line depreciation for fixed assets.

All branches use rented premises. These are accounted for under 'other costs' in the operating statement. Fixed assets are predominantly fixtures and fittings.

Each branch is individually responsible for ordering stock, the authorising of payments to creditors and the control of debtors. Cash management, however, is managed by Diamond's head office with any cash received by a branch being paid into a head office bank account twice daily.

You are employed in the head office of Diamond Ltd as a financial analyst monitoring the performance of all 30 branches. This involves calculating performance indicators for each branch and comparing each branch's performance with company standards. Financial data relating to Branch 24 is reproduced below.

Diamond Ltd - Branch 24 - Year ended 31 December 20X7					
Operating Statement					
	£'000	£'000		£'000	£'000
Turnover		720.0	*Fixed assets*		
Opening stock	80.0		Cost		225.0
Purchases	340.0		Accumulated depreciation		(90.0)
Closing stock	(60.0)		Net book value		135.0
		360.0			
Gross profit		360.0	*Working capital*		
Wages and salaries	220.6		Stocks	60.0	
Depreciation	45.0		Debtors	96.0	
Other costs	36.8		Creditors	(51.0)	
		302.4			105.0
Operating profit		57.6	*Net assets*		240.0

Tasks

Prepare a statement showing the following performance indicators for Branch 24.

(i)   The return on capital employed
(ii)   The gross profit margin as a percentage
(iii)   The asset turnover
(iv)   The sales (or net profit) margin as a percentage
(v)   The average age of debtors in months
(vi)   The average age of creditors in months
(vii)   The average age of the closing stock in months

(b)   The financial director of Diamond Ltd is Charles Walden. He is concerned that Branch 24 is not performing as well as the other branches. All other branches are able to meet or exceed most of the performance standards laid down by the company.

Charles is particularly concerned that branches should achieve the standards for return on capital employed and the asset turnover. He also feels that managers should try to achieve the standards laid down for working capital management. The relevant standards are:

- return on capital employed   40%
- asset turnover   4 times per annum
- average age of debtors   0.5 months
- average age of creditors   3 months
- average age of closing stock   1 month

Charles Walden has recently attended a course on financial modelling and scenario planning. Charles explains that scenario planning shows the likely performance of a business under different assumed circumstances. It requires an understanding of the relationship between the different elements within the financial statements and how these change as the circumstances being modelled change. As an example, he tells you that if the volume of branch turnover was to increase then the cost of sales would also increase but that all other expenses would remain the same as they are fixed costs.

He believes scenario planning would be particularly helpful to the manager of Branch 24, Angela Newton. Charles has previously discussed the performance of the branch with Angela and emphasised the importance of improving the asset turnover and maintaining control of working capital. However, Angela raised the following objections:

- Turning over assets is not important, making profit should be the main objective;
- Branch 24 has been in existence for two years less than all the other branches.

Task

Charles Walden asks you to write a memo to Angela Newton. Your memo should do the following.

(i)   Show the return on capital employed that Branch 24 would have achieved had it been able to achieve the company's asset turnover during the year to 31 December 20X7 while maintaining prices and the existing capital employed.

(ii)   Show the return on capital employed and the asset turnover for the year if Branch 24 had been able to achieve the company's standards for the average age of debtors, the average age of creditors and the average age of finished stock while maintaining its existing sales volume.

(iii)   *Using the data in task (a) and your solution to task (b)(i)*, address the issues raised by Angela Newton.

76   MICRO CIRCUITS LTD (85 mins)   *12/98*

(a)   You are employed by Micro Circuits Ltd as a financial analyst reporting to Angela Frear, the Director of Corporate Strategy. One of your responsibilities is to monitor the performance of subsidiaries within the group. Financial and other data relating to subsidiary. It is reproduced below.

SUBSIDIARY A						

Profit and loss account year to 30 November 20X8

	£'000	£'000
Sales		4,000
less returns		100
Turnover[1]		3,900
Material	230	
Labour	400	
Production overheads[2]	300	
Cost of production	930	
Opening finished stock	50	
Closing finished stock	(140)	
Cost of sales		840
Gross profit		3,060
Marketing	500	
Customer support	400	
Research and development	750	
Training	140	
Administration	295	2,085
Operating profit		975

Extract from balance sheet at 30 November 20X8

	£'000	£'000	£'000
Fixed assets	*Land and buildings*	*Plant and machinery*	*Total*
Cost	2,000	2,500	4,500
Additions	-	1,800	1,800
	2,000	4,300	6,300
Accumulated depreciation	160	1,700	1,860
	1,840	2,600	4,440
Raw material stock	15		
Finished goods stock	140		
	155		
Debtors	325		
Cash and bank	40		
Creditors	(85)		
			435
Net assets			4,875

Other information

Notes

1.   *Analysis of turnover*

	£'000		£'000
Regular customers	3,120	New products	1,560
New customers	780	Existing products	2,340
	3,900		3,900

2.   *Production overheads include £37,200 of reworked faulty production.*

3.   **Orders received in the year totalled £4,550,000.**

Task

Angela Frear asks you to calculate the following performance indicators in preparation for a board meeting.

(i)   The return on capital employed
(ii)   The asset turnover
(iii)   The sales (or operating profit) margin
(iv)   The average age of debtors in months
(v)   The average age of finished stock in months

(b)   One of the issues to be discussed at the board meeting is the usefulness of performance indicators. Angela Frear has recently attended a conference on creating and enhancing value.

Three criticisms were made of financial performance indicators.

•   They could give misleading signals.

- They could be manipulated.

- They focus on the short term and do not take account of other key, non-financial performance indicators.

At the conference, Angela was introduced to the idea of the balanced scorecard. The balanced scorecard looks at performance measurement from four perspectives.

The financial perspective

This is concerned with satisfying shareholders. Examples include the return on capital employed and sales margin.

The customer perspective

This asks how customers view the business and is concerned with measures of customer satisfaction. Examples include speed of delivery and customer loyalty.

The internal perspective

This looks at the quality of the company's output in terms of technical excellence and customer needs. Examples would be striving towards total quality management and flexible production as well as unit cost.

The innovation and learning perspective

This is concerned with the continual improvement of existing products and the ability to develop new products as customers' needs change. An example would be the percentage of turnover attributable to new products.

Task

Angela Frear asks you to prepare briefing notes for the board meeting. Using the data from part (a) where necessary, your notes should do the following.

(i) Suggest ONE reason why the return on capital employed calculated in (a) might be misleading.

(ii) Identify ONE way of manipulating the sales (or operating profit) margin.

(iii) Calculate the average delay in fulfilling orders.

(iv) Identify ONE other possible measure of customer satisfaction other than the delay in fulfilling orders.

(v) Calculate TWO indicators which may help to measure performance from an internal perspective.

(vi) Calculate ONE performance indicator which would help to measure the innovation and learning perspective.

77 ALV LTD (95 mins)   *6/99*

(a) You are employed by ALV Ltd as an accounting technician. Two companies owned by ALV Ltd are ALV (East) Ltd and ALV (West) Ltd. These two companies are located in the same town and make an identical electrical product which sells for £84.

Financial data relating to the two companies is reproduced below. In addition, performance indicators for ALV (East) Ltd are also shown. Both companies use the same straight-line depreciation policy and assume no residual value.

ALV (East) Ltd

				Income statement Year to 31 May 20X3	
Extract from balance sheet at 31 May 20X3					
		Accumulated	*Net book*		
	Cost	*depreciation*	*value*		
Fixed assets	£'000	£'000	£'000		£'000
Buildings	1,000	700	300	Turnover	840
Plant and machinery	300	240	60	Material and bought-in services	340
	1,300	940	360	Production labour	180
Net current assets				Other production expenses	52
Stock		45		Depreciation – buildings	20
Debtors		30		Depreciation – plant and machinery	30
Cash		5		Administration and other expenses	50
Creditors		(40)	40	Operating profit	168
			400		

Other data

Number of employees	18	Units produced	10,000

Performance indicators for ALV (East) Ltd

Asset turnover	2.1 times	Production labour cost per unit	£18.00
Net profit margin	20.00%	Output per employee	556
Return on capital employed	42.00%	Added value per employee	£27,778
Wages per employee	£10,000	Profit per employee	£9,333

ALV (West) Ltd

				Income statement Year to 31 May 20X3	
Extract from balance sheet at 31 May 20X3					
		Accumulated	*Net book*		
	Cost	*depreciation*	*value*		
Fixed assets	£'000	£'000	£'000		£'000
Buildings	1,500	120	1,380	Turnover	2,520
Plant and machinery	900	180	720	Material and bought-in services	1,020
	2,400	300	2,100	Production labour	260
Net current assets				Other production expenses	630
Stock		20		Depreciation – buildings	30
Debtors		30		Depreciation – plant and machinery	90
Cash		5		Administration and other expenses	112
Creditors		(55)	nil	Operating profit	378
			2,100		

Other data

Number of employees	20	Units produced	30,000

ALV Ltd is considering closing one of the companies over the next two years. As a first step, the board of directors wish to hold a meeting to consider which is the more efficient and productive company.

Task

In preparation for the board meeting, calculate the following performance indicators for ALV (West) Ltd.

- (i) Asset turnover
- (ii) Net profit margin
- (iii) Return on capital employed
- (iv) Wages per employee
- (v) Production labour costs per unit
- (vi) Output per employee
- (vii) Added value per employee
- (viii) Profit per employee

(b) Shortly after preparing the performance indicators for ALV (West) Ltd, the chief executive of ALV Ltd, Jill Morgan, issued a statement to a local newspaper. In that statement, she said that the workforce at ALV (West) Ltd was far less productive than at the other company despite both companies making an identical product. She concluded that it was up to the workforce to improve productivity. In response, the employees stated that the normal way of measuring efficiency is profit, and therefore, ALV (West) was more efficient than ALV (East).

Jill Morgan asks you to prepare a report for the next board meeting to explain the issues involved so that all board members can be properly briefed.

Task

Write a report to Jill Morgan for distribution to the board of directors. Your report should do the following.

- (i) Explain what is meant by the following.
  - (1) Productivity
  - (2) Efficiency

- (ii) Identify the best TWO performance indicators used by ALV Ltd to measure efficiency and use those indicators to identify which of the two companies is the more efficient.

- (iii) Identify the best TWO performance measures used by ALV Ltd to measure productivity and use those indicators to identify which of the two companies has the higher productivity.

- (iv) Use the NET FIXED ASSETS to derive a different measure of productivity for both companies.

- (v) Use the data in task (a) and your answer to task (b)(iv) to explain ONE reason why the productivity and efficiency measures might give different rankings.

Answers

1   PRACTICE QUESTION: COST BEHAVIOUR

> **Tutorial note**. Do not discuss the distinction between direct and indirect costs. This question is about cost behaviour - not cost classification - and you need to explain why it is necessary to classify costs by behaviour. For part (a) remember the following.
>
> - Costs are either variable or fixed, depending upon *how they behave* (whether they change) when the volume of production changes.
>
> - Costs are either direct or indirect, depending upon *how easily* they can be traced to a specific unit of production.
>
> The first point is a matter of fact; the second is a matter of practicality.

REPORT

To: Managing Director
From: Management Accountant
Date: 18 May 20X2
Subject: **Cost behaviour**

The classification of costs by their behaviour

Costs may be classified in many different ways, but one of the most important ways from the point of view of managing a business is classification according to how costs change in response to changes in the level of the business's activity. The main distinction is between fixed costs and variable costs.

Fixed costs are those that **do not change whatever the level of the business's activity**. The cost of rental of a business premises is a common example: this is a constant amount (at least within a stated time period) that does not vary with the level of activity conducted on the premises. Other examples are business rates, salaries, buildings insurance and so on.

A sketch graph of a fixed cost would look like this.

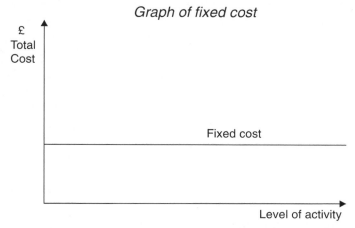

Graph of fixed cost

Variable costs, of course, are those that **do vary with the level of activity**: if a business produces two widgets, for example, it uses twice as many materials as it does for one widget. Similarly if it sells more goods, its sales administration costs like stationery and postage will vary proportionately.

A sketch graph of a variable cost would look like this.

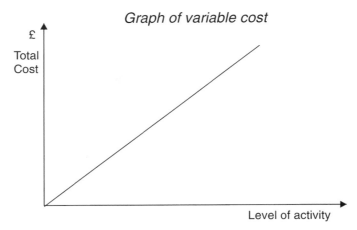

Graph of variable cost

£
Total
Cost

Level of activity

Many costs behave in a more complicated fashion than these simple models suggest. For example a telephone bill has a fixed element (the standing charge) and a variable element (the cost of calls). These are called **mixed costs** (or **semi-variable** or **semi-fixed costs**). Other costs are **stepped**: that is, they are fixed within a certain level of activity but increase above or below that level. For example, if a second factory has to be rented to produce the required volume of output the cost of rent will double. Other patterns are exhibited when quantity discounts are available.

Cost behaviour and total and unit costs

If the variable cost of producing a widget is £5 per unit then it will remain at that cost per unit no matter how many widgets are produced. However if the business's fixed costs are £5,000 then the fixed cost per unit will decrease the more units are produced: one unit will have fixed costs of £5,000 per unit; if 2,500 are produced the fixed cost per unit will be £2; if 5,000 are produced fixed costs per unit will be only £1. Thus as the **level of activity increases** the **total costs per unit (fixed costs plus variable costs)** will **decrease**.

In sketch graph form this may be illustrated as follows.

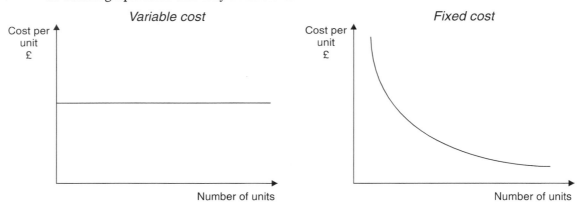

Variable cost

Cost per
unit
£

Number of units

Fixed cost

Cost per
unit
£

Number of units

The importance of cost behaviour

The classification of costs according to behaviour serves a number of purposes, notably the following.

(a) In **planning** it is necessary to know what costs will be at various possible levels of activity so that a level appropriate to the overall resources of the business may be chosen.

(b) To maintain **control** of the business it is necessary to compare actual results achieved to those expected and this will require adjustments depending upon actual and expected levels of activity.

(c) When **marginal costing** is used, for example for decision making, the distinction between fixed and variable costs is fundamental to this approach.

2 PRACTICE QUESTION: ABSORPTION COSTING

> **Tutorial note**. The trap in task (a) was failing to appreciate that an *overhead* analysis sheet was being asked for - direct wages and materials are not overheads. It would also have been a good idea in task (a) to rough out the table first to see how much space you needed. Machine hours are used for the absorption rates for extrusion and machining in (b) because they are much greater than labour hours in these departments; for finishing labour hours is used as the labour element is the most significant.

(a) **Analysis of overheads**

Overheads	Basis of analysis	Total £'000	A £'000	B £'000	C £'000	Service dept £'000
Indirect wages	Actual	102	15	21	8	58
Depreciation	Fixed assets	84	33.60	29.40	6.30	14.70
Rates	Floor area	22	4	6	5	7
Power	Machine hour	180	69.75	90	11.25	9
Personnel	Employees	60	10	14	23.50	12.50
Insurance	Fixed assets	48	19.20	16.80	3.60	8.40
Analysis by dept		496	151.55	177.20	57.65	109.60
Service dept	3:2:1	-	54.80	36.53	18.27	(109.60)
Analysis by production dept		496	206.35	213.73	75.92	-

(b) (i) *Dept A*

Using **machine hours**

$$\text{Absorption rate} = \frac{206,350}{15,500}$$

$$= £13.313 \text{ per machine hour}$$

(ii) *Dept B*

Using **machine hours**

$$\text{Absorption rate} = \frac{213,730}{20,000}$$

$$= £10.687 \text{ per machine hour}$$

(iii) *Dept C*

Using **direct labour hours**

$$\text{Absorption rate} = \frac{75,920}{15,000}$$

$$= £5.061 \text{ per labour hour}$$

(c) **Over recovery of overheads in dept A** = **Overheads absorbed – actual overheads**
= $(16,250 \times £13.313) - £211,820$
= $£216,336 - £211,820$
= $£4,516$

3   PRACTICE QUESTION: ABSORPTION COSTING AND MARGINAL COSTING

> **Tutorial note**. Several alternative methods of presenting the profit statement in task (a)(iii) would be acceptable. But remember than an absorption costing statement should include the overheads absorbed in production costs and the adjustment for under/over absorption of overhead.
>
> The difference between the profits in (a)(iii) and (b) of £7,500 is caused by the difference in closing stock values, which amounts to the fixed production overhead absorbed on the 3,000 units at £2.50 per unit. Had there been any opening stocks, the difference in their valuation would also have affected the comparative figures.

	Production costs £	Sales etc costs £
Total costs of 60,000 units (fixed plus variable)	510,000	150,000
Total costs of 36,000 units (fixed plus variable)	366,000	126,000
Difference = variable costs of 24,000 units	144,000	24,000
Variable costs per unit	£6	£1

	Production costs £	Sales etc costs £
Total costs of 60,000 units	510,000	150,000
Variable costs of 60,000 units	360,000	60,000
Fixed costs	150,000	90,000

The **rate of absorption** of fixed production overheads will therefore be:

$$\frac{£150,000}{60,000} = £2.50 \text{ per unit}$$

(a) (i)   The fixed production overhead absorbed by the products would be 16,500 units produced × £2.50 = £41,250.

(ii)   Budgeted annual fixed production overhead = £150,000

	£
Actual quarterly fixed production o/hd = budgeted quarterly production o/hd	37,500
Production o/hd absorbed into production (see (i) above)	41,250
Over absorption of fixed production o/hd	3,750

(iii)   **Profit for the quarter, using absorption costing**

	£	£	£
Sales (13,500 × £12)			162,000
Costs of production (no opening stocks)			
Value of stocks produced (16,500 × £8.50)		140,250	
Less value of closing stocks			
(3,000 units × full production cost of £8.50)		(25,500)	
		114,750	
Sales etc costs			
Variable (13,500 × £1)	13,500		
Fixed (¼ of £90,000)	22,500		
		36,000	
Total cost of sales		150,750	
Less over-absorbed production overhead		3,750	
			147,000
Profit			15,000

(b) Profit statement using marginal costing

	£	£
Sales		162,000
Variable costs of production (16,500 × £6)	99,000	
Less value of closing stocks (3,000 × £6)	18,000	
Variable production cost of sales	81,000	
Variable sales etc costs	13,500	
Total variable cost of sales (13,500 × £7)		94,500
Contribution (13,500 × £5)		67,500
Fixed costs: production	37,500	
sales etc	22,500	
		60,000
Profit		7,500

4   PRACTICE QUESTION: ABC

> **Tutorial note**. Although the question does not state that you have to use activity based costing techniques to deal with the indirect costs, the term 'cost driver' should have given you a very big hint as to how to proceed.
>
> When calculating the miles travelled by sales staff you should remember that each visit involves a return journey.

		Order JM3		Order AM5	
		£	£	£	£
Direct costs (given)			17,400		16,500
Indirect costs (W1)					
Sales	(£2.50 per mile travelled (W2) × 12 or 1,600 (W3))	30		4,000	
Design	(£20 per hour worked (W2) × 10 or 100 (W3))	200		2,000	
Sourcing	(£30 per item bought in (W2) × 3 or 16 (W3))	90		480	
Testing	(£15 per testing hour (W2) × 5 or 80 (W3))	75		1,200	
Training	(£15 per training hour (W2) × 10 or 150 (W3))	150		2,250	
Packaging (given)		-		200	
Delivery cost (given)		50		800	
Overtime premium	(AM5 only, 50% × £2,900)	-		1,450	
			595		12,380
Total costs			17,995		28,880

Workings

1   **Indirect costs** are calculated as **cost per unit of cost driver (see W2) × number of cost driver units associated with the order (see W3).**

2   **Calculation of cost per unit of cost driver**

Activity	*Cost driver*	*Cost per unit of cost driver*		
Sales	Miles travelled	£50,000 ÷ 20,000 =	£2.50 per mile
Design	Design hours worked	£40,000 ÷ 2,000 =	£20.00 per hour
Sourcing	Items bought in	£30,000 ÷ 1,000 =	£30.00 per item
Testing	Testing hours	£30,000 ÷ 2,000 =	£15.00 per hour
Training	Training hours	£30,000 ÷ 2,000 =	£15.00 per hour

3   **Calculation of number of cost driver units per order**

	JM3	*AM5*
Miles travelled	3 miles × 2 trips × 2(return) = 12	100 miles × 8 trips × 2(return) = 1,600
Design hours worked	10	100
Items bought in	3	16
Testing hours	5	80
Training hours	10	150

BPP PUBLISHING

5   PRACTICE QUESTION: BENEFITS OF ABC

> **Tutorial note**. Try to use the situation given in the question as the basis for your answer. The organisation is a law firm and so before you begin to write you will need to think about the type of activity that they might undertake.

ACTIVITY BASED COSTING (ABC)

A paper prepared for Lucy Thomson

Introduction

This paper will describe both how ABC works (illustrating the methodology with a simple illustration) and the advantages of ABC.

ABC arose from a dissatisfaction with the information that was provided by traditional overhead absorption methods. For example, in our firm we have always recovered our overhead costs on an hourly rate per client. ABC recognises that this may not be the most suitable basis for recovering overheads. An **ABC** system **looks more carefully at what actually causes overhead costs** and **attempts to allocate overheads more realistically** to the products produced/services provided.

How ABC works

The first step in an ABC exercise is to **analyse the activities** (rather than departments as required by absorption costing) that are undertaken in an organisation. Our activities include consulting with clients, maintaining client accounts, ordering stationery supplies and so on. All staff would therefore need to provide a description of exactly what they do and the way in which they do it.

Once the activities are identified the next step is to **determine the cost driver for the activity**. A cost driver causes the costs of the activity to alter. For example, the cost driver for maintaining client accounts might be the number of clients currently on our books. A client who simply requires a basic will to be drawn up may place as much burden on our resources for maintaining client accounts as one who requires detailed advice in a divorce case.

Each activity is treated as a cost pool and the costs are collected in much the same way as with a traditional cost centre system. Each total cost pool is then divided by the appropriate number of cost drivers to find the **cost per cost driver**. The number of cost drivers a product (or service) causes is then identified (which is equivalent to the degree by which the product/service has caused the costs of the activity to change). The cost per cost driver is then multiplied by the appropriate number of cost drivers to determine the share of the activity's cost the product/service must bear.

Illustration

For purposes of illustration assume that our organisation has two activities and that the relevant cost drivers are as follows.

Activity	Cost of activity during period £	Cost driver	Cost per unit of cost driver
Consulting with clients	20,000	250 consultant hours	£80 per hour
Client account maintenance	4,000	400 clients	£10 per client

The costing system would therefore charge each client £80 per consultant hour for consulting time, and £10 per period for account maintenance regardless of the number of hours they have spent with our legal consultants.

The benefits of ABC

The benefits of ABC include the following.

(a) Staff will have a better understanding of the firm's overhead costs and what causes them, instead of simply assuming that all overhead costs are incurred at an hourly rate.

(b) Clients will be charged an appropriate amount which more closely relates to the burden that they have placed on the firm's resources.

(c) The process of describing activities will provide a focus for cost reduction exercises, forcing all of the firm's employees to look more closely at the way that they do things.

(d) A better understanding of overhead costs will improve budgeting and planning in the future.

(e) A carefully determined cost driver rate can provide the basis for improved cost control and perhaps some form of performance assessment.

(f) A client profitability exercise may be carried out, resulting in more of an idea of what it is costing to service each type of client. This may provide the basis for a reassessment of fees charged and may even lead to a decision to discontinue a particular type of business.

6 PRACTICE QUESTION: DATA COLLECTION

> **Tutorial note**. It is important that you not only understand the differences between the various sampling methods but also that you can relate the ideas to the particular scenario.

(a) (i)   **Simple random sampling**

A simple random sample is one in which **every member of the population has an equal chance of being included**. A sampling frame of the entire adult population of the Northern sales territory would have to be drawn up if this method were to be used. Such a sampling frame would probably be constructed by combining the electoral registers for the area in question. Each person on the electoral register would then need to be allocated a number and a sample of 10,000 (500,000 × 2%) would be selected using random number tables or a random number generator on a computer.

(ii) **Cluster sampling**

Cluster sampling involves **selecting one definable subsection of the population** as the sample, that subsection taken to be **representative of the population in question**. In the Northern sales territory, where a sample of 10,000 is required, the regions might be split into groups (or clusters) of size 10,000 each. Northia would, for instance, contain 9 clusters while Eastis would contain only one. In total there would be 50 clusters from which one would be selected randomly by numbering them and using random number tables as in (i). Every member of the selected cluster would then be surveyed. A more representative cluster sample could be obtained at greater cost by dividing the population into 500 geographic groups of 1,000 people each and then randomly selecting ten groups to be surveyed.

(iii) **Stratified sampling**

It is possible that people's responses to the survey will depend on the region in which they live and so, in order to obtain a representative sample, it is important to ensure that all regions contribute to the sample in proportion to their population sizes. This is achieved by **dividing the total population into strata**

(the regions in this case), **sampling separately in the** six **strata** (regions) and then pooling the samples. Regional samples must be proportional to regional sizes so, for instance, Northia's population of 90,000 would require a sample of 2% of 90,000 which is 1,800 people. The members of this sample would be selected randomly from the population of Northia by numbering and using random numbers as outlined in (i). The other sample sizes required would be as follows.

Wester	2% of 10,000	=	200
Southam	2% of 140,000	=	2,800
Eastis	2% of 40,000	=	800
Midshire	2% of 120,000	=	2,400
Centrasia	2% of 100,000	=	2,000

The total of the six smaller samples is 10,000.

(iv) **Systematic sampling**

This method selects the sample by **choosing every nth person from a list of the population,** having first made a **random start** at some point between 0 and fifty on the list (we require a sample of 2% of the population so every fiftieth (500,000 ÷ 2% of 500,000) name will be chosen). Assuming that the territory does not have a single list of the adult population but does have electoral registers spanning the entire area, these could constitute a single list provided agreement could be reached on the order they were to be taken. A computer could randomly select one number between 0 and 50 and the person on the list in that position could be the random start. Thereafter every fiftieth person would be selected, with counting running on from one electoral list to the next until the total sample of 10,000 was selected.

(b) The method likely to give the **most representative** sample is **stratified sampling** since this method deliberately selects from the different groups in the population in a representative fashion. The groups used in this case would be geographic, however, and it may be that people's characteristics regarding sales intentions do not vary according to the region in which they live. It may be that the sample would be more representative were it stratified by age or by gender. It would be very difficult, perhaps impossible, to stratify in such a way, however. With the caveat therefore that the **basis of stratification needs to be relevant to the subject of the survey,** stratification can be expected to give the most representative sample. Its disadvantages are that both the initial division of the sampling frame into strata and the process of numbering all population members, generating the required random numbers and identifying the corresponding people are **difficult** and **time-consuming** and therefore very **costly.**

The **disadvantage of simple random sampling** is that it is **theoretically possible,** although unlikely, to **select highly unrepresentative samples.** For example, every single sample member could live in Northia. Additional problems are that a **sampling frame** for the entire country could be **difficult to construct** and, as for stratified sampling, the method of number and selecting by random numbers is **cumbersome** and **costly**.

In general, **systematic sampling** is just as likely to give unrepresentative samples as simple random sampling, but it has the added problems of **bias** if the sampling frame contains any cyclical patterns which correspond to the cycle of selection, such as every fiftieth person being elderly. The method we have suggested above would at least remove the danger of geographic imbalance, however. The combination of electoral registers into a single sampling frame would also be difficult.

Cluster sampling, although a relatively simple and cheap process by comparison with the other methods, is very open to **bias**. Indeed it would be surprising if one single geographic group could possibly be representative of the entire population. Even the selection of ten groups could easily prove to be very unrepresentative. There would also be some difficulty in dividing the population into clusters of exactly 10,000 each.

7   PRACTICE QUESTION: INDEX NUMBERS

> **Tutorial note**. It would not be practical to show all your workings to task (a) but it is important to give the assessor one or two examples showing how you obtained your results.

(a)

		Average earnings index (June 20X5 = 100)	Retail prices index (June 20X5 = 100)	Real earnings (June 20X5 = 100)
20X5	June	100.0	100.0	100.0
	July	102.1	101.5	100.6
	August	103.9	108.9	95.4
	September	105.8	114.2	92.6
	October	109.0	117.4	92.8
	November	111.2	121.6	91.4
	December	113.0	124.0	91.1

		Average earnings index (June 20X5 = 100)	Retail prices index (June 20X5 = 100)	Real earnings (June 20X5 = 100)
20X6	January	115.4	127.3	90.7
	February	121.9	129.3	94.3
	March	124.3	131.9	94.2
	April	126.9	135.1	93.9
	May	129.6	138.6	93.5

Both indices are **rebased by dividing each monthly index by the June 20X5 index and multiplying by 100,** ie divide by 243.2 for the average earnings index and by 151.8 for the retail prices index.

(b) The **index for average earnings** (June 20X5 = 100) is **converted into an index of real earnings at constant June 20X5 prices by multiplying each monthly index by 100** (the RPI for June 20X5) and **dividing by the RPI for the month in question**. For example, $129.6 \times 100/138.6$ is the calculation for May 20X6.

The retail price index shows prices rising by a massive 38.6% over the year starting June 20X5 whilst average earnings rose by only slightly less (29.6%). Throughout the whole of the year under consideration, increases in earnings lagged behind increases in prices (with the sole exception of July 20X5 when the purchasing power of earnings rose by 0.6% (102.1 – 101.5)). As can be seen from the index of real earnings, the low point in terms of purchasing power of earnings occurred in January 20X6, when real earnings were down by 9.3% compared to the level in June 20X5. By the end of the year, however, real earnings had picked up somewhat and were only 6.5% less than those of June 20X5.

8   PRACTICE QUESTION: Z CHARTS

> **Tutorial note.** The values of the annual moving total and the cumulative values are plotted on month-end positions on the graph whereas the values for the current monthly figures are plotted on mid-month positions.

(a) The data required to draw a Z chart are as follows.

Month	Costs 20X6 £'000	Costs 20X7 £'000	Cumulative costs 20X7 £'000	Annual moving total £'000
January	35.8	43.9	43.9	434.0
February	33.6	40.1	84.0	440.5
March	35.5	46.0	130.0	451.0
April	37.5	48.7	178.7	462.2
May	37.2	48.9	227.6	473.9
June	34.6	46.0	273.6	485.3
July	36.3	48.3	321.9	497.3
August	36.0	47.9	369.8	509.2
September	35.4	48.2	418.0	522.0
October	30.4	47.0	465.0	538.6
November	36.1	49.4	514.4	551.9
December	37.5	51.6	566.0	566.0
	425.9			

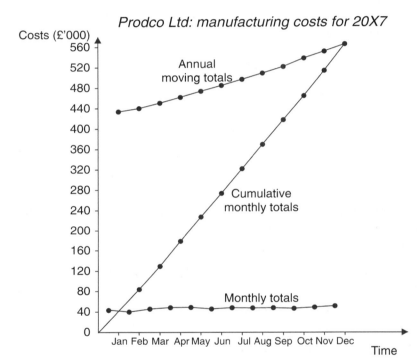

Prodco Ltd: manufacturing costs for 20X7

(b) The purpose of a Z chart is to **display simultaneously**:

(i) **monthly totals** which show the monthly results together with any seasonal variations;

(ii) **cumulative totals** which show the performance for the year to date, and can be easily compared with planned or budgeted performance by superimposing a budget line;

(iii) **annual moving totals** which compare the current levels of performance with those of the previous year and disclose any long-term trend.

The graph drawn in part (a) shows a fairly stable pattern of monthly costs. The annual moving total line shows a significant increase in monthly costs for 20X7 as compared to 20X6.

9   PRACTICE QUESTION: STANDARD COSTING

> **Tutorial note**. This is a very straightforward introduction to standard costing. The three types of variance required in task (b) are calculated as follows.
>
> • The total labour variance is calculated as the difference between what the actual output should cost in terms of labour and what it did cost.
>
> • The labour rate variance is calculated as the difference between what the actual labour hours should cost and what they did cost.
>
> • The labour efficiency variance is calculated as the difference between the number of hours the actual output should have taken and the number of hours actually taken, valued at the standard rate per hour.

(a)   **Standard production cost per unit**

		Major			Minor	
		£	£		£	£
Direct materials	(2.2kgs × £15.00)		33.00	(1.4kgs × £15.00)		21.00
Direct labour						
Machining dept	(4.8 hrs × £6.00)	28.80		(2.9hrs × £6.00)	17.40	
Assembly dept	(3.6hrs × £5.00)	18.00		(3.1hrs × £5.00)	15.50	
			46.80			32.90
Standard direct cost			79.80			53.90
Overheads						
Machining dept	(3.5hrs × £16.00)	56.00		(0.9hrs × £16.00)	14.40	
Assembly dept	(3.6hrs × £9.50)	34.20		(3.1 hrs × £9.50)	29.45	
			90.20			43.85
Standard product cost per unit			170.00			97.75

(b)   **Major**

Total - machining department

	£
650 units should cost (× £28.80)	18,720
but did cost	18,239
	481 (F)

Total - assembly department

	£
650 units should cost (× £18.00)	11,700
but did cost	11,700
	-

Rate - machining department

	£
2,990 hrs should have cost (× £6)	17,940
but did cost	18,239
	299 (A)

assembly department

	£
2,310 hrs should have cost (× £5)	11,550
but did cost	11,700
	150 (A)

Efficiency - machining department

650 units should have taken (× 4.8 hrs)	3,120 hrs
but did take	2,990 hrs
Efficiency variance in hrs	130 hrs (F)
× standard rate per hour	× £6
Efficiency variance in £	£780 (F)

assembly department

650 units should have taken (× 3.6 hrs)	2,340 hrs
but did take	2,310 hrs
Efficiency variance in hrs	30 hrs (F)
× standard rate per hour	× £5
Efficiency variance in £	£150 (F)

Minor

Total - machining department £

842 units should cost (× £17.40)	14,650.80
but did cost	15,132.00
	481.20 (A)

Total - assembly department £

842 units should cost (× £15.50)	13,051
but did cost	12,975
	76 (F)

Rate - machining department £

2,480 hrs should have cost (× £6)	14,880
but did cost	15,132
	252 (A)

assembly department £

2,595 hrs should have cost (× £5)	12,975
but did cost	12,975
	-

Efficiency - machining department

842 units should have taken (× 2.9 hrs)	2,441.8 hrs
but did take	2,480.0 hrs
Efficiency variance in hours	38.2 hrs (A)
× standard rate per hour	× £6
Efficiency variance in £	£229.20 (A)

assembly department

842 units should have taken (× 3.1 hrs)	2,610.2 hrs
but did take	2,595.0 hrs
Efficiency variance in hours	15.2 hrs (F)
× standard rate per hour	× £5
Efficiency variance in £	£76 (F)

(c) **Direct labour rate variances indicate whether rates of pay above standard rates have been paid**. An adverse variance would indicate that rates were higher, perhaps because of a wage increase or perhaps because labour with a higher rate of pay than the type of labour anticipated in the standard were used. A favourable variance might indicate that less skilled, and therefore lower paid, labour were used than anticipated in the standard.

Direct labour efficiency variances indicate whether labour took more time or less time than anticipated by the standard to produce the output. An adverse variance might indicate that less skilled labour were used, who consequently took more time than allowed by the standard or that the labour had to use poor quality materials and could not work so quickly. A favourable variance would indicate that labour took less time than standard, possibly because a more skilled labour force was used.

In the example above, the analysis of variances by both product and department will enable management to **pinpoint more accurately the areas of operations which need investigation** because they are not operating to standard and to **capitalise on the benefits offered by those areas which are operating above standard**.

10 PRACTICE QUESTION: MORE STANDARD COSTING

> **Tutorial note**. Task (b) involves 'working backwards' to determine standards, given actual data and variances. The majority of central assessment questions provide you with data about actual and standard results and you have to calculate variances.
>
> The approach adopted in this question is one way in which your depth of understanding of variance calculations can really be assessed, however. You must be able to understand the link between standard data, actual data and the resulting variances if you are to prove yourself competent at variance analysis questions in the central assessments.

(a)

Cost element	Product EM - April		Standard cost for 600 units
		£	£
Direct material E	Actual cost	6,270	
	Price variance	330	
	Usage variance	(600)	
			6,000
Direct material M	Actual cost	650	
	Price variance	(50)	
			600
Direct labour	Actual cost	23,200	
	Rate variance	(800)	
	Efficiency variance	(1,400)	
			21,000
Fixed production overhead	Actual cost	27,000	
	Expenditure variance	500	
	Volume variance	2,500	
			30,000
Total standard costs for 600 units of produce EM			57,600

Note . Variances in brackets are adverse.

(b) *Initial workings*

(i) **Calculation of standard material price**

	Material E	Material M
Actual price of material	£6,270	£650
Price variance	£330 (F)	£50 (A)
∴ Standard price of material used	£6,600	£600
÷ Actual usage (metres)	660	200
Standard price per metre	£10	£3

(ii) **Calculation of material E standard usage**

Excess usage in metres standard price	=	£600 adverse variance ÷ £10
	=	60 metres
Actual usage for 600 units	=	660 metres
∴ Standard usage for 600 units	=	600 metres
∴ Standard usage for 1 unit	=	1 metre

There is no usage variance for material M, therefore standard usage is equal to actual usage (0.33 metres per unit).

(iii) **Calculation of standard labour rate**

Actual wages paid	£23,200
Rate variance	£800 (A)
∴ Standard rate for actual hours	£22,400
÷ Actual hours	3,200
Standard rate per hour	£7

(iv) **Calculation of standard labour hours**

Excess labour hours	=	£1,400 adverse variance ÷ £7 standard rate	
	=	200 hours	
Actual hours for 600 units	=	3,200 hours	
∴ Standard hours for 600 units	=	3,000 hours	
∴ Standard hours for 1 unit	=	5 hours	

We now have all the information needed to compile a standard cost sheet.

Product EM
Standard product cost for one unit

	Standard quantity	Standard price £	Total standard cost £
Direct material E	1 metre	10	10
Direct material M	0.33 metres	3	1
Direct labour	5 hours	7	35
Fixed production overhead			50 (note 1)
			96

Note. The total standard fixed overhead for 600 units is £30,000 (from (a)) and therefore the standard cost for one unit is £50.

(c) **Fixed production overhead volume variance = (actual units – budgeted units) × standard fixed overhead per unit.**

∴ £2,500 = (600 – budgeted units) × £50
∴ Budgeted units = 550

The number of units of product EM which were budgeted for April was 550.

(d) Material and labour cost standards would originally have been determined by establishing a standard price and quantity for each type of material and for labour.

Technical specifications would be prepared by production experts, either in the production department or the work study department.

The specification for materials would take account of the required finished quality of the product and may include allowances for wastage, losses and so on.

The standard operation sheet for labour will specify the operating methods to be used, detailing the expected hours required by each grade of labour to make one unit. This may be determined by method study and work measurement and may include allowances for idle time and other inefficiencies.

The **standard price for material** would take account of factors such as the availability of bulk discounts, and any purchase contracts already agreed. Forecasts will be made of future price movements, for incorporation into the standard.

The **standard rate of labour** would be set with advice from the personnel department, taking account of factors such as the level of skill required, trade union agreements, any bonus schemes and so on.

11 PRACTICE QUESTION: CALCULATING COST VARIANCES

> **Tutorial note.** Variance calculations are a *very* popular central assessment topic and so it is vital that you are completely happy with calculating all the variances explained in the BPP Interactive Text.

(a) **Materials price variance**

	£	£
37,100 metres of wood should cost (× £0.30)	11,130	
but did cost	11,000	
wood price variance		130 (F)
29,200 metres of gut should cost (× £1.50)	43,800	
but did cost	44,100	
gut price variance		300 (A)
wood and gut price variance		170 (A)

(b) **Material usage variance**

3,700 units of Henman should use	(× 7)	25,900 m	(× 6)	22,200 m	
1,890 units of Lendl should use	(× 5)	9,450 m	(× 4)	7,560 m	
		35,350 m		29,760 m	
but together they did use		37,100		29,200 m	
Material usage variance in metres		1,750 m (A)		560 m (F)	
× standard cost per metre		× £0.30		× £1.50	
Material usage variance in £					
Wood		£525 (A)			
Gut				£840 (F)	

(c) **Other materials cost variance**

	£
3,700 units of Henman should cost (× £0.20)	740.00
1,890 units of Lendl should cost (× £0.15)	283.50
	1,023.50
but together they did cost	1,000.00
Other materials cost variance	23.50 (F)

(d) **Direct labour rate variance**

	£
2,200 hours of labour should cost (× £3)	6,600
but did cost	6,850
Direct labour rate variance	250 (A)

(e) **Direct labour efficiency variance**

3,700 units of Henman should take (× 30 minutes)	1,850 hrs
1,890 units of Lendl should take (× 20 minutes)	630 hrs
	2,480 hrs
but together they did take	2,200 hrs
Efficiency variance in hrs	280 hrs (F)
× standard rate per hour	× £3
Efficiency variance in £	£840 (F)

(f) **Fixed overhead**

		Hours
Budgeted hours:	Henman	2,000
	Lendl	500
		2,500
Budgeted fixed costs		£21,000
Budgeted hours		2,500 hrs
Absorption rate per hour		£8.40

(g) **Fixed overhead price variance**

	Budgeted expenditure £	Actual expenditure £	Variance £
Supervision	8,000	7,940	60 (F)
Heating and lighting	1,200	1,320	120 (A)
Rent	4,800	4,800	
Depreciation	7,000	7,000	-
Total	21,000	21,060	60 (A)

(h) **Fixed overhead usage variance**

(Same as labour efficiency) 280 hours (F) × £8.40 per hour £2,352 (F)

(i) **Fixed overhead capacity variance**

Budgeted hours worked	2,500 hrs
Actual hours worked	2,200 hrs
Volume capacity variance in hours	300 hrs (A)
× standard rate per hour	× £8.40
	£2,520 (A)

12 PRACTICE QUESTION: RECONCILIATION STATEMENT

> **Tutorial note.** The key test for you here is to establish how readily you can calculate the variances. This solution tries to explain the calculations in case you have any difficulties with them.

(a) **Direct materials variances**

The variance for leather can be divided into a materials price and a materials usage variance.

(i) **Leather: price variance**

	£
9,200 units of leather were purchased and cost	45,400
but should cost (× £ 5)	46,000
Price variance	600 (F)

(ii) **Leather: usage variance**

3,200 units of TS3 were made and used	9,200 units of materials
but 3,200 units should use (× 3)	9,600 units of materials
Usage variance in units	400 units (F)
× standard cost per unit of leather	× £5
Usage variance in £	£2,000 (F)

(iii) **Other materials**

We are not given a breakdown into units of material and price per unit of material, and so the only materials variance we can calculate is the total cost variance.

	£
3,200 units of TS3 did cost	9,500
but should cost (× £3)	9,600
Other materials cost variance	100 (F)

(b) **Direct labour variances**

(i) **Direct labour rate variance**

	£
5,100 hours cost	24,100
but should cost (× £4)	20,400
Labour rate variance	3,700 (A)

(ii) **Direct labour efficiency variance**

3,200 units of TS3 took	5,100 hours
but should take (× $1^1/_2$ hrs)	4,800 hours
Efficiency variance in hours	300 hours (A)
× standard cost per labour hour	× £4
Efficiency variance in £	£1,200 (A)

(c) **Fixed production overhead variances**

Fixed production overhead variances **measure the total under- or over-absorbed production overhead** in the period.

In our example, we have a standard fixed overhead cost of £9 per unit and budgeted production of 3,000 units, which means that the budgeted fixed overheads for the period must be £9 × 3,000 units = £27,000. In standard costing, the fixed overhead absorption rate is the standard cost per unit, for the actual number of units made: 3,200 units × £9 per unit. This gives us the following.

	£
Actual fixed overheads absorbed (3,200 × £9)	28,800
Actual fixed overheads incurred	31,500
Total fixed overhead variance	2,700 (A)

Variance analysis then goes on to establish why the total under- or over-absorbed fixed overhead occurred.

(i) **Fixed overhead price variance**

This is under or over absorption of overhead because **actual fixed overhead expenditure differed from budgeted expenditure.**

	£
Budgeted fixed overhead	27,000
Actual fixed overhead	31,500
Price variance	4,500 (A)

The price variance also indicates over-spending above budget by £4,500, and a control report should attempt to pinpoint the source of this excessive overhead spending more specifically.

(ii) **Fixed overhead usage variance**

This is the same variance in hours as the direct labour efficiency variance and is valued in £ at the standard fixed overhead rate per hour.

300 hrs (A) × £6 per hour	£1,800 (A)

(iii) **Fixed overhead capacity variance**

This is the difference between actual and budgeted production hours.

Budgeted production hours (3,000 units × 1.5 hrs)	4,500 hours
Actual production hours, ignoring idle time	5,100 hours
Capacity variance in hours	600 hours (F)
× standard fixed overhead rate per hour	× £6
Capacity variance in £	£3,600 (F)

The variances can now be summarised in an **operating statement**.

OPERATING STATEMENT FOR PERIOD 7 20X8

		£	£
Standard cost of actual production (3,200 × £33)			105,600

Cost variances	£(F)	£(A)	
Leather price	600		
usage	2,000		
Other materials	100		
Direct labour: rate		3,700	
efficiency		1,200	
Fixed overhead price		4,500	
Fixed overhead usage		1,800	
Fixed overhead capacity	3,600		
	6,300	11,200	
Total cost variances			4,900 (A)
Actual costs			110,500

13   STATELY HOTELS PLC

> **Tutorial note**. Don't be put off by the non-manufacturing slant of the variance analysis. Pen and notepaper sets are just like widgets and conference rooms are just like product X.
>
> According to the assessor there was clear evidence of competence in handling variances and explaining the possible reasons for the variances but a noticeable lack of understanding about possible management controls or actions.

			£
(a)	(i)	4,280 pen and notepaper sets should have cost (× £2.50)	10,700
		but did cost (W1)	11,207
		Pen and notepaper set **price variance**	507 (A)

	(ii)	4,100 conference delegates should have used	4,100 sets
		but did use	4,280 sets
		Usage variance in sets	180 sets (A)
		× standard cost per set	× £2.50
		Pen and notepaper set **usage variance** in £	£450 (A)

			£
	(iii)	1,240 hours should have cost (× £5)	6,200
		but did cost (W2)	5,684
		Cleaning labour **rate variance**	516 (F)

	(iv)	70 cleaning sessions should have taken (× 15 hours)	1,050 hrs
		but did take	1,240 hrs
		Labour efficiency variance in hours	190 hrs (A)
		× standard rate per hour	× £5
		Cleaning labour **efficiency variance**	£950 (A)

Workings

1			£
2,800 × £2.50	=		7,000
1,060 × £2.80	=		2,968
420 × £2.95	=		1,239
			11,207

			£
2	900 × £4.20	=	3,780
	340 × £5.60	=	1,904
			5,684

(b) The **adverse price variance** could be due to an increase in pen and notepaper set prices above the price used in the standard or careless purchasing by the purchasing department.

Management should investigate to see whether cheaper supplies are available. If they are not, the standard should be changed so that it represents a realistic target.

The **adverse usage variance** may be due to a delivery of low quality pen and notepaper sets (perhaps sets have items missing or the packaging is ripped) or there may be theft or pilferage of the sets from stores. Checks should be made to see whether there have been any problems with recent deliveries and management should ensure that the stocks of sets are kept securely locked and that the correct number are issued each day.

The **favourable rate variance** has probably arisen because the proportion of weekday hours worked was greater than anticipated. A more detailed standard cost may have to be established which includes two elements for labour rate, one for weekday working and one for weekend working. A separate variance could then be calculated for each.

The **adverse efficiency variance** may be due to a level of idle time greater than that allowed for in the standard, perhaps because conferences did not finish on time and cleaners were unable to enter conference rooms. The management should ensure that cleaners do not commence work until after the time set for conferences to finish.

14   OMEGA

> **Tutorial note**. Remember that the fixed overhead volume variance is the sum of the fixed overhead efficiency and capacity variances. You should therefore not include all three variances in the reconciliation in task (b) since you will be double counting the volume variance.
>
> According to the assessor, candidates who were adequately prepared had no problems with tasks (a) and (b) but it was clear that many candidates had chosen to ignore this area in their studies. The assessor also remarked that a worrying feature in some candidates' solutions to task (c) was their inability to explain fixed overhead variances in simple language.

(a) (i)

	£
Budgeted fixed overhead expenditure (4,100 × 40 × £12.50)	2,050,000
Actual fixed overhead expenditure	2,195,000
Fixed overhead **expenditure variance**	145,000 (A)

(ii)

	£
Actual production at standard rate (3,850 × 40 × £12.50)	1,925,000
Budgeted production at standard rate (4,100 × 40 × £12.50)	2,050,000
Fixed overhead **volume variance**	125,000 (A)

(iii)

Budgeted hours (4,100 × 40)	164,000 hrs
Actual hours	159,000 hrs
Fixed overhead capacity variance in hours	5,000 hrs (A)
× standard rate per hour	× £12.50
Fixed overhead **capacity variance**	£62,500 (A)

(iv)

3,850 units should have taken (× 40 hrs)	154,000 hrs
but did take	159,000 hrs
Fixed overhead efficiency variance in hours	5,000 hrs (A)
× standard rate per hour	× £12.50
Fixed overhead **efficiency variance**	£62,500 (A)

(b)

REPORT

To: Production Director
From: Assistant Management Accountant
Date: 14 April 20X8
Subject: **Performance of Division Omega** – 4 weeks ended 1 April 20X8

Set out below is a **reconciliation** of the **standard cost** of production **to the actual cost of production** in Division Omega for the four-week period ended 1 April 20X8.

	(F) £	(A) £	£
Standard cost of production (3,850 units × £975)			3,753,750
Variances			
Material price		45,000	
Material usage		76,250	
Labour rate		32,500	
Labour efficiency		37,500	
Fixed overhead expenditure		145,000	
Fixed overhead capacity		62,500	
Fixed overhead efficiency	———	62,500	
	-	461,250	461,250 (A)
Actual cost of production (W)			4,215,000

Working

	£
Materials	795,000
Labour	1,225,000
Fixed overheads	2,195,000
Actual cost of production	4,215,000

(c)

MEMORANDUM

To: Production Director
From: Assistant Management Accountant
Date: 14 April 20X8
Subject: **Fixed overhead variances**

This memorandum provides information on fixed overhead variances. In particular it covers the similarities between fixed overhead variances and other cost variances, the meaning of the various fixed overhead variances and the ways in which such variances can be of assistance in the planning and the controlling of the division.

Similarities between fixed overhead variances and other variances

The fixed overhead expenditure variance is the difference between the budgeted fixed overhead expenditure and actual fixed overhead expenditure. It is therefore similar to the material price and labour rate variances in that it shows the effect on costs and hence profit of paying more or less than anticipated for resources used.

Material usage and labour efficiency variances show the effect on costs and hence profit of having used more or less resource than should have been used for the actual volume of production. Fixed overheads should remain constant within the relevant range of production, however; they should not change simply because budgeted and actual production volumes differ. Fixed overhead variances similar to material usage and labour efficiency variances (reflecting the difference between the actual fixed overhead expenditure and the fixed overhead expenditure which should have been incurred at the actual volume of production) cannot therefore occur.

The meaning of fixed overhead variances

Whereas labour and material total variances show the effect on costs and hence profit of the difference between what the actual production volume should have cost and what it did cost (in terms of labour or material), if an organisation uses standard absorption costing (as we do), the fixed overhead total variance is the difference between actual fixed overhead expenditure and the fixed overhead absorbed (the under- or over-absorbed overhead).

The total under or over absorption is made up of the fixed overhead expenditure variance and the fixed overhead volume variance. The volume variance shows that part of the under- or over-absorbed overhead which is due to any difference between budgeted production volume and actual production volume.

The volume variance can be further broken down into an efficiency variance and a capacity variance. The capacity variance shows how much of the under- or over-absorbed overhead is due to working the labour force or plant more or less than planned whereas the efficiency variance shows the effect of the efficiency of the labour force or plant.

The volume variance and its two subdivisions, the efficiency variance and the capacity variance, measure the extent of under or over absorption due to production volume being different to that planned. Material usage and labour efficiency variances, on the other hand, measure the effect of usage being different from that expected for the actual volume achieved.

Fixed overhead variances and planning and control

The fixed overhead volume variance and its subdivisions are perhaps misleading as variances for management control, because unlike expenditure variances or variable cost efficiency variances, they are not a true reflection of the extra or lower cash spending by an organisation as a result of the variance occurring. However, the fixed overhead efficiency and capacity variances are of some relevance for planning and control. They provide some measure of the difference between budgeted production volume and actual production volume, and management should obviously be interested in whether budgeted output was achieved, and if not, why not. A favourable efficiency variance might indicate an efficient workforce whereas an unfavourable capacity variance might indicate plant breakdowns or strikes. The existence of a fixed overhead volume variance can therefore be important; it is only the monetary value given to it that can be misleading.

The fixed overhead expenditure variance highlights the effect on costs and hence profit of changes to the level of overheads. For overhead expenditure variances to have any practical value as a planning or control measure, the variance for each overhead cost centre needs to be calculated, and reported to the manager responsible. Within each overhead cost centre, the manager should be able to analyse the total variance into indirect material cost variances, indirect labour cost variances and excess or favourable spending on other items, such as depreciation, postage, telephone charges and so on. Managers can then, for example, consider other suppliers, reconsider pricing structures of products and the like.

15   GRANSDEN LTD

> **Tutorial note**. In task (a)(i) you were not provided with the actual cost per metre of wood. By adding the variance to the standard cost you can determine the actual cost, however, and by dividing this actual cost by the actual usage of wood you can determine the actual cost per metre.

(a) (i)

		£
Standard cost of 5,000 cabinets		2,500,000
Variance		200,000 (A)
Actual cost		2,700,000

Actual usage	22,500 metres
∴ Actual cost per metre	£2,700,000 ÷ 22,500 = £120

	£
22,500 metres of wood should have cost (× £100)	2,250,000
but did cost (× £120)	2,700,000
Material price variance	450,000 (A)

5,000 cabinets should have used (× 5m)	25,000 m
but did use	22,500 m
Material usage variance in metres	2,500 m (F)
× standard cost per metre	× £100
Material usage variance	£250,000 (F)

(ii)

Current index	168
Index when standards agreed	160

$$\therefore \text{Increase} = 8 \text{ index points}$$
$$= 8/160 \times 100\% = 5\%$$

∴ Price inflation = increase in RPI = 5%

(b)

	Usage Metres	Price £
Standard cost of 5,000 cabinets	25,000	100
Actual cost of 5,000 cabinets	22,500	120
Difference	2,500	20

Part of the difference of £20 in price per metre is due to inflation. This element = £100 × 5% = £5. The remaining increase of £15 is due to other factors.

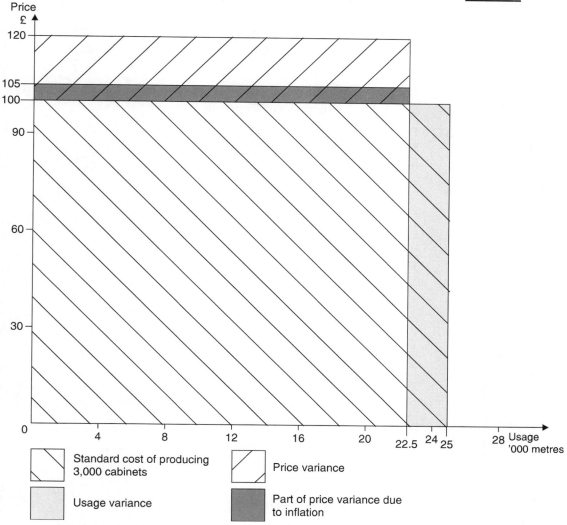

Standard cost of producing 3,000 cabinets	Price variance
Usage variance	Part of price variance due to inflation

(c) **Difficulties in interpreting the price variance**

(i) The original standard may have been inappropriate given the conditions in May.

(ii) There may be an interrelationship between the adverse price variance and the favourable usage variance. If a superior but more expensive material is used (resulting in an adverse price variance), wastage should be less (and a favourable usage variance should occur).

(iii) The Retail Prices Index (RPI) is a measure of the cost of living of the average household in the UK. It may not reflect changes in prices in manufacturing generally or of wood in particular.

16   PRIORY LTD

> **Tutorial note**. The additive model for time series analysis is $Y = T + S$. In task (a)(i) we want to calculate T and so we deduct S from Y. The signs of the seasonal variations as provided in the question therefore change. For example, if $Y = 10$ and $T = -1$, then $T = Y - S = 10 - -1 = 10 + 1$.
>
> In task (a)(ii), we want to calculate a forecast Y as $T + S$, so the signs of the seasonal variations provided in the question do not change.

			Quarter 1	Quarter 2	Quarter 3	Quarter 4
(a)	(i)	Actual price	£90	£105	£80	£75
		Seasonal variation	−+£10	−+£20	−−£10	−−£20
			£80	£85	£90	£95

The **seasonally-adjusted price shows an increase of £5 per quarter**. The **trend** is therefore an **increase of £5 per quarter**.

	(ii)	Trend	£100	£105	£110	£115
		Seasonal variation	+£10	+£20	−£10	−£20
		Forecast price	£110	£125	£100	£95

(b) (i) (1)

	£
18,200 l should have cost (× £110)	2,002,000
but did cost	2,003,100
Material **price variance**	1,100 (A)

(2)

	£
950 units should have used (× 21 l)	19,950 l
but did use	18,200 l
	1,750 l (F)
× standard cost per litre	× £110
Material **usage variance**	£192,500 (F)

(3)

	£
7,100 hours should have cost (× £7)	49,700
but did cost	41,200
Labour **rate variance**	8,500 (F)

(4)

	£
950 units should have taken (× 7 hrs)	6,650 hrs
but did take	7,100 hrs
	450 hrs (A)
× standard rate per hour	× £7
Labour **efficiency variance**	£3,150 (A)

(ii) **STATEMENT RECONCILING STANDARD COST OF ACTUAL PRODUCTION WITH ACTUAL COST OF ACTUAL PRODUCTION**
(WEEK 7, CONTROL PERIOD 2)

	(F) £	(A) £	£
Standard cost of production (950 × £2,653)			2,520,350
Cost variances			
Material price		1,100	
Material usage	192,500		
Labour rate	8,500		
Labour efficiency		3,150	
Fixed overhead expenditure		81,900	
Fixed overhead efficiency		18,900	
Fixed overhead capacity		39,900	
	201,000	144,950	56,050 (F)
Actual cost of production			2,464,300

(c)   MEMORANDUM

To: Production Director
From: Assistant Management Accountant
Date: XX July 20X8
Subject: **Meaning of variances**

(i)   **What variances are attempting to measure**

Most organisations have targets which they aim to reach in the course of one or more accounting periods. These targets are generally identified when an organisation plans for the future. Budgeting and standard costing are two methods whereby an organisation plans for the future.

Once an accounting period has been completed, it is useful to compare the actual results for the period with the budgeted results or standard costs for the same period. Any differences which arise are known as *variances*.

Variances are therefore attempting to measure any deviation between actual results and the original plan of action of the organisation.

(ii)   **Ways in which production variances can arise**

There are three main ways in which production variances can arise.

(1)   The actual cost per unit is different from the planned cost per unit
(2)   The actual input usage is different from the planned input usage
(3)   The actual production volume is different from the planned production volume

(iii) **Reasons for errors in reporting variances**

There are a number of ways in which errors may arise when reporting variances.

(1)   If the original standards used are unrealistic or out-of-date.

(2)   If the actual results are recorded incorrectly.

(3)   If expenses are posted incorrectly, then the costs will not be matched with the budgeted costs.

(4)   If costs which have been incurred, but not invoiced are not accrued, then the costs will be understated, giving rise to an incorrect favourable variance.

(5)   If costs incurred by one department are due to the actions of another department, then the costs should be charged to the department responsible for them. If these costs are not identified correctly, then an incorrect adverse variance is likely to arise in the department which is not responsible for the costs.

(iv)   **Material price variance query**

Material A was forecast at a price of £125 per litre during control period 2. The standard price for material A is £110 per litre. During control period 2, the actual price paid per litre of A was £110.06 (£2,003,100 ÷ 18,200). The purchasing manager appears to have been efficient when buying litres of A, since he paid £110.06 per litre, when the standard cost was £110 per litre. The standard cost per litre of A may not be appropriate, however, since a forecast price of £125 per litre of A indicates that the purchasing manager may well have been very efficient when buying litres of A in control period 2. The standard price should possibly be higher.

17 MALTON LTD

> **Tutorial note**. Task (a) was very straightforward but task (b) was more difficult.
>
> Task (b) required you to recalculate the same variances for a subsection of the original data. This is just like being asked to calculate the variances for different types of material and different classes of labour.
>
> According to the assessor the weakest answers were to task (b)(iv). Too many candidates gave no consideration to the data in, or the requirements of, the question. For example, some candidates blamed the workforce for the adverse material usage variance on the special order even though it was specifically stated in the question that the additional material was below specification.

(a) (i) (1)

	£'000
78,000 litres of material should have cost (× £20)	1,560
but did cost	1,599
Material **price variance**	39 (A)

(2)

9,500 units of Beta should have used (× 8L)	76,000 L
but did use	78,000 L
	2,000 L (A)
× standard cost per litre	× £20
Material **usage variance**	£40,000 (A)

(3)

	£
39,000 hours of labour should have cost (× £6)	234,000
but did cost	249,600
Labour **rate variance**	15,600 (A)

(4)

9,500 units of Beta should have taken (× 4)	38,000 hrs
but did take	39,000 hrs
Labour efficiency variance in hours	1,000 (A)
× standard rate per hour	£6
Labour **efficiency variance**	£6,000 (A)

(ii) **STATEMENT RECONCILING ACTUAL MARGINAL COST OF PRODUCTION TO STANDARD MARGINAL COST OF PRODUCTION**

	(F) £	(A) £	£
Standard marginal cost of production (9,500 × £184)			1,748,000
Cost variances			
Material price		39,000	
Material usage		40,000	
Labour rate		15,600	
Labour efficiency		6,000	
	-	100,600	100,600 (A)
Actual marginal cost of production May 20X7			1,848,600

(b) (i) Since 20% of the special purchase was scrapped *prior* to being issued to production, then the **amount of material purchased in order to make 1,500 units** is as follows.

1,500 × 8L × 1/0.8 = 15,000L

(∴ 20% of 15,000L was scrapped = 3,000L scrapped and not issued to production)

	£
15,000L of material should have cost ($\times$ £20)	300,000
but did cost ($\times$ £22)	330,000
Material price variance due to extra order	30,000 (A)

Since 20% of the special purchase was scrapped prior to being issued to production, then of the 15,000L purchased for the extra order, 20% $\times$ 15,000L = 3,000L were scrapped. Therefore 78,000L – 3,000L = 75,000L were issued to production.

1,500 units of Beta should have used ($\times$ 8L)	12,000	L
but did use	15,000	L
	3,000	L (A)
$\times$ standard cost per litre	$\times$ £20	
Material usage variance due to extra order	£60,000	(A)

	£
1,500 units of Beta should have cost (1,500 $\times$ 4 $\times$ £6)	36,000
but did cost (1,500 $\times$ 4 $\times$ £6 $\times$ 150%)	54,000
Labour rate variance due to extra order	18,000 (A)

(ii) (1) Standard price for materials was set with an index measuring 240.0.

Revised standard price for materials in May is

$$£20 \times \frac{247.2}{240.0} = £20.60$$

(2) **Materials price variance caused by general change in prices** is therefore calculated as follows.

Total material used for 9,500 units	78,000 L
less: material used for special order	15,000 L
	63,000 L
$\times$ price increase	$\times$ £0.60
	£37,800 (A)

(iii) **REVISED COSTING STATEMENT RECONCILING ACTUAL MARGINAL COST OF PRODUCTION WITH STANDARD MARGINAL COST OF PRODUCTION**

	Variances controllable by R Hill	*Variances not controllable by R Hill*	£
Standard marginal cost of production (9,500 $\times$ £184)			1,748,000
Cost variances			
Material price - due to inflation		37,800 (A)	
Material price - due to extra order		30,000 (A)	
Material price (W)	28,800 (F)		
Material usage	20,000 (F)	60,000 (A)	
Labour rate	2,400 (F)	18,000 (A)	
Labour efficiency	6,000 (A)		
	45,200 (F)	145,800 (A)	100,600 (A)
Actual marginal cost of production			1,848,600

Working

	£	£
Total variance		39,000 (A)
Variance due to inflation	37,800 (A)	
Variance due to extra order	30,000 (A)	
		67,800 (A)
Remaining variance		28,800 (F)

(iv) NOTE TO RICHARD HILL

Following my review of the standard cost report for the Eastern Division, I should like to make the following comments.

The actual marginal cost of production was found to be £100,600 more than the standard marginal cost of production for May 20X7.

Inflation

There was an overall adverse materials price variance of £39,000. This was partly due to the fact that the original standard cost of material did not take into account inflation in May 20X7 (which caused a £37,800 (A) variance). This variance was out of your control, and I would like to suggest that the company revise standard material prices as soon as the indices for each month are known.

Extra order

The extra order which was accepted at late notice by the sales director was responsible for a number of adverse variances.

Firstly, materials for the extra order were purchased at a higher than normal price, giving rise to a material price variance (net of inflation) of £30,000.

Secondly, the extra material purchased was not up to normal specification and 20% of it had to be scrapped before being issued to production. This in turn gave rise to an adverse variance of £60,000.

Lastly the workforce could only produce the special order by working overtime. This overtime was in turn responsible for an adverse variance of £18,000.

All of the variances associated with the extra order were not within your control.

I would suggest that the company agrees to meet special orders at short notice only if the extra costs incurred (higher material prices, overtime costs) are recovered by charging a higher sales price.

18 DEBUSSY LTD

> **Tutorial note**. Did you read the instructions carefully? Let's hope so. In task (b) you were told to calculate *total* variances (not variances for individual elements of fixed overhead). In task (c) you had to provide *one* possible reason for each of the variances that occurred.

(a) (i)

Budgeted labour cost for quarter 4	=	£48,000
Budgeted rate per hour	=	£8
∴ **Budgeted labour hours** for quarter 4	=	£48,000 ÷ £8
	=	6,000 hours

(ii)

Actual labour cost for quarter 4	=	£42,240
Actual rate per hour	=	£8
∴ **Actual labour hours** for quarter 4	=	£42,240 ÷ £8
	=	5,280 hours

(iii) Budgeted output for quarter 4   =   3,000 tonnes
Budgeted labour hours   =   6,000 hours
∴ **Budgeted hours per tonne of fertiliser**   =   6,000 ÷ 3,000
  =   2

(iv) Actual output for quarter 4   =   2,400 tonnes
Actual labour hours   =   5,280 hours
∴ **Actual hours per tonne of fertiliser**   =   5,280 ÷ 2,400
  =   2.2

(b) We need to **begin by calculating the fixed overhead absorption rate per labour hour and per tonne.**

Budgeted fixed overheads   =   £81,000
Budgeted labour hours   =   6,000
∴ Overhead absorption rate per hour   =   £13.50
Budgeted hours per tone of fertiliser   =   2
∴ Overhead absorption rate per tonne   =   2 × £13.50
  =   £27

		£
(i)	Budgeted fixed overheads	81,000
	Actual fixed overheads	90,000
	Fixed overhead expenditure variance	9,000 (A)

(ii)	Budgeted production	3,000 tonnes
	Actual production	2,400 tonnes
		600 tonnes (A)
	× standard absorption rate per tonne	× £27
	Fixed overhead volume variance	16,200 (A)

(iii)	Budgeted hours of work	6,000 hrs
	Actual hours of work	5,280 hrs
		720 hrs
	× standard absorption rate per hour	× £13.50
	Fixed overhead capacity variance	£9,720 (A)

(iv)	2,400 tonnes should have taken (× 2 hrs)	4,800 hrs
	but did take	5,280 hrs
	Efficiency variance in hours	480 hrs (A)
	× standard rate per hour	× £13.50
	Fixed overhead efficiency variance	£6,480 (A)

(c) MEMORANDUM

To: Claude Debussy
From: Accountant
Date: 13 December 20X8
Subject: **Fixed overhead variances**

(i) **Fixed overheads and changes in activity level**

Fixed overheads do not vary with changes in the level of production but remain fixed within a relevant range of production levels. For example, our plant and machinery can produce up to 15,000 tonnes of fertiliser per annum and so the insurance on this machinery should remain fixed provided output is 15,000 tonnes or less. If we were to produce 18,000 tonnes, however, we would need to invest in additional plant and machinery and hence the cost of insurance would increase.

Rather than vary in line with changes in output, fixed overheads vary with time. Rent and rates increase with time, the cost of leasing machinery increases the longer the machinery is leased and so on.

As actual output is within the relevant range of output, it is therefore most unlikely that fixed overheads have increased because actual output was greater than budgeted output. The difference between actual and budgeted fixed overheads is therefore due to either increases in the cost of fixed overheads since when the budget was set or to poor planning and budgeting.

(ii) **Possible reasons for variances** (You were only required to provide one per variance.)

(1) The fixed overhead **expenditure variance** occurred because the overhead costs were actually higher than anticipated. This may be due to a rate of inflation that was higher than anticipated, the use of non-standard suppliers of insurance and power, sudden increase in costs or inappropriate standards.

(2) The fixed overhead **capacity variance** occurred because actual hours of work were less than budgeted hours of work. This may be due to a reduction in demand for fertiliser compared with budget (and so the production workers were not required to work so many hours), a strike by workers or poor planning.

(3) The fixed overhead **efficiency variance** occurred because the production workers worked less efficiently than anticipated. This may be due to poor motivation, weak supervision, machine breakdowns, production bottlenecks, poor quality materials that were difficult to work with or an inappropriate standard.

(d) (i)

	Quarter 1	Quarter 2	Quarter 3	Quarter 4
Current budget	£30,000	£30,000	£30,000	£30,000
Seasonal variation (%)	+ 5%	– 10%	– 20%	+ 25%
Seasonal variation (£)	+ £1,500	– £3,000	– £6,000	+ £7,500
Revised budget	£31,500	£27,000	£24,000	£37,500

(ii) **Use of revised budget for calculating variances**

The power which provides the heating for our ovens does not vary with changes in production output but it does depend on the outside temperature. If we take account of the seasonal variation in temperature and its effect on power consumption when budgeting, we will produce more accurate budgeted costs against which actual costs can be compared for control purposes. For example, the current figures shows an adverse power expenditure variance of £6,000 in quarter 4 but, by using the revised budget figure of £37,500, the variance is converted to a favourable variance of £1,500. Overall fixed overheads for the quarter would increase to £88,500, resulting in an overall adverse variance of £1,500, making it clear that the level of expenditure on fixed overheads was actually very close to the level budgeted.

The use of the revised figures for power costs would, however, increase the fixed overhead absorption rate in quarters when the seasonal variation is positive and decrease it in quarters when the seasonal variation is negative. This would in turn increase and decrease fixed overhead volume variances. The same volume variance in tonnes could therefore have a different monetary value in different quarters which would be extremely confusing and misleading for managers.

Given that the seasonal variations balance each other out over the four quarters it would seem **more appropriate to use an annual fixed overhead absorption rate for calculating the volume variance.**

19   HAMPSTEAD PLC

> **Tutorial note**. Task (b) contained the tricky part of this question. You had to calculate the variances due to the machine breakdown and the price index change and then work out the variance due to normal operations. For example, if the total variance is £6,000 (F) and the variance due to the material shortage is £10,000 (A), the variance due to normal operations is *not* £4,000 (F) but £16,000 (F).

(a)   (i)   (1)   **Standard marginal cost of a unit of Alpha**

	£
Material (36,000m ÷ 12,000) 3m × (£432,000 ÷ 36,000) £12 per m	36.00
Labour (72,000 hrs ÷ 12,000) 6 hours × (£450,000 ÷ 72,000) £6.25 per hr	37.50
	73.50

(2)   **Standard cost of producing 10,000 units of Alpha**

	£
Material (£36 × 10,000)	360,000
Labour (£37.50 × 10,000)	375,000
Fixed overheads	396,000
	1,131,000

(ii)   (1)

	£
32,000 m should have cost (× £12)	384,000
but did cost	377,600
Material price variance	6,400 (F)

(2)

10,000 units should have used (× 3 m)	30,000 m
but did use	32,000 m
Material usage variance in metres	2,000 m (A)
× standard cost per metre	× £12
Material usage variance in £	£24,000 (A)

(3)

	£
70,000 hrs should have cost (× £6.25)	437,500
but did cost	422,800
Labour rate variance	14,700 (F)

(4)

10,000 units should have taken (× 6 hrs)	60,000 hrs
but did take	70,000 hrs
Efficiency variance in hours	10,000 hrs (A)
× standard rate per hour	× £6.25
Labour efficiency variance in £	£62,500 (A)

(5)

	£
Budgeted fixed overhead expenditure	396,000
Actual fixed overhead expenditure (£(330,000 + 75,000))	405,000
Fixed overhead expenditure variance	9,000 (A)

(iii)

REPORT

To: Managing Director
From: Assistant Management Accountant
Date: 18 June 20X8
Subject: The **use of standard marginal costing** at Finchley Ltd

As discussed at our earlier meetings, because all companies within the Hampstead Group use standard marginal costing, Finchley Ltd will need to adopt the system from 1 August 20X8. This report is intended to **demonstrate and describe the use of standard marginal costing** in your company.

(1)   Set out below is a **statement reconciling the standard cost of production** for the three months ended 31 May 20X8 **with the actual cost of production** for that period.

	(A) £	(F) £	£
Standard cost of output ((see (a)(i)(2))			1,131,000
Variances			
Material price		6,400	
Material usage	\24,000		
Labour rate		14,700	
Labour efficiency	62,500		
Fixed overhead expenditure	9,000		
	95,500	21,100	74,400 (A)
Actual cost of output			1,205,400

(2)   The total labour variance in the statement above (£47,800 (A)) differs from that in your absorption costing management report for the three months ended 31 May 20X8 because the **original report compares the actual cost of producing 10,000 units and the budgeted cost of producing 12,000 units**. It therefore fails to compare like with like. The **report above, however, compares actual costs of producing 10,000 units and what costs should have been given the actual output of 10,000 units**. The total material variances in the two reports differ for this reason. There is very little point comparing a budgeted cost with an actual cost if the production level upon which the budgeted cost was based in not achieved.

The fixed overhead expenditure variance in the statement above also differs from the fixed overhead variance reported in the absorption costing statement. This is because the **absorption costing statement compares overhead absorbed whereas the marginal costing statement compares overhead expenditure.**

(3)   There are other **reasons why the marginal costing statement provides improved management information**.

    (i)   It separates total variances into their components and so you will be able to determine whether, for example, the total material variance is the responsibility of the purchasing manager (price variance) or the production manager (usage variance).

    (ii)   It avoids the use of under-or over-absorbed overhead, which is simply a bookkeeping exercise and does not reflect higher or lower cash spending.

    (iii) It allows management by exception.

(iv) The original statement conveys the wrong message (that the overall variance was favourable).

I hope this information has proved useful. If I can be of further assistance or you have any questions, please do not hesitate to contact me.

(b)

	(A)	(F)	£
Standard cost of output			1,131,000
Variances	£	£	
Labour rate due to machine breakdown (W1)		2,520	
Labour rate due to normal working (W1)		12,180	
Labour efficiency due to machine breakdown (W2)	75,000		
Labour efficiency due to normal working (W2)		12,500	
Material price due to change in price index (W3)	32,000		
Material price due to other reasons (W3)		38,400	
Material usage	24,000		
Fixed overhead expenditure	9,000		
	140,000	65,600	74,400 (A)
Actual cost of output			1,205,400

Workings

1		£
	Total labour rate variance	14,700 (F)
	Labour rate variance due to machine breakdown	
	$(12,000 \times £14,700/70,000)$	2,520 (F)
	Labour rate variance due to normal working (balance)	12,180 (F)

2		£
	Total labour efficiency variance	62,500 (A)
	Labour efficiency variance due to machine breakdown	
	$(12,000 \text{ hrs} \times £6.25)$	75,000 (A)
	Labour efficiency variance due to normal production	12,500 (F)

3		£	£
	Total material price variance		6,400 (F)
	Variance due to price index change		
	32,000 m should have cost $(\times £12 \times 420.03/466.70)$	345,600	
	but did cost	377,600	
			32,000 (A)
	Variance due to other reasons		38,400 (F)

(c) (i) The four general headings making up the **cost of quality** are as follows.

    (1) **Prevention** costs
    (2) **Appraisal** costs
    (3) **Internal failure** costs
    (4) **External failure** costs

(ii) **Examples** of types of cost likely to be found in each category are as follows.

    (1) Prevention costs: maintenance of quality control and inspection equipment, training in quality control

    (2) Appraisal costs: inspection of goods inwards, inspection costs of in-house processing

    (3) Internal failure costs: losses from failure of purchased items, losses due to lower selling prices for sub-quality goods

    (4) External failure costs: costs of customer complaints section, cost of repairing products returned from customers

(iii) **Implications for the existing costing system**

(1) If there are fixed price contracts with guaranteed levels of quality there are likely to be few, if any, material price variances or material usage variances due to poor quality.

(2) The cost of labour will effectively become a fixed cost, the actual unit cost of labour simply depending on the volume produced. Labour efficiency variances could therefore be calculated but they will not reflect costs saved or excess wages paid. Labour rate variances are likely to be minimal if there is a guaranteed weekly wage.

(3) Predetermined standards conflict with the TQM philosophy of continual improvement.

(4) Continual improvements should alter prices, quantities of inputs and so on, whereas standard costing systems are best used in stable, standardised, repetitive environments.

(5) Standard costing systems often incorporate a planned level of scrap in material standards. This is at odds with the TQM aim of 'zero defects'.

Results of these implications

(1) There is less need for a standard costing system: variances are likely to be small or non-existent and, if incurred, non-controllable; the use of standards is inappropriate in a TQM environment.

(2) With the flexible work practices, capture of actual labour costs by individual jobs would be very difficult. Only material costs could be collected in the normal way. It is therefore unlikely that the full marginal cost of individual jobs could be collected.

(iv) **A cost saving not recorded in the existing costing system**

With the introduction of a system of just-in-time, the cost of having money tied up in high levels of stocks will be saved. This cost would not normally be captured by Barnet Ltd's existing costing system.

20 COUNTRYSIDE COMMUNICATIONS PLC

> **Tutorial note.** One of the assessor's favourite types of task is to split a variance into a number of components, as is required in (b)(iii). In this instance you have to split the total labour rate variance into one due to faulty planning and standard setting and one due to other (operational) reasons.

(a) (i) (1)

	£
11,440 hours should have cost ($\times$ £5.25)	60,060
but did cost	59,488
Labour rate variance	572 (F)

(2)

1,040 Betas should have taken ($\times$ 10 hours)	10,400 hrs
but did take	11,440 hrs
	1,040 hrs (A)
$\times$ standard rate per hour	$\times$ £5.25
Labour efficiency variance	£5,460 (A)

(3)

	£
Budgeted expenditure (£157.50 × 1,200)	189,000
Actual expenditure	207,000
Fixed overhead expenditure variance	18,000 (A)

(4)

	£
Budgeted production at standard rate (1,200 × £157.50)	189,000
Actual production at standard rate (1,040 × £157.50)	163,800
Fixed overhead volume variance	25,200 (A)

(5)

Budgeted hours of work (10 hrs × 1,200)	12,000 hrs
Actual hours of work	11,440 hrs
	560 hrs (A)
× standard rate per hour	× £15.75
Fixed overhead capacity variance	£8,820 (A)

(6)

Labour efficiency variance in hrs	1,040 hrs (A)
× standard rate per hour	× £15.75
Fixed overhead efficiency variance	£16,380 (A)

(ii)

	£
Standard cost of actual production (1,040 × £570)	592,800

Variances	(A) £	(F) £	
Labour rate		572	
Labour efficiency	5,460		
Fixed overhead expenditure	18,000		
Fixed overhead capacity	8,820		
Fixed overhead efficiency	16,380		
	48,660	572	48,088 (A)
Actual cost of actual production			640,888

(b)
MEMO

To: Ann Green, Production Director
From: Assistant Management Accountant
Date: 7 December 20X8
Subject: **Labour rate variance** - four weeks ended 27 November 20X8

Following our telephone conversation, I set out below the information you requested.

(i) The **original labour rate**, before allowing for the 5% increase, was £5.25/1.05 = £5.

(ii) The percentage increase in the labour rate was ((104.04 – 102.00)/102.00) × 100% = 2%, not the 5% allowed for. The **revised standard hourly rate** should therefore be based on the rate of £5 and the increase of 2%, giving £5 × 1.02 = £5.10.

(iii)

	£	£
Variance due to change in index		
Actual hours worked at original standard cost (11,440 × £5.25)	60,060	
Actual hours worked at revised standard cost (11,440 × £5.10)	58,344	
		1,716 (F)
Variance due to other reasons		
Actual hours worked at revised standard cost	58,344	
Actual cost	59,488	
		1,144 (A)
Total labour rate variance		572 (F)

BPP PUBLISHING

(iv) The subdivision of the **labour rate variance** in (iii) above suggests that the variance was **only favourable because of an incorrectly-set standard rate** (assuming that the index of labour rates is applicable to Eastern Division). If the standard has been set correctly, the variance would have been £1,144 adverse, indicating that more stringent control is needed over the setting of wage rates.

(v) The **index of labour rates might not be valid in explaining part of the labour rate variance** for a number of reasons.

(1) The index is a weighted average of many different labour rates for many different levels of skill. The rate of increase may depend on skill level and hence the weighted average, represented by the index, may not be appropriate for the level of skill demonstrated by Eastern Division's employees.

(2) Indices are based on data gathered from across the country but regional variations in wage rates are very likely.

(3) The 5% increase allowed for by Eastern Division may be tied to a productivity agreement or flexible working arrangements.

(4) Eastern Division may have decided to increase wage rates by 5% in an attempt to improve quality or reduce labour turnover.

The subdivision of the labour rate variance should therefore be interpreted with caution.

(vi) (1) The **fixed overhead expenditure variance** indicates that the actual expenditure on fixed overheads was greater than the budgeted expenditure. This may be due to poor budgeting or to unexpected increases in costs.

(2) The **fixed overhead capacity variance** indicates that, because the number of hours worked was less than budgeted, the level of fixed overheads absorbed was not as high as anticipated. Fewer hours may have been worked than budgeted because of a strike or shortage of material or because the original budgeted volume of output was incorrectly estimated.

(3) The **fixed overhead efficiency variance** indicates that, because labour did not work as efficiently as anticipated, the level of fixed overheads absorbed was not as high as anticipated. This may be due to the original standard hours per unit being underestimated or because the workforce were not adequately trained or were poorly motivated.

I hope this information is useful. If I can be of any further assistance please do not hesitate to contact me.

21 ORIGINAL HOLIDAYS LTD

> **Tutorial note**. You may have had trouble with task (a) but exchange rates should be one of the most familiar of all indices to you. Exchange rates are merely a special form of price index - the cost of one currency in terms of another (rather than the price of a product in terms of its price at a particular point in time).

		Quarter 1	Quarter 2	Quarter 3	Quarter 4
(a)	UK cost	£102.400	£137.760	£134.480	£68.921
	Exchange rate (francs (F) to £)	2,000 F	2,000 F	2,800 F	3,000 F
	(i) Cost in F (UK cost × exchange rate)	204,800 F	275,520 F	376,544 F	206,763 F
	Seasonal variation*	− 20%	+ 5%	+ 40%	− 25%

* **Seasonal variations are expressed as a % of the trend**. If the trend is 100% and the seasonal variation is – 20%, the forecast (a) is 80%. To determine the trend you therefore need to multiply the forecast by 100/80 = 125% (*not* 120%).
Quarter 2 - multiply forecast by 100/105%
Quarter 3 - multiply forecast by 100/140%
Quarter 4 - multiply forecast by 100/75%

(ii)

	Quarter 1	Quarter 2	Quarter 3	Quarter 4
Trend in F	256,000F	262,400 F	268,960 F	275,684 F
Increase in F		6,400 F	6,560 F	6,724 F

(iii) Increase as %

		★★2.5%	2.5%	2.5%

Annual rate of increase $= (1 + 0.025)^4 – 1$

$= 10.38\%$

★★6,400/256,000 × 100%

(iv)

Trend cost in F for quarter 4	275,684 F
Add quarterly increase of $2^{1}/_2$ %	6,892 F
	282,576 F
Seasonal adjustment (- 20%)	(56,515) F
Forecast in F (i)	226,061 F
Exchange rate (ii)	3,000 F
Forecast in £ ((i) ÷ (ii))	£75.35

(b) (i) **Standard absorption cost per holiday**

	£
Accommodation (£840,000 ÷ 6,000)	140
Air transport (£720,000 ÷ 6,000)	120
	260

(ii) **Standard absorption cost of 7,800 holidays** $= £260 × 7,800$
$= £2,028,000$

(iii) (1)

	£
Accommodation for 7,800 holidays should have cost (× £140)	1,092,000
but did cost	1,048,944
Material price variance (accommodation)	43,056 (F)

(2)

	£
Budgeted fixed overhead expenditure variance	720,000
Actual fixed overhead expenditure variance	792,000
Fixed overhead expenditure variance (air transport)	72,000 (A)

(3)

Budgeted number of return flights	80 flights
Actual number of return flights	78 flights
Fixed overhead capacity variance in flights	2 flights (A)
× standard overhead absorption rate per flight (£120 × 75)	× £9,000
Fixed overhead capacity variance in £	£18,000 (A)

(4)

7,800 holidays should have used (÷ 75)	104 flights
but did use	78 flights
Fixed overhead efficiency variance in flights	26 flights (F)
× standard overhead absorption rate per flight	× £9,000
Fixed overhead efficiency variance in £	£234,000 (F)

(iv) **Original Holidays Cost Reconciliation Statement - 3rd quarter 20X7**

£

Standard absorption cost for 7,800 holidays
(7,800 × £260)   2,028,000

Variances	A	F	
	£	£	
Material price		43,056	
Fixed overhead expenditure	72,000		
Fixed overhead capacity	18,000		
Fixed overhead efficiency		234,000	
	90,000	277,056	187,056 (F)
Actual absorption cost			1,840,944

(v) The single most important **reason for the difference between budgeted and actual cost** is the more **intensive use of the aircraft**. 104 flights should have been used to transport 7,800 passengers but only 78 were required. This is represented by the favourable fixed overhead efficiency variance of £234,000.

(c)   MEMORANDUM

To: Jane Armstrong
From: Accounting Technician
Date: 11 November 20X7
Subject: **Fixed overhead variances**

Following our earlier telephone conversation, I set out below the information about fixed overhead variances that you requested.

(i)   **Fixed overhead expenditure variance**

Provided that an organisation's activity level remains within what is known as the relevant range, fixed overheads remain the same regardless of the level of activity. The only reason they will therefore change is if the price paid for the overhead changes. This is represented by a fixed overhead expenditure variance. We reported an adverse fixed overhead expenditure variance of £72,000 in the third quarter of 20X7, caused by one or more of the costs associated with providing air transport increasing above the level budgeted. Maintenance, for example might have been more expensive than anticipated or the cabin crews might have had a salary increase which was not accounted for in the budget.

(ii) **Fixed overhead capacity variance**

The capacity variance is a measure of resource usage. If it is favourable, a resource was used more than budgeted and so we would expect output to be greater than budgeted. If, on the other hand, a resource was used less than budgeted, there would be an adverse variance because we would expect output to be lower than budgeted.

The £18,000 adverse fixed overhead capacity variance reported in quarter 3 reflects the fact that there were actually two fewer flights than budgeted and hence, given budgeted passengers per flight, one would expect the total number of passengers carried to be lower than budgeted. There are a number of reasons why there were two fewer flights than budgeted: for example the aircraft may have been taken out of service to await spare parts that were not readily available; there may have been air traffic controller strikes which prevented the plane from taking off; or bad weather may have halted flights.

(iii)   **Fixed overhead efficiency variance**

The efficiency variance is a measure of resource productivity. If it is favourable, a resource was more productive than planned whereas if it is adverse, a resource was less productive than planned. In our case, the variance shows how intensively the aircraft was being used while it was operating.

The £234,000 favourable fixed overhead efficiency variance reported in quarter 3 reflects the fact that, for each of the 78 return flights which actually took place, 100 passenger (7,800 passengers ÷ 78 flights) were carried compared with the budgeted 75 passengers per return flight. In other words, the aircraft was used far more intensively than anticipated. More passengers may have been carried per return flight than planned because of the rising popularity of the island of Zed.

22   PRONTO LTD

> **Tutorial note**. Remember in task (b)(ii)(3) that fixed overheads absorbed is based on the standard hours for actual production.

(a)

MEMO

To: Richard Jones, Managing Director
From: Accounting Technician
Date: 11 December 20X8
Subject: **Variations in kit prices**

(i)   (1)   **UK cost per kit at the time the contract was agreed**

$54,243 ÷ $9.80 = £5,535

(2)   **UK cost of kits delivered**

	September	October	November
Kits delivered	2,000	2,100	2,050
Contract cost in $ (× $54,243)	$108,486,000	$113,910,300	$111,198,150
Exchange rate	$9.00	$10.00	$10.25
Contract cost in £($ cost/exchange rate)	£12,054,000	£11,391,030	£10,848,600

(3)   **Price variance due to exchange rate differences**

	September £	October £	November £
Contract cost of kits delivered should have been (from (2) ÷ $9.8)	11,070,000	11,623,500	11,346,750
but cost of kits delivered was (from (2))	12,054,000	11,391,030	10,848,600
Variance	984,000 (A)	232,470 (F)	498,150 (F)

(4)   Total variance = price variance + usage variance

∴ If price variance is as in (3) above, usage variance is total variance minus price variance in (3).

Usage variance

	September £	*October* £	*November* £
Kits delivered should have cost (see (3))	11,070,000	11,623,500	11,346,750
but did cost (given)	12,059,535	11,385,495	10,848,600
	989,535 (A)	238,005 (F)	498,150 (F)
less: price variance (see (3))	984,000 (A)	232,470 (F)	498,150 (F)
	5,535 (A)	5,535 (F)	Nil

(ii) The price variances due to exchange rate differences should be excluded from any standard costing report prepared for the production manager of Pronto Ltd because they are not controllable by him and so he can do nothing to influence their occurrence. They do need to be recognised and monitored, however.

(b) (i) (1) Budgeted overheads per machine (or track) hour
= £840,000 ÷ 140 = £6,000 per hour

(2) Budgeted number of cars produced per machine (or track) hour
= 560/140 = 4 per hour

(3) Standard hours of actual production = 500 cars ÷ 4 per hour = 125 hours

(ii) (1) **Fixed overhead expenditure variance**

	£
Budgeted expenditure	840,000
Actual expenditure	842,000
	2,000 (A)

(2) Fixed overhead absorption rate per unit = £6,000/4 = £1,500

Fixed overhead volume variance

	£
Budgeted production at standard rate (560 × £1,500)	840,000
Actual production at standard rate (500 × £1,500)	750,000
	90,000 (A)

(3) **Fixed overhead efficiency variance**

500 cars should have taken (from (a)(i)(3))	125 hrs
but did take	126 hrs
Variance in hours	1 hr (A)
× standard absorption rate per hour	×£6,000
	£6,000 (A)

(4) **Fixed overhead capacity variance**

Budgeted hours of work	140 hrs
Actual hours of work	126 hrs
	14 hrs (A)
× standard absorption rate per hour	× £6,000
	£84,000 (A)

(iii) **Reconciliation of fixed overheads incurred to fixed overheads absorbed**

	£	£	£
Fixed overheads incurred			842,000
Variances			
Expenditure		2,000 (A)	
Volume efficiency	6,000 (A)		
Volume capacity	84,000 (A)		
Volume		90,000 (A)	
			92,000 (A)
Fixed overheads absorbed (125 hrs × £6,000)			750,000

23 BRIGHTER CHEMICALS LTD

> **Tutorial note.** Part (a)(i) requires you to determine some basic data that you will need in order to calculate the variances in part (a)(ii). Lay out your answer to part (a)(i) clearly and neatly. This will help the marker, and it will help you to find the relevant part of the data quickly when you need it.

(a) (i)

(1) Actual litres of material used = £338,283 ÷ £40.20 = 8,415 litres

(2) Actual labour hours worked = £110,330 ÷ £5.90 = 18,700 hours

(3) Standard litres of material to produce 1,700 tins of Zed = 1,700 × 5 litres = 8,500 litres

(4) Standard labour hours to produce 1,700 tins of Zed = 1,700 × 10 hours = 17,000 hours

(5) Standard hours of fixed overheads charged to budgeted production = 1,750 × 10 hours = 17,500 hours

(6) Standard hours of fixed overheads charged to actual production = 1,700 × 10 hours = 17,000 hours

(ii)

(1)
	£
From (a)(i)(1), 8,415 litres used should cost (× £40)	336,600
but did cost	338,283
Material price variance	1,683 (A)

(2)
From (a)(i)(3), 1,700 tins should use	8,500 litres
but did use ((a)(i)(1))	8,415 litres
Material usage variance in litres	85 litres (F)
× standard price per litre	× £40
Material usage variance	£3,400 (F)

(3)
	£
From (a)(i)(2), 18,700 hours worked should cost (× £6)	112,200
but did cost	110,330
Labour rate variance	1,870 (F)

(4)
From (a)(i)(4), 1,700 tins should take	17,000 hours
but did take ((a)(i)(2))	18,700 hours
Labour efficiency variance in hours	1,700 hours (A)
× standard rate per hour	× £6
Labour efficiency variance	£10,200 (A)

		£	
(5)	Budgeted fixed overhead expenditure	420,000	
	Actual fixed overhead expenditure	410,000	
	Fixed overhead expenditure variance	10,000	(F)

(6)	Actual number of tins produced	1, 1,700 tins	
	Budgeted number of tins	1,750 tins	
	Volume variance in number of tins	50 tins	(A)
	× standard overhead per tin	× £240	
	Fixed overhead volume variance	£12,000	(A)

(7)	Budgeted hours of work ((a)(i)(5))	1, 17,500 hours	
	Actual hours of work ((a)(i)(2))	18,700 hours	
	Capacity variance in hours	1,200 hours	(F)
	× standard overhead rate per hour	× £24	
	Fixed overhead capacity variance	£28,800	(F)

(8)	From (a)(ii)(4), efficiency variance in hours	1,700 hours	(A)
	× standard overhead rate per hour	× £24	
	Fixed overhead efficiency variance	£40,800	(A)

(iii) Brighter Chemicals Ltd May 20X2
Standard cost reconciliation statement for production of Zed

Budgeted production of Zed	1,750 tins
Actual production of Zed	1,700 tins

	£		£	
Standard cost of actual production (1,700 × £500)			850,000	
Cost variances				
Material price variance	1,683	(A)		
Material usage variance	3,400	(F)		
			1,717	(F)
Labour rate variance	1,870	(F)		
Labour efficiency variance	10,200	(A)		
			8,330	(A)
Fixed overhead expenditure variance	10,000	(F)		
Fixed overhead capacity variance	28,800	(F)		
Fixed overhead efficiency variance	40,800	(A)		
			2,000	(A)
Actual cost of actual production			858,613	

Note. (A) denotes adverse variance; (F) denotes favourable variance.

(b)

MEMORANDUM

To:	Production director
From:	Management accountant
Date:	12 June 20X2
Subject:	**Material variances on production of Zed, May 20X2**

Further to your comments concerning the material variances for May, there are a number of factors to consider.

(i) **The subdivision of the material price variance**

The adverse material price variance for May indicates that the materials used cost £1,683 more than the standard cost. Part of this variance reflects the efficiency or inefficiency of the purchasing department. Part of it, however, is caused by the fact that material prices in general increased, as indicated by the change in the material price index.

If we **restated the standard price to take account of the general price increase**, the revised standard price would be higher.

Revised standard price per litre = £40 × (125.86/124.00) = £40.60 per litre

The increase in the standard price is therefore £0.60 per litre (£40.60 – £40).

The part of the price variance caused by the change in standard price is therefore calculated as follows.

Change in standard price per litre	£0.60
× number of litres used	× 8,415
Variance caused by change in standard price	£5,049 (A)

The performance of the purchasing department can now be monitored using the higher, more realistic standard price.

	£
8,415 litres used should cost (× £40.60)	341,649
but did cost	338,283
Price variance caused by efficiency of purchasing department	3,366 (F)

Total price variance = £5,049 (A) + £3,366 (F) = £1,683 (A)

The purchasing department's **efficiency** was therefore masked by the general increase in material prices.

(ii) **Three possible reasons for the material usage variance**

(1) Each drum of material contains a *minimum* of 50 litres. Several may have contained more than this, but were recorded as 50 litres. Actual usage of materials may in fact have been higher than the usage recorded, resulting in an apparent favourable usage variance.

(2) The machine which measures the output of Zed may be inaccurate. The actual material usage per tin was 8,415/1,700 = 4.95 litres per tin. The acceptable measurement error is 0.5% × 5 litres = 0.025 litres, measured contents per tin therefore being 4.975 litres. This may indicate inaccuracies in the machine's measurements.

(3) Spillage or wastage of the material may have been lower than the allowance in the standard.

(iii) Every variance is potentially worthy of investigation, whether it is adverse or favourable. There are a number of **reasons why it might be worth investigating a favourable material usage variance.**

(1) A favourable usage variance may be inter-related with an adverse variance elsewhere in the business. For example, the use of more highly skilled labour may lead to favourable usage, but may result in an adverse labour rate variance.

(2) Unrealistic standard costs causing favourable variances need to be identified so that planning and control can be improved in future.

(3) The variance may be caused by data recording errors, so that management is working with inaccurate information and is therefore unable to exercise effective control.

24 PRACTICE QUESTION: RESPONSIBILITY CENTRES

> **Tutorial note**. We have discussed generic types of responsibility centre but you might equally validly have answered by talking about specific centres, for example, a painting department, which is part of process department which is part of subsidiary X.

A responsibility centre is a function or department of an organisation that is headed by a manager who has direct responsibility for its performance. Three types of responsibility centre often identified are the cost centre, the profit centre and the investment centre.

(a) **Cost centres**

A cost centre is **any unit of an organisation to which costs can be separately attributed**. A feature of a cost centre is that it relates to **costs only**, not to revenues nor to capital employed.

A cost centre should be a location, activity, function or item for which costs should be separately identifiable and attributable. The person responsible for the cost centre should then be made responsible for the controllable parts of those costs.

Cost centres can be quite small, sometimes one person or one machine or one expenditure item. They can also be quite big, for example an entire department. An organisation might establish a **hierarchy** of cost centres. For example, within a transport department, individual vehicles might each be made a cost centre, the repairs and maintenance section might be a cost centre, the lorries section and the vans sections might be cost centres, there might be cost centres for expenditure items such as rent or buildings depreciation on the vehicle depots, vehicle insurance and road tax, vehicle depreciation, or heating and lighting in the vehicle depots. The transport department as a whole might be a cost centre at the top of this hierarchy of sub-cost centres.

The **performance** of cost centres might be measured in terms of **total actual costs, total budgeted costs** and **total cost variances sub-analysed** perhaps into efficiency, usage and expenditure variances. In addition, performance might be measured in terms of **ratios** such as:

(i)   cost per unit produced (budget and actual);

(ii)   hours per unit produced (budget and actual);

(iii)   efficiency ratio;

(iv)   selling cost per £ of sales (budget and actual);

(v)   transport costs per tonne/mile (budget and actual).

(b) **Profit centres**

A profit centre is **any unit of an organisation to which both revenues and costs are assigned** so that the **profitability** of the unit **may be measured**. Profit centres differ from cost centres in that they are related to both costs and revenues, although not capital employed and the key performance measure of a profit centre is therefore profit.

For profit centres to have any validity in a control system based on responsibility accounting, the **manager** of the profit centre must have some control over both revenues and costs. This should imply the need for some **control over**:

(i)   **sales policy**, for example sales price decisions, sales promotion decisions, advertising decisions, the marketing budget, and sales force organisation, distribution facilities; and

(ii)   **production facilities**.

A profit centre manager is likely to be a fairly senior person within an organisation, and a profit centre is likely to cover quite a **large area of operation**. A profit centre might be an entire division within the organisation, or there might be a separate profit centre for each product, product range, brand or service that the organisation sells.

In the hierarchy of responsibility/budget centres within an organisation, there are likely to be several cost centres within a profit centre.

(c) **Investment centres**

An investment centre is a **profit centre whose performance is measured by its return on capital employed**.

An investment centre is different from a profit centre because it is made **accountable for capital employed, as well as for costs and revenues**. This should imply that the investment centre manager has some control over investment policy in his area of operations, although in some organisations, investment centre managers might be made accountable for capital employed without having any authority to make investment decisions.

Several profit centre's might share the same capital items, for example, the same buildings, stores or transport fleet, and so investment centres are likely to include several profit centres, and provide a basis for control at a very senior management level, perhaps at the level of a subsidiary company within a group.

Control can be exercised by feedback of a variety of other subsidiary performance measures, such as **profit/sales ratio, asset turnover ratios, cost/sales ratios**, and **cost variances**. In addition, the performance of investment centres can be measured by **interfirm comparisons**.

25 PRACTICE QUESTION: FORECASTING

> **Tutorial note**. In computing the seasonally adjusted sales, we must remember that data = trend + seasonal adjustment, so trend = data − seasonal adjustment. Thus a positive seasonal adjustment must be subtracted, and a negative one added.

(a)

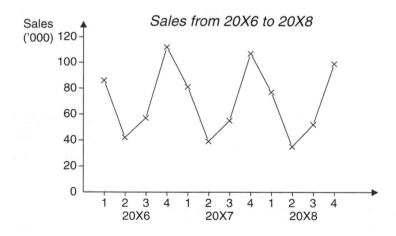

There are very **marked seasonal fluctuations**, with the fourth quarter of each year showing the highest sales and the second quarter the lowest sales. There does appear to be a **steadily falling trend**, with each peak and each trough slightly lower than the previous one.

BPP
PUBLISHING

Answers

(b)

Year	Quarter	Data £'000	4-quarter total £'000	Moving average of 4-quarter total £'000	Trend £'000
20X6	1	86			
	2	42			
	3	57	297	74.25	73.625
	4	112	292	73.00	72.625
20X7	1	81	289	72.25	72.000
	2	39	287	71.75	71.125
	3	55	282	70.50	70.000
	4	107	278	69.50	69.000
20X8	1	77	274	68.50	68.125
	2	35	271	67.75	66.750
	3	52	263	65.75	
	4	99			

(c)

20X8

Quarter	Data £'000	Adjustment £'000	Adjusted data £'000
1	77	−9	68
2	35	+32	67
3	52	+16	68
4	99	−39	60

(d) We can **forecast sales by extrapolating the trend and then making seasonal adjustments.**

Over the period from 20X6, quarter 3 to 20X8, quarter 2 (a duration of seven quarters, not eight) the trend fell by 73.625 − 66.75 = 6.875, giving an average fall per quarter of 6.875/7 = 0.982.

Forecasts can then be prepared as follows, extrapolating the trend at this rate from the value for 20X8, quarter 2. Forecasts have been **rounded to avoid giving a false impression of great precision.**

20X9

Quarter	Trend £'000	Adjustment £'000	Forecast £'000
1	*63.804	+9	73
2	62.822	−32	31
3	61.840	−16	46
4	60.858	+39	100

* $66.750 − 3 \times 0.982$

These forecasts should **not be assumed to be reliable.** Although the decline in the trend has been steady, and the pattern of seasonal variations consistent, from 20X6 to 20X8, it is always dangerous to extrapolate into the future. The trend or seasonal patterns may break down, or random variations may have a substantial effect.

26 PRACTICE QUESTION: FORECASTING AGAIN

Tutorial note. Because the moving total is made up of four quarters' revenue, you must centre the trend but adding two four-quarter totals together and dividing by eight. *Don't* use both the additive and multiplicative model. It won't impress the examiner - you will simply waste precious time.

In task (c) you could also suggest using the commonsense 'rule-of-thumb' approach or linear regression analysis.

(a)

Year	Quarter	Revenue £'000	Moving total of 4-quarters' revenue £'000	Moving average of 4-quarters' total £'000	Mid-point of two moving averages Trend £'000	Actual minus trend £'000	Actual as % of trend
20X5/X6	1	49					
	2	37					
			211	52.75			
	3	58			52.875	+5.125	109.7
			212	53.00			
	4	67			53.125	+13.875	126.1
			213	53.25			
20X6/X7	1	50			53.375	−3.375	93.7
			214	53.50			
	2	38			53.625	−15.625	70.9
			215	53.75			
	3	59			53.875	+5.125	109.5
			216	54.00			
	4	68			54.250	+13.750	125.3
			218	54.50			
20X7/X8	1	51			54.625	− 3.625	93.4
			219	54.75			
	2	40			55.000	−15.000	72.7
			221	55.25			
	3	60			55.125	+4.875	108.8
			220	55.00			
	4	70			55.250	+14.750	126.7
			222	55.50			
20X8/X9	1	50			55.625	−5.625	89.9
			223	55.75			
	2	42					
	3	61					

(b) **Additive model**

			Quarter			
Year	1 £'000	2 £'000	3 £'000	4 £'000	Total £'000
20X5/X6			+5.125	+13.875	
20X6/X7	−3.375	−15.625	+5.125	+13.750	
20X7/X8	−3.625	−15.000	+4.875	+14.750	
20X8/X9	−5.625				
Total	−12.625	−30.625	15.125	42.375	
Average	−4.208	−15.313	+5.042	+14.125	= −0.354
Seasonal variation	−4	−15	5	14	= 0

No adjustment was made to the average since the total was too small.

Multiplicative model

			Quarter			
Year	1 %	2 %	3 %	4 %	Total %
20X5/X6			109.7	126.1	
20X6/X7	93.7	70.9	109.5	125.3	
20X7/X8	93.4	72.7	108.8	126.7	
20X8/X9	89.9				
Total	277.0	143.6	328.0	378.1	
Average	92.30	71.80	109.30	126.00 =	399.40
Adjustment ((400−399.4)/4)	0.15	0.15	0.15	0.15	0.60
Adjusted average variation	92.45	71.95	109.45	126.15	400.00

(c) One would need to take the following steps **to forecast** the revenue for quarter 4 20X8/X9 and quarters 1, 2, 3 of 20X9/X0.

(i) **Plot by eye the trend values calculated, to produce a trend line.**

(ii) **By eye, establish a forecast of the trend for the relevant quarters (by continuing the trend line on the time series graph).**

(iii) **Adjust these forecast trends by the appropriate seasonal variation as follows.**

Additive model

Forecast value = value forecast from trend + appropriate seasonal variation.

Multiplicative model

Forecast value = value forecast from trend × appropriate seasonal variation.

27 PRACTICE QUESTION: TIME SERIES ANALYSIS

> **Tutorial note.** In this question you need to calculate a moving total of four quarters' sales. The moving average calculated from this moving total does not 'line up' with actual time periods, however, and so you need to take a second set of moving averages (which will be the mid-points of two of the first moving averages).

(a)

Year	Revenue	Sales	Moving total of 4-quarters' sales	Moving average of 4-quarters' sales	Mid-point of two moving averages Trend	Variation
20X2	1	200				
	2	110				
	3	320	870	217.5	219	+101
	4	240	884	221.0	222	+18
20X3	1	214	892	223.0	225	-11
	2	118	906	226.5	229	-111
	3	334	926	231.5	232	+102
	4	260	932	233.0	234	+26
20X4	1	220	938	234.5	235	-15
	2	124	944	236.0	238	-114
	3	340	962	240.5		
	4	278				

(b)

Year Quarter	1	2	3	4	Total
20X2			+101	+18	
20X3	-11	-111	+102	+26	
20X4	-15	-114			
	−26	−225	+203	+44	−4
Unadjusted average	-13.0	-112.5	+101.5	+22.0	-2
Adjustment	+0.5	+0.5	+0.5	+0.5	+2
Adjusted average	−12.5	−112.0	+102.0	+22.5	0

28 HENRY LTD

> **Tutorial note.** A positive seasonal variation is deducted from actual results to determine the deseasonalised data (trend). Remember to check who you are meant to be so that the memorandum (in task (c)) comes from the correct person.
>
> In his report, the assessor noted that many candidates had difficulty understanding the basic rudiments of seasonal variations and trends despite the detailed workings having been provided for tasks (a) and (b). However, they showed less difficulty in task (c) in explaining the concepts.

(a)

	Quarter 1 Units	Quarter 2 Units	Quarter 3 Units	Quarter 4 Units
Actual sales volumes	420,000	450,000	475,000	475,000
Seasonal variation	+25,000	+15,000	0	−40,000
Deseasonalised sales volumes	395,000	435,000	475,000	515,000

(b) The deseasonalised sales volumes (trend) show an increase of 40,000 units per quarter.

	Quarter 1 Units	*Quarter 2* Units	*Quarter 3* Units	*Quarter 4* Units
Trend	555,000 (W1)	595,000 (W2)	635,000 (W3)	675,000 (W4)
Seasonal variations	+25,000	+15,000	0	–40,000
Forecast sales volumes	580,000	610,000	635,000	635,000

Workings

1   515,000 + 40,000
2   555,000 + 40,000
3   595,000 + 40,000
4   635,000 + 40,000

(c) MEMORANDUM

To: Marketing Assistant
From: Assistant to the Management Accountant
Date: XX June 20X8
Subject: **Time series analysis and forecasting**

Following our meeting yesterday, at which you expressed concern over your level of understanding of time series analysis and forecasting, I set out below explanations of some of the principal terms used in preparing sales forecasts and analysing sales trends and the role of these concepts in analysing a time series and preparing forecasts.

(i)   **Explanation of terminology**

Seasonal variations are short-term fluctuations in sales around the trend in sales, due to different circumstances which affect sales at different times of the year. For example, a quarter 2 seasonal variation of 15,000 units for product P means that in quarter 2 sales volumes are 15,000 units higher than the underlying trend in sales whereas in quarter 4 sales volumes are 40,000 units below the underlying trend in sales. Of course, for other organisations, seasonal variations occur with the days of the week, weeks of the month and so on. A supermarket, for example, is likely to experience higher sales on a Saturday than a Monday.

Data from which the seasonal variations have been removed are termed **deseasonalised (seasonally-adjusted) data** and represent the trend, the underlying long-term movement in the values of the data recorded. The deseasonalised sales volumes for product P show an upward trend, the rate of increase being 40,000 units per quarter. When just one year's actual data are viewed in isolation, the seasonal variations hide this upward trend. Before seasonally adjusting the data there appears to be a decreasing rate of growth in sales volumes.

(ii) **The role of seasonal variations and deseasonalised data in time series analysis and forecasting**

Forecasts using seasonal variations and deseasonalised data rely on one major assumption: that the trend will continue in the future, outside the time period for which actual data is available. There are various methods of extrapolating (projecting) the trend into the future. For the purposes of project P we can assume that the trend in sales volume will be an increase of 40,000 units per quarter and therefore for every quarter after that for which we have data (quarter 4 of last year) we add 40,000 to the deseasonalised data value for quarter 4 to determine the trend value for the future quarter. We then adjust this trend value by the appropriate seasonal variation (upward for a positive variation, downward for a negative variation) to give us the actual forecast.

I hope this information is useful. If I can be of any further assistance please do not hesitate to contact me.

29   ALAN DUNN

MEMORANDUM

To: Alan Dunn
From: Management Accountant
Date: XX December 20X8
Subject: **Sales forecasting**

Thank you for your recent memo. I have made the following brief notes which I hope you that will find useful.

(a) **Ways of forecasting future sales volumes**

There are a number of methods which may be used to forecast future sales volumes. Different methods will be suitable for different organisations, product ranges and customers.

If the number of potential customers is relatively small, then it is possible to **ask them directly** what they expect their likely demand to be in the future. It is also possible to discuss customers' likely requirements with members of the sales team (who are likely to have knowledge which may be useful for sales forecasts).

If the number of potential customers is not small enough to ask them directly, it is possible to carry out a **survey** or **use market research methods**. If a market research is specially commissioned by the company, potential customers may be asked what their future requirements are likely to be.

If there is information available which relates to past sales, it may be possible to **identify a trend using time series analysis**. Any trend which is identified in past sales is assumed to continue in the future, and is used to forecast future sales demand.

By studying the general economic climate, it is often possible to predict what might happen to future demand of a product. Any organisation which is sensitive to changes in the economy may be able to use this information as an aid to forecasting. For example, it may be possible to establish a pattern of demand when changes occur in another economic indicator. An economic indicator may be leading, coincident, or lagging. A leading indicator indicates change, a coincident indicator follows the general trend and a lagging indicator follows the general trend but only after a timing delay.

(b) **Applicability**

Obtaining estimates of future demand **directly from customers** is likely to be the most appropriate method when wishing to **increase sales to existing customers**.

Market research techniques are best suited to the **development of new products**. This is because market research methods enable an organisation to get a clear idea of whether it is worth developing new products, and which products to develop. The results of such a survey are an invaluable tool in deciding whether or not to develop a new product (and thereby potentially increasing sales volumes).

Time series are based on past sales data, and are therefore most applicable to **existing customers**. (New customers have not been included in the past sales data which gave rise to the time series).

Economic conditions may give an indication of sales demand in the market as a whole since general economic conditions have an effect on the overall market. This may therefore be most suitable to forecasting sales demand from **existing customers** (and also new customers since they are part of the whole market).

(c) **Limitations of forecasting methods**

Obtaining information from existing customers is limited by the fact that they may not wish to be completely open and honest. There is **no guarantee therefore that the information received is totally accurate**.

Market research also has limitations, such as the use of samples in order to draw conclusions about the population as a whole. If a small sample is selected, then it is possible that a **statistical error** will occur, and incorrect conclusions will be drawn from the survey. It is also possible that information given by the **people** taking part in the market research **do not give accurate answers**.

Time series are limited by the fact that they **assume that a linear relationship exists** (between time and demand) **and that any past patterns will repeat themselves in the future**.

Economic conditions are limited as an aid to forecasting in the short-term, since **economic indicators depend upon recent information**. One further limitation of economic indicators is that they **assume that past patterns repeat themselves in the future** (as do time series).

30   ESKAFIELD INDUSTRIAL MUSEUM

> **Tutorial note**. In task (a) the seasonal variations sum to zero and so no averaging or adjustments are required. In task (d), discuss the product life cycle in general *and* in relation to the museum.

(a)

Year	Quarter	Number of visitors (actual)	Moving annual total	Moving average	Midpoint of two moving averages (trend)	Seasonal variations
20X7	1	5,800				
	2	9,000				
			35,200	8,800		
	3	6,000			8,900	– 2,900
			36,000	9,000		
	4	14,400			9,100	+ 5,300
			36,800	9,200		
20X8	1	6,600			9,300	– 2,700
			37,600	9,400		
	2	9,800			9,500	+ 300
			38,400	9,600		
	3	6,800				
	4	15,200				

(b)

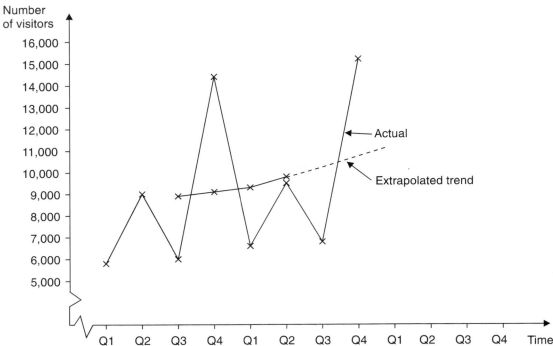

Number of visitors

(c) The **trend figures calculated above indicate an increase of 200 visitors per quarter. (Alternatively you could read the figures from the graph.)**

Year	Quarter	Trend		Seasonal variation	Forecast
20X9	1	$9,500 + (3 \times 200)^\star$	= 10,100	– 2,700	7,400
	2	10,100 + 200	= 10,300	+300	10,600
	3	10,300 + 200	= 10,500	– 2,900	7,600
	4	10,500 + 200	= 10,700	+5,300	16,000

$\star$For the three quarters between 20X8 Quarter 2 and 20X9 Quarter 1

(d) **Notes on forecasting for John Derbyshire**

(i) There are a number of steps that we can take to **improve the forecasting** of visitor numbers.

We should attempt to **analyse the visitor numbers in more detail,** perhaps by day of the week, week or month of the year. Time series analysis could then be applied to this more detailed data and a more accurate trend determined. The use of time series analysis assumes that the pattern of trend and seasonal variations will continue into the future, however, and this may not necessarily be true.

We could also consider **surveying past, present and future visitors** to the museum to obtain information about their possible plans to visit the museum in the future. Visitors may not always tell the truth when questioned, however.

Secondary sources of data could also be examined. Tourist industry data, data obtained by other museums and so on could be analysed with a view to determining future visitor numbers. But it should be borne in mind that such data will have been collected for another purpose and we will not be aware of its limitations.

(ii) If we wish to **obtain the views of past, present and future visitors** to the museum (as suggested above), we could use either **telephone sampling or postal**

questionnaires. Telephone sampling might be preferable for a number of reasons.

(1) The response is rapid.

(2) It is relatively cheap.

(3) A wide geographical area can be covered from a central location without the need for an interviewer to travel between respondents.

(4) The interview does not take up so much of the respondent's time.

(5) Large numbers of postal questionnaires may not be returned or may be returned only partly completed.

(6) Misunderstanding is more likely with postal questionnaires because there is nobody to explain questions that the respondent does not understand.

(7) Interviewers can ask for clarification of answers given.

(8) Additional questions can be asked if necessary.

(iii) Information about the stage the museum has reached in its product life cycle may provide an important indicator of likely future visitor numbers.

The **product life cycle** is an attempt to recognise distinct stages in a product's (in this case a museum's) sales history.

The **introduction phase** of a product requires heavy investment; this would have been the situation when the museum opened ten years ago, the major investment being in working exhibits. Significant marketing expenditure would have been necessary to bring the museum to the public's attention.

During the **growth phase,** a product gains a bigger market as demand build up. The museum's growth phase would have seen a significant increase in visitor numbers as a result of the marketing activity and early investment.

The growth in demand for a product will slow down and enter a period of relative maturity during the **maturity stage**. The number of visitors to the museum would have reached a peak and then levelled off. Modifications and/or improvements to exhibits may be required as a means of sustaining visitor numbers.

At some stage, the market will have bought enough of a product and it will reach 'saturation point'. Demand will start to fall. During this stage visitor numbers would have started to fall off as interest in the museum waned; this is probably the phase faced by the museum in recent years.

In order **to ensure continuous demand** for a product, **regular investment** is necessary so that each investment has its own product life cycle, overlapping with that of the previous investment, thereby resulting in sustained growth. As a result of the recent improvements which you made, the museum has completed the introduction phase of a life cycle and is at the beginning of a period of growth after a number of years of decline.

31   STAR FUELS

> **Tutorial note**. Calculate residuals (the difference between actual values and forecast values) in task (b) to determine the best method of estimating turnover.

(a)   **Calculation of trend sales values from the regression line**

Quarter

17	£(2,000,000 + (40,000 × 17)) =	£2,680,000
18	£(2,000,000 + (40,000 × 18)) =	£2,720,000
	or £(2,680,000 + 40,000) =	£2,720,000
19	£(2,720,000 + 40,000) =	£2,760,000
20	£(2,760,000 + 40,000) =	£2,800,000

Calculation of seasonally-adjusted sales

Quarter	Trend value £	Seasonal variation	Absolute variation £	(i) Forecast £	Percentage variation %	(ii) Forecast £
17	2,680,000	A	+350,000	3,030,000	+15	3,082,000★
18	2,720,000	B	+250,000	2,970,000	+10	2,992,000
19	2,760,000	C	–400,000	2,360,000	–15	2,346,000★★
20	2,800,000	D	–200,000	2,600,000	–10	2,520,000

*   £2,680,000 × 115%
** £2,760,000 × 85%

(b)   (i)

Quarter	Actual £	Absolute forecast £	Residual error £	Percentage forecast £	Residual error £
17	3,079,500	3,030,000	+49,500	3,082,000	–2,500
18	3,002,400	2,970,000	+32,400	2,992,000	+10,400
19	2,346,500	2,360,000	–13,500	2,346,000	+500
20	2,490,200	2,600,000	–109,800	2,520,000	–29,800

In each of the four quarters, the residual error associated with percentage seasonal variations is lower than that associated with absolute seasonal variations. On the basis of the sample of four quarters, the **percentage seasonal variations method appears to be the more accurate forecasting method**.

(ii)

Quarter	Season	Trend £	Seasonal variation %	Forecast £
21	A	2,840,000★	+15	3,266,000
22	B	2,880,000	+10	3,168,000
23	C	2,920,000	–15	2,482,000
24	D	2,960,000	–10	2,664,000

★Trend for Q20 + £40,000

(c)   MEMORANDUM

To: Managing Director
From: Assistant Management Accountant
Date: 17 June 20X8
Subject: **Forecasting, seasonal variations and seasonally-adjusted data**

I have recently tested a statistical software package which can be used for estimating demand for fuel oil. I set out below some information which you may find useful.

(i)   **Seasonal variations** are regular, predictable and consistent changes in recorded values due to different circumstances which affect results at different times of the year, on different days of the week, at different times of day or whatever. For oil distribution, it is likely that demand will be higher in winter than in summer and this is reflected in the seasonal variations for our organisation produced by the software package. The sales revenue in Quarter A, which includes the winter months, is 15% above the average quarterly sales revenue whereas the sales revenue in Quarter C, which includes the summer months, is 85% of the average quarterly sales revenue.

Seasonally-adjusted data is actual data from which seasonal variations (derived from historic data) have been removed, to leave a figure which might be taken to indicate the trend (if we assume that any random variations are negligible). For example, the estimated seasonal variations within the actual sales revenue for Quarter 17 = $15/115 \times £3,079,500 = £401,674$, say £402,000. Deducting this from the actual sales revenue leaves an underlying figure of $£(3,079,500 - 402,000) = £2,677,500$.

(ii) The **percentage seasonal variations method of seasonal adjustment might be more accurate than the absolute seasonal variations method because the trend in sales turnover is increasing over time**. When a trend is increasing, it is likely that absolute seasonal variations are also increasing. The absolute seasonal variations method simply adds absolute and unchanging seasonal variations to the trend figures whereas the percentage seasonal variations method, by multiplying the increasing trend values by a constant factor, produces seasonal variations which increase in time with the trend in sales.

(iii) There are a number of ways in which an **understanding of seasonal variations and seasonally-adjusted data** can help us to be more efficient. For example, it **helps in stock control**. If we are able to forecast demand we will not have to hold excessive stock. This helps cash flow in two ways.

(1) It reduces cash tied up in stocks.
(2) It minimises the interest charges on amounts owing to Star Fuels.

Accurate forecasts of demand will also enable us to forecast future profit levels more accurately.

(iv) There are, however, a number of **limitations** to this forecasting technique

(1) The use of the least squares regression equation assumes that there is a linear relationship between sales turnover and time.

(2) The use of the equation also assumes that sales turnover is dependent only upon time. In reality it might depend on several other variables such as the actions of competitors or the state of the economy.

(3) It assumes that what has happened in the past will provide a reliable guide for what will happen in the future. If, for example, a new competitor has entered the market, this will not be the case.

(4) The data used was measured in monetary terms but part of any increase in sales turnover may be due to rising prices rather than increased demand. It might therefore be better to measure sales in litres rather than value.

(5) The choice of a quarterly seasonal variation may be inappropriate. Forecasting on a weekly basis may be more suitable.

32 PRACTICE QUESTION: BUDGETS

> **Tutorial note**. It is worth setting out standard product costs for the two products before you begin preparing your budgets; they will help you to organise the data provided in the question.

Budgeted production overhead	£3,717,000
Budgeted labour hours	1,062,000 hrs
Absorption rate per direct labour hour	£3.50

This is applied to Torks at the rate of £(3.50 × 16) = £56 per unit
and to Larfs at the rate of £(3.50 × 18) = £63 per unit

Standard costs

	Tork	Larf
	£	£
Direct material:		
Cri	12	6
Showt	20	40
Direct wages:		
Sobbers	21	42
Screamers	10	6
Production overhead	56	63
Standard factory cost	119	157

Budgeted opening stocks	£238,000	£628,000
	ie 2,000 units	4,000 units
Budgeted closing stocks	£595,000	£1,413,000
	ie 5,000 units	9,000 units

Budgeted sales

	£'000	£'000
Division 1	1,808	1,280
Division 2	600	1,600
Division 3	900	2,600
Division 4	500	800
Total	3,808	6,280

At factory cost (75%)	£2,856,000	£4,710,000
	ie 24,000 units	30,000 units

(a) **Production budget**

	Tork	Larf
	Units	Units
Closing stock, finished goods	5,000	9,000
Less opening stock	2,000	4,000
Stock increase, finished goods	3,000	5,000
Sales	24,000	30,000
Production requirement	27,000	35,000

(b) **Direct materials cost budget**

(See workings for standard cost per unit to be multiplied by production quantities in units).

	Cri	Showt	Total
	£'000	£'000	£'000
Torks	324	540	864
Larfs	210	1,400	1,610
	534	1,940	2,474

(c) **Purchases budget**

	Cri £'000	*Showt* £'000	*Total* £'000
Closing stock	40	180	
Opening stock	120	160	
Increase/(decrease) in stock	(80)	20	
Production requirements	534	1,940	
Purchase requirements	454	1,960	2,414

(d) **Direct wages budget**

(See workings for standard cost per unit to be multiplied by production units)

	Sobbers Hours ('000)	£'000	*Screamers* Hours ('000)	£'000
Torks (27,000 units)	162	567	270	270
Larfs (35,000 units)	420	1,470	210	210
	582	2,037	480	480

(*Note.* The total hours, 582,000 + 480,000 = 1,062,000 agrees with the total figure given for the budget in the question.)

(e) **Budgeted profit and loss account:** *year to 31 December 20X3*

	£'000	£'000
Sales		10,088
Less costs of production:		
Direct materials	2,474	
Direct labour	2,517	
Production overhead	3,717	
less: increase in finished good stock	(1,142)	
		7,566
		2,522
Administration, sales and distribution (see note)		1,261
Budgeted profit		1,261

Note

Factory cost of sales	= 75% of £10,088,000 = £7,566,000
Added overheads	= $16^2/_3$% of £7,566,000 = £1,261,000

33 PRACTICE QUESTION: BUDGET PREPARATION

> **Tutorial note**. You may think it's not worth the bother of writing out workings such as those in tasks (b) and (c). But, as we have said so often, if you make a mistake while putting numbers into your calculator, the assessor will not be able to see that, although you made an arithmetic mistake, you did know what to do.

(a)

Production budget
Cases

	June	*July*	*August*	*September*
Sales quantity	6,000	7,500	8,500	7,000
Closing stocks	750	850	700	650
	6,750	8,350	9,200	7,650
Less opening stocks	(750)	(750)	(850)	(700)
Budgeted production	6,000	7,600	8,350	6,950

(b)

Ingredients purchase budget

	June	July	August
	kg	kg	kg
Budgeted material usage (W)	15,000	19,000	20,875
Closing stocks	9,500	10,438	8,688
Less opening stocks	(5,800)	(9,500)	(10,438)
Budgeted ingredients purchases	18,700	19,938	19,125

Working

June	= 6,000 kg × 2.5 = 15,000 kg
July	= 7,600kg × 2.5 = 19,000 kg
August	= 8,350kg × 2.5 = 20,875 kg

(c) **Budgeted gross profit** for the quarter June - August

	June	July	August	Total
	£	£	£	£
Sales (W1)	150,000	187,500	212,500	550,000
Cost of sales (W2)	90,000	112,500	127,500	330,000
Budgeted gross profit	60,000	75,000	85,000	220,000

Workings

1	June	6,000 × £25 = £150,000
	July	7,500 × £25 = £187,500
	August	8,500 × £25 = £212,500

2	June	6,000 × £15 = £90,000
	July	7,500 × £15 = £112,500
	August	8,500 × £15 = £127,500

(d) A **flexible budget** is a budget which **recognises different cost behaviour patterns**, and therefore **changes as the volume of activity changes**. The **advantages** of adopting a system of flexible budgeting are therefore as follows.

(i) At the planning stage an organisation may wish to know what the consequences would be if the actual outcome differs from the prediction. For example, an organisation may prepare budgets at the planning stage to sell 100,000 units of product L, and it may also prepare flexible budgets based upon sales of say, 75,000 and 125,000 units of product L. Contingency plans could then drawn up if considered necessary.

(ii) Managers are likely to have a more positive attitude to flexible budgets since they will feel that they are more realistic as they are adjusted for different volumes of activity.

(iii) At the end of a period, the actual results obtained by the organisation may be compared with the flexible budget. This comparison acts as a control procedure.

(iv) Since flexible budgets recognise whether costs are fixed, variable or semi-variable, such information can be used in the decision making process.

34 PRODUCT Q

Tutorial note. In task (a) you need to ensure that you take account of the losses and idle time correctly. In part (i) for example, the loss is 1/99 of the finished units required not 1/100. Likewise in part (ii) the idle time represents 7.5% of total hours, not 7.5% of worked hours.

The assessor reported that many candidates had great difficulty deriving a gross figure from a net figure in task (a) but that many were able to use their general business and commercial awareness to explain the implications of a shortage of material in task (b).

(a) (i) **Production budget for product Q**

	Units	Units
Budgeted sales		18,135
Closing stocks (1,200 × 115%)	1,380	
Opening stocks	1,200	
Increase in stocks		180
Finished units required		18,315
Loss through quality control check (1/99 × 18,315)		185
Budgeted production		18,500

(ii) **Direct labour budget for product Q**

	Hours
Worked hours (18,500 × 5 hours)	92,500
Idle time (7.5/92.5 × 92,500)	7,500
Budgeted paid hours	100,000
Budgeted labour cost (100,000 hrs × £6)	£600,000

(iii) **Material usage budget for material M**

	Kgs
Material for production (18,500 × 9kg)	166,500
Wastage (166,500 × 10/90)	18,500
Budgeted material usage	185,000

(iv) **Material purchases budget for material M**

	Kgs	Kgs
Required for production		185,000
Closing stocks (8,000 × 112%)	8,960	
Opening stocks	8,000	
Increase in stocks		960
Loss		1,000
Budgeted material purchases		186,960

(b) To achieve the budgeted production level of 18,500 units of product Q, 186,960 kgs of material M need to be purchased. If sufficient supplies are not available, however, budgeted production levels cannot be met, Alfred Ltd's plans cannot be achieved and material M is a limiting factor. **If the limiting factor cannot be alleviated material M will become the principal budget factor and the budget will need to be revised, the materials purchases budget being prepared first and all other budgets based around it.**

There are, however, a number of **ways in which this problem could be overcome.**

(i) Stock levels in the store could be kept as low as possible so that deterioration of material M is not possible. This would reduce the purchases requirement by 1,000 kg. Associated with such a policy, however, is the risk of stockouts (having insufficient stock when it is required for production) leading to disruptions to production and loss of sales and customer goodwill.

(ii) The planned closing stock levels of material M and product Q could be lowered. Again this could lead to stockouts (as in (a) above).

(iii) The rate of rejects due to the quality control check could be lowered, either by lowering the quality requirements or by improving the quality of the finished product. Alfred Ltd may be loath to reduce the quality requirements of product Q, however, as this could lead to a drop in sales. By implementing a programme of Total Quality Management, however, the company could attempt to raise the quality of the finished product, thereby reducing the number of units rejected.

(iv) The implementation of the TQM programme should also reduce that part of the 10% wastage rate due to spillage.

(v)   The company could attempt to find alternative suppliers of material M but potential suppliers would need to be carefully vetted to ensure that they could guarantee the appropriate level of quality and reliability of supply.

(vi) The budgeted level of sales could be reduced. Valuable customers may, however, move to competition on a permanent basis, affecting profits both next year and in subsequent years.

35   ARDEN ENGINEERING LTD

> **Tutorial note.** In task (a), don't forget to calculate the fixed production overhead on the basis of gross production during the year rather than good production.
>
> In task (b) you need to compare the marginal cost of production in Period 3 with the supplier's price for proposal 1. Since the labour cost is a fixed cost, the marginal labour cost is the £1.50 overtime payment.
>
> The assessor reported that candidates had few problems with task (a) but were ill-prepared for task (b).

(a) *Ardern Engineering Ltd*
     Production cost budget for periods 1 to 3 20X6

	Period 1 Units	Period 2 Units	Period3 Units	Total Units
Gross production per period (W1)	240,000	280,000	320,000	840,000
Good production per period	228,000	266,000	304,000	798,000
	£	£	£	£
Wages	270,000	270,000	270,000	810,000
Overtime (W2)	-	-	45,000	45,000
Total labour cost	270,000	270,000	315,000	855,000
Material (W3)	840,000	980,000	1,120,000	2,940,000
Direct costs	1,110,000	1,250,000	1,435,000	3,795,000
Fixed production overheads (W4)	480,000	560,000	640,000	1,680,000
Production cost	1,590,000	1,810,000	2,075,000	5,475,000
Production cost per unit (based on good production)	£6.97	£6.80	£6.83	

Workings

1

	Period 1 Units	Period 2 Units	Period3 Units	Period 4 Units
Sales	190,000	228,000	266,000	304,000
Good production	228,000	266,000	304,000	
Gross production (good production × 100/95)	240,000	280,000	320,000	

2   (320,000 – 290,000) units × £1.50 = £45,000

3   Material for period 1 = 240,000 × £3.50 = £840,000

4   Over the year, units sold equals good units produced = 3,296,500 units

    ∴ Gross production = 3,296,500 × 100/95 = 3,470,000

    ∴ Fixed production overhead per unit = £6,940,000 ÷ 3,470,000 = £2

    ∴ Fixed production overhead per period = gross production × £2

(b) **Evaluation of proposal 1: outsourcing**

This is **not a viable proposal** because the marginal cost per unit is less than the price charged by the outside suppliers, even in the period when overtime is worked, as the working below shows.

Unit marginal cost in period 3 (with no wastage) =

	£
Material	3.50
Labour	1.50
	5.00

Note that the £270,000 labour cost is a fixed cost and hence will be paid regardless of the number of units produced. We included the £1.50 per unit overtime cost in our calculation above since this is what it costs in terms of labour to produce a unit over and above 290,000 units.

We need to adjust this unit cost to take account of wastage, however, since at the moment it represents the cost of producing a unit in a situation where all production is good.

∴ Unit marginal cost in Period 3 = £5 × 100/95 = £5.26

Evaluation of proposal 2: bringing forward production

30,000 of the units which it is planned to produce in Period 3 need to be produced in Periods 1 and 2. **Financing costs will be minimised if as many units as possible are produced in Period 2** since those produced in Period 1 will incur financing costs over two periods. We can produce another 10,000 units in Period 2 before the limit of 290,000 is reached.

Financing costs

	£
10,000 units in Period 2 × £0.50	5,000
20,000 units in Period 1 × (2 × £0.50)	20,000
	25,000

Savings

	£
Savings of overtime cost	45,000
Extra financing costs	25,000
Overall saving from proposal	20,000

Revised production schedule

	Period 1 Units	Period 2 Units	Period 3 Units
Planned production	240,000	280,000	320,000
Change to planned production	+20,000	+10,000	−30,000
Revised production schedule	260,000	290,000	290,000

36   ALDERLEY LTD

> **Tutorial note**. If employees are only able to work at 95% efficiency, standard hours must be multiplied by 100/95 to determine budgeted hours.

Alderley Ltd
Budget statements for the 13 weeks to 4 April 20X8

(a) **Production budget**

	Elgar Units	Holst Units
Budgeted sales volume	845	1,235
Add closing stock (W1)	78	266
Less opening stock	(163)	(361)
Units of production	760	1,140

(b) **Material purchases budget**

	Elgar Kg	Holst Kg	Total Kg
Material consumed (W2)	5,320	9,120	14,440
Add raw material closing stock (W3)			2,888
Less raw material opening stock			(2,328)
Purchases (kg)			15,000

(c) **Purchases (£)(W4)**   £180,000

(d) **Production labour budget**

	Elgar Hours	Holst Hours	Total Hours
Standard hours required for budgeted production (W5)	6,080	5,700	11,780
Productivity adjustment (W6)			620
Total hours employed			12,400
Normal hours employed (W7)			11,544
Overtime hours			856

(e) **Labour cost budget**

	£
Normal hours (11,544 × £8)	92,352
Overtime (856 × £8 × 125%)	8,560
Total cost of labour for budgeted production	100,912

Workings

1. $\text{Elgar} = \dfrac{6\,\text{days}}{(13\,\text{weeks}\times 5\,\text{days})} \times 845\,\text{units} = 78\,\text{units}$

       $\text{Holst} = \dfrac{14\,\text{days}}{(13\,\text{weeks}\times 5\,\text{days})} \times 1{,}235\,\text{units} = 266\,\text{units}$

2.   Elgar = 760 units × 7 kg = 5,320 kg

       Holst = 1,140 units × 8 kg = 9,120 kg

3. $\dfrac{13\,\text{days}}{13\,\text{weeks}\times 5\,\text{days}} \times 14{,}440 = 2{,}888\,\text{kg}$

4.   15,000 kg × £12 = £180,000

5.   Elgar = 760 units × 8 hrs = 6,080 hrs

       Holst = 1,140 units × 5 hrs = 5,700 hrs

6.   **11,780 hours are required for budgeted production. Since employees are only able to work at 95% efficiency compared to standard, actual hours required for budgeted production = 12,400 (11,780 ÷ 0.95)).**

7.   13 weeks × 37 hrs × 24 employees = 11,544 hrs

37   PICKERINGS CANNING COMPANY

> **Tutorial note**. If there is 50% waste in production and the net amount of apples in 1,000 cans is 100kgs, 200kgs of apples are actually required to produce 1,000 cans.

(a) (i)   **Materials purchases budget**

Apples required for 84,211 cans (W2)	16.8422	tonnes
Cost per tonne (basic)	× £200	
Purchase cost	£3,368.44	

(ii) **Labour budget**

Production for September 20X7 (**W1**)	84,211	cans
Hours required per can	× 0.006	
Labour hours required to produce 84,211 cans	505.266	hrs
Hours worked per month per employee (**W3**)	136.8	hrs
Number of employees required for September 20X7 (505.266 ÷ 136.8)	4 employees	

(iii) **Cost of materials purchased**

16.8422 tonnes at £208.33 per tonne (W4) = £3,508.74

Workings

1   **80,000 cans per month are required by customers. 5% of cans are damaged in the final stages of production, we therefore need to budget production of 84,211 cans (84,211 × 95% = 80,000).**

2   Per (W1) 84,211 cans need to be produced

1,000 cans require 100kg of apple (net) (or 0.1 tonnes)

1,000 cans require 200kg of apple (gross) (or 0.2 tonnes)

84,211 cans require 8.4211 tonnes of apple (net) or 16.8422 tonnes of apples (gross)

3   **Each employee works a 38 hour week. 10% absenteeism means that on average each employee will only work 38 hrs × 0.9 = 34.2 hours per week, or 136.8 hours (34.2 × 4) per month.**

4    $£200 \times \dfrac{125}{120} = £208.33$ per tonne

(b)   MEMORANDUM

To:	C. Hathaway, Production Manager
From:	M. Greene, Assistant Cost Accountant
Date:	XX August 20X8
Subject:	**Short-term budget for September 20X8**

Internal index of apple prices

The **usefulness** of the materials price indices supplied by the buyer for budgeting the costs of materials will probably **depend on whether the crop of apples last year was similar to this year**. For example, a poor crop of apples may cause the price of apples to rise, whereas a bumper crop may cause the price of apples to be lowered so that they can all be sold. If the conditions in 20X7 were the same as in 20X8, and the supply and demand were similar then the internal index of apple prices may be a useful means of predicting prices.

Estimates based on **actual figures for last year are not likely to be very useful**, as costs are likely to have risen, even if only by the amount of **inflation**. Last year's costs will

147

not include any increases due to inflation, and are therefore not likely to be very reliable.

An **alternative method** for predicting material prices might be to use a **special published index** such as the Retail Prices Index (**RPI**). The RPI is a measure of the change in the cost of living and its principal use is as a measure of inflation. It is a weighted index which is published every month and which has a base date of January 20X7. Since the cost of apples will be affected by inflation (wages of apple pickers, transport costs, storage costs) the RPI is a useful index for predicting costs of materials.

Wages

Wages costs are a significant part of the company's expenditure. It is important therefore that there is adequate control in this area. The type of information which should be supplied is summarised as follows.

On a **daily** basis, it would be useful to have a **log of absentees**, along with the reasons (sickness, holiday and so on). On a **weekly** basis it is important that **timesheets** are completed (showing hours worked per week by each employee).

On a **monthly** basis, **performance reports** should be prepared which compare actual results with budgets. For example, labour rate, efficiency and total variances should be calculated and any significant variances should be investigated. It would also be useful to supply an idle time report on a monthly basis with reasons of why these non-productive periods have occurred.

38   GEORGE PHILLIPS

> **Tutorial note**. In task (a)(iii), given that there is a shortage of raw materials the original production and sales budget cannot be achieved and so revised profit-maximising budgets need to be prepared. These budgets need to be based on the contribution per limiting factor (raw materials) from the two products.

(a)   (i)   **Material purchases budget** - *weeks 1 to 13 20X8*

20,000 kgs × £5 per kg = £100,000.

(ii)   **Materials issued to production budget** - *weeks 1 to 13 20X8*

	Kgs	£
Opening stock	6,000	30,000
Purchases	20,000	100,000
Closing stock	(6,600)	(33,000)
Issues to production	19,400	97,000

(iii)   **Sales volume and turnover budget** - *weeks 1 to 13 20X8*

		Alpha		*Beta*
		£		£
Selling price		36.00		39.00
Variable costs				
material	(2 kgs × £5)	10.00	(1.5kg × £5)	7.50
labour	(2.5 hrs × £4*)	10.00	(2.785 hrs × £4*)	11.14
		20.00		18.64
Contribution per unit		16.00		20.36
Kgs of material required per unit		2 kgs		1.5 kgs
Contribution per kg of material		£8		£13.57
Priority for production		2nd		1st

* £169,260 ÷ 42,315 hrs = £4 per hour

The calculations above indicate that the Beta should be produced up to its maximum demand and then the Alpha produced using the remaining raw material.

We therefore need to produce the 9,000 units of Betas, which will use 9,000 × 1.5 kgs = 13,500 kgs of raw material. This leaves (19,400 (see (b)) – 13,500) 5,900 kgs with which to make 5,900 ÷ 2 kgs = 2,950 units of Alpha, a reduction of (6,900 – 2,950) 3,950 units compared with the original budget. If the closing stocks have to remain the same the sales budget for Alphas will have to be reduced by 3,950 units (ie to 6,500 – 3,950 = 2,550 units).

Revised sales budget

	Sales volume	Selling price per unit	Sales revenue
	Units	£	£
Alpha	2,550	36.00	91,800
Beta	7,800	39.00	304,200
			396,000

(iv) **Labour hours and cost budget** - *weeks 1 to 13 20X8*

Product	Production	Labour hours per unit	Total labour hours	Labour cost per hour	Total labour cost
	Units	Hrs	Hrs	£	£
Alpha	2,950	2.500	7,375	4	29,500
Beta	9,000	2.785	25,065	4	100,260
			32,440		129,760

(v) **Number of employees required budget** - *weeks 1 to 13 20X8*

Labour hours required	32,440
Number of weeks work this represents (÷ 35)	926.86
Within a 13-week period, this requires (÷ 13)	71.3 employees

(b) REPORT

To: George Phillips
From: Trainee Accountant
Date: 20 November 20X7
Subject: **Issues raised at budget meeting**

This report contains information on a number of issues raised at the recent management meeting to discuss the 20X8 budget.

(i) **Reducing staff numbers**

The use of labour standards implies that our organisation's labour costs are variable. This would be the case if the workforce were paid on a piecework basis but, in common with most organisations, we pay our employees either weekly or monthly a certain amount regardless of the volume of output achieved. Labour costs are fixed but only in the short term. The size of the workforce can always be reduced or increased within, say, two or three months (subject to notice periods and the pool of available workers). Theoretically an organisation would not continue to employ workers that were surplus to requirements in the longer term but in practice a number of factors would have to be considered.

(1) The **financial costs of making employees redundant** and possible **recruitment and retraining** in the future **versus the financial cost of continuing to employ idle employees** needs to be borne in mind.

(2)   As pointed out by the production manager, those **staff made redundant may be loathe to work for us again** if there is a chance that they will be made redundant again.

(3)   It could be **difficult** and/or it would **take time** to **replace** such highly-trained staff.

(4)   If **new employees** had to be taken on, the **quality of output** may not be up to our normal standard during their training period. This would have a detrimental effect on our efforts to re-enter the market.

(5)   It may be possible to purchase the raw material from **another source** and meet sales demand for both products, in which case all current employees would be required.

(6)   It may be possible to use an **alternative raw material**.

Given the above it would probably be **inadvisable to lay off workers**, especially as it is quite likely that the shortage is not long term or an alternative supplier can be found.

(ii)   **Key factors**

It is true that in most instances sales is an organisation's key factor. Most businesses only produce as many products as they can sell. But sales demand is by no means the only key factor. **Any of an organisation's resources can be a key factor** and so machine capacity, distribution and selling resources, the availability of trained personnel or the availability of cash could limit the number of units an organisation can produce. What's more, **key factors can change over time**. An organisation might usually be limited by the number of units it can sell but if specialised machinery suddenly breaks down and cannot be repaired or replaced immediately, machine capacity will become the key factor.

It is therefore vital that an organisation's **key factor is identified before the budget is prepared** so that the managers can work towards a budget that is actually achievable. There is little point in the sales department having targets that can never be attained because the budgeted production levels cannot be met due to shortage in machine capacity.

An organisation should **attempt to overcome the constraints of the key factor**, however. If machine capacity is the key factor, an organisation should look into the possibility of subcontracting work, of looking for alternative suppliers or of looking for alternative machinery that will perform the same task. Such solutions will of course impact on other resources which then become key factors. For example, an alternative machine may exist but may be far too expensive and so cash will become the key factor.

Key factors must therefore be identified before the budget is set and the situation must be **continuously reviewed** in case another resource has become the key factor, in which case the key factor must be overcome or the budget amended to reflect what is actually achievable.

(iii)   **Budgeting using spreadsheets**

The production of a budget requires a great many numerical manipulations. When first prepared, functional budgets are often out of balance with each other and require modification so that they are compatible. The revision of one budget often leads to the revision of all the budgets. The **manual preparation** of a master budget is nothing short of **daunting**.

Computers in general and **spreadsheet** packages in particular can, however, **take the hard work out of budgeting**.

A mathematical model of the budget is built on the **spreadsheet** in rows and columns format. An **input area** of the spreadsheet contains the data which can change and therefore influence the budget. The input area for a labour budget might contain details of the labour hours required per unit of product and the labour cost per hour.

The **calculation section** of the spreadsheet model contains the formulae that act upon the data in the input section (for example, total labour cost of product Alpha = labour hours per unit × labour cost per hour).

In a complex spreadsheet it is a good idea to have a separate **output section** for the results of the calculations.

The actual budget would then collect together, in a single area of the spreadsheet, the results of the numerous calculations in the calculation area.

The more sophisticated spreadsheet packages can handle information in '3D' format (a 'pad' of paper as it were, rather than a single sheet) and present results as charts or graphs.

Spreadsheets have a number of important **benefits**.

(1) Spreadsheet packages have a facility to perform 'what if' calculations at great speed. For example, the consequences throughout the organisation of sales growth per period of nil, 1%, 2% and so on can be calculated at the touch of a button.

(2) If one or two figures need to be changed, it is only the cells in the input area that need to be changed and the computer will automatically make all the computational changes to the figures in the output area.

(3) A spreadsheet model will ensure that the preparation of the functional budgets and master budget is co-ordinated. Data and information from the functional budgets will be automatically fed through to the master budget model, ensuring that the master budget is an accurate reflection of the subsidiary budgets.

(4) Key performance ratios can be automatically calculated; the computer simply picks the relevant data straight from the spreadsheet model.

(5) Constraints (such as closing stock of product Alpha not to exceed a certain number of units) could be automatically built into the formulae.

Given the **time savings** possible, the **huge increase in accuracy** that can be achieved and their relatively **low cost**, I recommend that a spreadsheet package be used for budget preparation in the future.

If I can provide any further information on the matters covered in this report, please do not hesitate to contact me.

39 GARDEN EQUIPMENT LTD

Tutorial note. In task (a)(iii), don't forget that the output of Wye has changed and so labour and material input will have changed.

BPP PUBLISHING

(a) (i) (1) Litres per Exe = 8,740 l/2,185 units   =   4 litres per unit
Litres per Wye = 13,300 l/2,660 units   =   5 litres per unit

      (2) Labour hours per Exe = 4,370 hrs/2,185 units   =   2 hours per unit
Labour hours per Wye = 21,280 hrs/2,660 units   =   8 hours per unit

      (3) Raw material cost per litre = £26,220/8,740 litres   =   £3 per litre

      (4) Labour rate per hour = £21,850/4,370 hours   =   £5 per hour

      (5) Selling price per Exe = £152,070/2,055 units   =   £74 per unit
Selling price per Wye = £248,920/2,540 units   =   £98 per unit

      (6) *Budgeted raw material purchases*

	Litres
Opening stock	(3,040)
Issued to production	
Exe	8,740
Wye	13,300
Closing stock	6,200
Purchases	25,200

(ii) **STATEMENT OF PRODUCTION**
5 WEEKS ENDING 5 FEBRUARY 20X9

	Litres
Opening stock of raw material	3,040
Revised purchases of raw material (80% × 25,200)	20,160
Closing stock of raw material	(6,200)
Raw material before issue to production	17,000
Less: **loss in issue (5% × 17,000)**	(850)
Raw material issued to production	16,150
Raw material required for Exe production	8,740
Raw material available for Wye production	7,410

∴   Production of Wye   = 7,410 litres/5 litres   = 1,482 units
      Production of Exe   = 2,185 units

(iii) **REVISED PRODUCTION BUDGET**
5 WEEKS ENDING 5 FEBRUARY 20X9

	Exe		Wye	
	Quantity	£	*Quantity*	£
Raw material (at £3 per litre)	9,200 l (W1)	27,600	7,800 l (W2)	23,400
Labour (at £5 per hour)	4,370 hrs	21,850	11,856 hrs (W3)	59,280
Production	2,185 units	49,450	1,482 units	82,680

Workings

1   8,740 ÷ 0.95 = 9,200 litres
2   7,410 ÷ 0.95 = 7,800 litres
3   1,482 units × 8 hrs = 11,856 hrs

(b)   MEMO

To: Production Director
From: Management Accountant
Date: 5 December 20X8
Subject: **Performance of the Agricultural Division**

Following our recent telephone conversation, I set out below the information you requested.

(i)   **Possible ways of overcoming the shortage of raw material in the future**

   (1) **In the short term**

   - Search for other suppliers
   - Reduce stock levels (if this has no adverse impact on production)

   (2) **In the longer term**

   - Build up stocks when demand for the raw material is low, to be run down when demand is high

   - Set up contracts with suppliers which include penalty clauses for non-delivery

   - Search for alternative raw materials which could be used instead (which may involve redesigning the product)

   - Redesign the product so that less material is needed per unit

(ii) **Possible consequences for the division if the raw material shortages continue**

   (1) A breach of contract with the large retail company if deliveries of Exe cannot be met. A competitor may be asked to supply instead.

   (2) Loss of the market for Wye to a competitor if demand cannot be met.

   (3) Redundancies if production levels have to be cut back (or payments to idle labour).

   (4) Loss of customer goodwill and reputation if goods cannot be supplied.

I hope this has proved useful. If I can provide any further information please contact me.

40   AMBER LTD

Tutorial note. You may have got confused with the rejection rate. Remember that if units are rejected, more units must initially be made than sold, and so sales is less than gross production.

(a)

		Week 1 Units	Week 2 Units	Week 3 Units	Week 4 Units
	Forecast sales	23,520	27,440	28,420	32,340
	Good production needed (W1)	27,440	28,420	32,340	
(i)	**Gross production required** (W2)	28,000	29,000	33,000	

		£	£	£
	Weekly labour cost	21,280	21,280	21,280
(ii)	**Cost of overtime** (W3)	-	-	5,200
	Total labour cost	21,280	21,280	26,480
	Cost of material (W4)	140,000	145,000	165,000
	Fixed production overhead (W5)	63,000	65,250	74,250
(iii)	**Cost of production**	224,280	231,530	265,730

Workings

1   Based on following week's sales

2   **There is a 2% rejection rate and so production has to be greater than sales.**

   ie 98% of production units = sales units

$\therefore$ **0.98 production = sales**

$\therefore$ **production = sales $\div$ 0.98**

3   (Units in excess of weekly capacity) $\times$ £2

Week 1 - nil $\times$ £2

Week 2 - nil $\times$ £2

Week 3 - (33,000 – 30,400) units $\times$ £2 = £5,200

4   Gross production units $\times$ £5 per unit

5   Budgeted annual fixed overheads = £3,792,825

Estimated annual production = 1,685,700 units

$\therefore$ Budgeted fixed overhead absorption rate per unit
= £3,792,825/1,685,700 = £2.25 per unit

$\therefore$ Overheads absorbed per week = gross production volume $\times$ £2.25

(b) (i)

	Week 1 Units	Week 2 Units	Week 3 Units
Gross production	28,000	29,000	33,000
Capacity	30,400	30,400	30,400
(Spare capacity)/overtime units	(2,400)	(1,400)	2,600
Additional production/(reduced production)	1,200	1,400	(2,600)
Revised production plan	29,200	30,400	30,400

Units will be made in week 2 before week 1 to minimise the financing costs.

(ii) **Net savings if revised production plan accepted**

	£	£
Overtime costs saved (from task (a)(ii))		5,200
Financing costs : week 1 (1,200 $\times$ £0.20 $\times$ 2 wks)	480	
week 2 (1,400 $\times$ £0.20 $\times$ 1 wk)	280	
		(760)
Net saving		4,440

41   WILMSLOW LTD

> **Tutorial note.** Take care when you are calculating the budgeted labour hours in part (a)(iv). If efficiency levels are 80% you cannot simply add another 20% to determine the hours required. The hours lost due to inefficiency are 20% of the **final** total, and so you need to multiply by (20/80) to arrive at the 'gross' hours required.

(a) (i)   **Production budget** for quarter 3, 12 weeks to 17 September

		Alphas Units		*Betas* Units
Sales demand		2,000		2,400
Required closing stock (see working)		200		480
		2,200		2,880
Less opening stock		(500)		(600)
Budgeted production		1,700		2,280
Working				
Sales for quarter 4	(2,000 $\times$ 1.2)	2,400	(2,400 $\times$ 1.2)	2,880
Sales per day in quarter 4	($\div$ 60)	40	($\div$ 60)	48
$\therefore$ Stock at end of quarter 4	($\times$ 5)	200	($\times$ 10)	480

(ii) **Material purchases budget** for quarter 3, 12 weeks to 17 September

		Kilograms
Material required for production:	Alphas (1,700 × 8 kg)	13,600
	Betas (2,280 × 12 kg)	27,360
		40,960
Required closing stock (see working)		16,384
		57,344
Less opening stock		(12,000)
Material purchases		45,344

Working

Material required for production in quarter 4	(40,960 × 1.2)	49,152 kgs
Material required per day	(÷ 60)	819.2 kgs
∴ Stock sufficient for 20 days production	(× 20)	16,384 kgs

(iii) Budgeted cost of material purchases in quarter 3 = 45,344 kg × £10 per kg = £453,440.

(iv) **Labour budget** for quarter 3, twelve weeks to 17 September

		Hours
Labour hours required for production:	Alphas (1,700 × 3 hours)	5,100
	Betas (2,280 × 6 hours)	13,680
		18,780
Adjust for 80% efficiency level (see tutorial note)		4,695
		23,475

(v) **Budgeted cost of labour** in quarter 3

	Weeks		Hours		Labour cost £
Basic hours					
(50 employees × 12 weeks)	600	(× 35hrs)	21,000	(600 weeks × £210)	126,000
Overtime hours (balance)			2,475	(× £9 per hour)	22,275
			23,475		148,275

(b)

Tutorial note. You may have thought of other, equally valid, limitations of, and alternatives for, linear regression analysis.

MEMORANDUM

To: Margaret Brown, financial director
From: Management accountant
Date: 15 April 20X5
Subject: **The quality of sales forecasting**

This memorandum deals with your queries concerning the quality of sales forecasting within Wilmslow Ltd.

(i) **Two limitations of the use of linear regression as a forecasting technique**

(1) Linear regression analysis **assumes that there is a linear relationship** between two variables, in this instance time and sales demand. This may not be the case. For example, if sales demand grows by, say, ten per cent each quarter (which does not represent a linear pattern) rather than by, say, 1000 units a quarter (a linear pattern), linear regression analysis would not be an appropriate technique to use.

(2) Linear regression analysis **assumes that what has happened in the past will provide a reliable guide to the future**. This may not hold. For

example, there may be technological advances or changes in fashion or taste which affect the future demand for Alphas and Betas.

(ii) **Two other ways of sales forecasting**

Although linear regression analysis can be a useful technique, it does have limitations. Other methods of forecasting should be considered.

(1) **Market research** could be used. This could be primary research carried out specifically for our company, perhaps by interviews or postal questionnaires. Alternatively we could use a secondary source, which means that the information would not be collected specifically for our company. Examples of secondary sources include government statistics and trade journals.

(2) **Sales personnel could be asked to provide estimates.** The sales team will have up-to-date first hand knowledge of current sales patterns and will have a 'feel for the market'. They will be able to talk directly to customers and will know how well our products are selling and how many orders are on the order books.

I hope that this information will be useful to you in your forthcoming meeting.

42 PRACTICE QUESTION: FLEXED BUDGETS

> **Tutorial note**. In task (b) remember to check the unit cost rate at every level of activity in case the cost is semi-variable.

(a) **Calculation of budgeted production** (units)

	Period 1	*Period 2*	*Period 3*	*Period 4*
Sales	15,000	20,000	16,500	21,000
Closing stock	2,500	3,300	2,500	3,000
	17,500	23,300	19,000	24,000
Less opening stock	4,000	2,500	3,300	2,500
Budgeted production	13,500	20,800	15,700	21,500

(b) **Direct labour**

Production in period 4 will be above 18,000 units so we **need to know the bonus rate which applies** above that level.

Direct labour rate below 18,000 units	=	as periods 1 and 3
	=	£20 per unit
∴ Basic labour cost for period 2 production	=	£20 × 20,800
	=	£416,000
Actual labour cost	=	£444,000
∴ Bonus paid for extra 2,800 units (£444,000 – £416,000)	=	£28,000
∴ Bonus per unit above 18,000 units	=	£10

Direct materials

Constant rate per unit for all levels of output $= \dfrac{£108,000}{13,500} = £8$

Production overhead

The rate per unit is not constant for all levels of output so this is a semi-variable cost. Using the **high-low method**:

	Units	£
Period 2	20,800	154,000
Period 1	13,500	117,500
Change	7,300	36,500

$\therefore$ Variable cost per unit $= \dfrac{£36,500}{7,300} = £5$

$\therefore$ Fixed cost $= £154,000 - (£5 \times 20,800) = £50,000$

Administration overhead

Using the **high-low method** again:

	Units	£
Period 2	20,800	106,600
Period 1	13,500	92,000
Change	7,300	14,600

$\therefore$ Variable cost per unit $= \dfrac{£14,600}{7,300} = £2$

$\therefore$ Fixed cost $= £106,600 - (£2 \times 20,800) = £65,000$

Selling overhead

Using the **high-low method** again, based on sales volume:

	Units	£
Period 2	20,000	65,000
Period 1	15,000	60,000
Change	5,000	5,000

$\therefore$ Variable cost per unit $= £1$

$\therefore$ Fixed cost $= £65,000 - (£1 \times 20,000)$
$\qquad\qquad\;\; = £45,000$

COST BUDGET FOR PERIOD 4
PRODUCTION VOLUME 21,500 UNITS

		£'000	£'000
Direct labour - basic rate	$21,500 \times £20$	430.0	
- bonus	$3,500 \times £10$	35.0	
			465.0
Direct materials	$21,500 \times £8$		172.0
Production overhead - variable	$21,500 \times £5$	107.5	
- fixed		50.0	
			157.5
Depreciation			40.0
Administration overhead - variable	$21,500 \times £2$	43.0	
- fixed		65.0	
			108.0
Selling overhead - variable	$21,000 \times £1$	21.0	
- fixed		45.0	
			66.0
Total budgeted cost			1,008.5

(c) **VARIANCE REPORT FOR PERIOD 4**

	Budget £'000	Actual £'000	Variance £'000	
Direct labour	465.0	458	7.0	Favourable
Direct material	172.0	176	4.0	Adverse
Production overhead	157.5	181	23.5	Adverse
Depreciation	40.0	40	-	
Administration overhead	108.0	128	20.0	Adverse
Selling overhead	66.0	62	4.0	Favourable
	1,008.5	1,045	36.5	Adverse

43   PRACTICE QUESTION: FLEXIBLE BUDGETING

> **Tutorial note**. We begin the preparation of a flexible budget by splitting total budgeted costs into fixed and variable components on the basis of 2,000 occupied room nights and 4,300 visitors.

(a) and (b)

Budget centre	Variable cost analysis	Variable costs* £	Fixed costs ** £
Cleaning	£2.50 per ORN	5,000	8,250
Laundry	£1.75 per V	7,525	7,500
Reception	£0.5 per ORN	1,000	12,100
Maintenance	£0.8 per ORN	1,600	9,500
Housekeeping	£2 per V	8,600	11,000
Administration	£0.2 per ORN	400	7,300
Catering	£2.20 per V	9,460	12,000
General overheads		-	11,250

* 2,000 or 4,300 × variable cost rate. For example: variable cost of cleaning = 2,000 × £2.50 = £5,000.

** Budgeted expenditure – variable costs. For example: fixed costs of cleaning = £13,250 – £5,000 = £8,250.

The **flexible budget** for period 9 (1,850 ORN and 4,575 V) is as follows.

Budget centre	Fixed budget £	Flexible budget £	Actual results £	Budget variance £	
Cleaning (W1)	13,250	12,875	13,292	417	(A)
Laundry (W2)	15,025	15,506	14,574	932	(F)
Reception (W3)	13,100	13,025	13,855	830	(A)
Maintenance (W4)	11,100	10,980	10,462	518	(F)
Housekeeping (W5)	19,600	20,150	19,580	570	(F)
Administration (W6)	7,700	7,670	7,930	260	(A)
Catering (W7)	21,460	22,065	23,053	988	(A)
General overheads	11,250	11,250	11,325	75	(A)
	112,485	113,521	114,071	550	(A)

Workings

1   £8,250 + (1,850 × £2.50) = £12,875

2   £7,500 + (4,575 × £1.75) = £15,506.25

3   £12,100 + (1,850 × £0.50) = £13,025

4   £9,500 + (1,850 × £0.80) = £10,980

5   £11,000 + (4,575 × £2.00) = £20,150

6   £7,300 + (1,850 × £0.20) = £7,670

7   £12,000 + (4,575 × £2.20) = £22,065

(c)   The **advantages of a budgeting system** at the Arcadian Hotel are as follows.

Control

When actual results are compared with the flexible budget at the end of each period this acts as a control procedure. It is likely therefore that the Hotel will develop a greater awareness towards costs when a budgeting system is in operation.

Responsibilities

Expenditure is budgeted over eight separate budget centres at the Hotel. Such budget centres clarify who is responsible for which costs since the budget managers in charge of the costs will need to explain any significant variances which arise.

Motivation

With a budgeting system such as the one in place at the Arcadian Hotel, it is likely that staff will become more motivated to achieve the goals of the business. This is because a flexible budget recognises the different cost behaviour patterns, and is designed to change as the volume of activity changes.

Co-ordination and communication

The use of budget centres at the Arcadian Hotel means that the Hotel's business activities are likely to be more co-ordinated, and since a budget manager is likely to be responsible for each budget centre, communication will probably be improved also.

44   PRACTICE QUESTION: FLEXIBLE BUDGETS AND VARIANCES

> **Tutorial note**. A common error in this type of question is to automatically assume that costs relating to material and labour are variable. If the question does not specifically mention fixed costs and variable costs then it is likely that you have to calculate the split between them yourself.

(a)

	Flexed budget at 75% activity (W4)	*Actual*	*Variance*
	£	£	£
Costs (W4)			
Material costs	281,250	311,750	30,500 (A)
Labour costs	372,500	351,500	21,000 (F)
Production overhead costs	191,250	171,250	20,000 (F)
Administration costs	105,000	117,500	12,500 (A)
Selling and distribution costs	62,500	66,500	4,000 (A)
	1,012,500	1,018,500	6,000 (A)

Note. (F) denotes favourable variance, (A) denotes adverse variance.

Workings

1   Number of units sold at 100% = 50,000

∴ If 37,500 units have been sold, this represents 37,500/50,000 = 75% activity.

90% activity represents 90% × 50,000 = 45,000 units.

2   **Variable costs**

	90% £'000	*100%* £'000	*Difference* £'000	**Variable cost per unit*** £
Material	337.5	375	37.5	7.50
Labour	440.0	485	45.0	9.00
Production overhead	217.5	235	17.5	3.50
Administration	120.0	130	10.0	2.00
Selling and distribution	70.0	75	5.0	1.00
Number of units	45,000	50,000	5,000	

* Difference ÷ 5,000 units

3   **Fixed costs**

	Total cost at 100% £'000	Variable cost at 100% £'000	Fixed costs £'000
Material	375	375	-
Labour	485	450	35
Production overhead	235	175	60
Administration	130	100	30
Selling and distribution	75	50	25

4   **Total cost at 75%**

Cost = (37,500 units × variable cost per unit (W2)) + fixed cost (W3).

(b)   Actual costs are £6,000 greater than the costs budgeted at 75% activity. The majority of this difference is accounted for by variances for material costs, labour costs and production overhead costs.

The **favourable labour cost variance** of £21,000 and the **favourable production overhead cost variance** of £20,000 suggest that fewer hours have been worked, perhaps because overtime has been controlled. The favourable labour cost variance could, on the other hand, have arisen because wage rates were decreased, a less skilled and therefore lower paid workforce was used or not so much labour was used. The production overhead cost variance may be favourable due to a more economical use of services such as repairs and maintenance or a change in overhead such as a different supervisory structure.

Management should encourage further similar variances provided the quality of output is not affected.

The **adverse material cost variance** of £30,500 should be investigated. It could have arisen because of a price increase beyond the control of the company or because of careless purchasing or a change or error in the material standard. The material may have been defective, some may have been stolen or the use of less skilled labour may have led to excessive waste. All possible reasons for the variance need to be investigated to assess whether the variance is controllable or uncontrollable and whether it can be corrected next year.

45   GEORGE LTD

> **Tutorial note**. You were required to use your own examples and figures as illustrations in task (c). The key here is to keep it simple. Use 'round' numbers that can easily be divided and multiplied by each other such as 1,000, 100 or 10,000, for example.

MEMORANDUM

To: Marketing Assistant
From: Assistant to the Management Accountant
Date: XX June 20X8
Subject: **Flexible budgets**

Following our recent conversation I set out below a response to your query concerning the usefulness of flexible budgets.

(a)   A **fixed budget** is one which **remains unaltered regardless of whether or not the actual activity level achieved** by the organisation **corresponds to the budgeted activity level** upon which the budget was based. Fixed budgets are **useful for planning** because they provide the basis for all plans and subsidiary budgets and assist in the coordination of all of the organisation's activities.

It is unlikely, however, that actual activity levels will correspond with those upon which the fixed budget was based. In such circumstances a fixed budget provides little assistance in exercising effective control over distribution costs. If, for example, the fixed budget is based on an activity level of 100,000 units but the actual level is 150,000 units then we should expect certain costs (those that vary with activity level) to be above the level budgeted. Such variable costs might include petrol and drivers' wages. A **comparison of actual costs with the fixed budget is meaningless** for the purposes of cost control. Actual costs should be higher than the fixed budget costs because activity levels have increased. No information is provided to show whether control action is needed for any costs. A **flexible budget** should therefore be prepared to **show what the** distribution **costs should have been at the actual activity level**. Flexible budgets recognise the fact that variable costs should increase or decrease in line with increases or decreases in activity level and that fixed costs should remain unchanged. They therefore provide a higher budget cost allowance for variable costs such as petrol if activity levels increase and a lower one if activity levels decrease. Actual costs can be compared with the flexible budget costs. The resulting variances (the differences between actual and budget data) are more meaningful for cost control purposes since the effects of changes in activity levels are taken into account.

(b) The formulation of a flexible budget requires an appropriate measure of activity with which to flex variable costs. There are a number of **possible indicators which could be used as a basis for flexing the budget** for distribution costs.

    (i)   Miles/kilometres travelled
    (ii)   Tons/tonnes carried
    (iii)   Tonne-kilometres (ton-miles)
    (iv)   Journeys made
    (v)   Deliveries made

(c) Once a basis for flexing the budget has been established a flexible budget cost allowance can be calculated. Since we **assume** that **fixed costs remain the same regardless of the level of activity** the flexible budget cost allocation is calculated by adding the expected variable cost at the actual activity level to the original budgeted fixed cost.

Flexible budget cost allowance = budgeted fixed cost + number of units of activity (actual activity level) × budgeted variable cost per unit

For example suppose that the lorries used by the distribution department travel 100,000 kilometres, the budgeted fixed distribution costs are £20,000 and the variable cost per kilometre is £2 (kilometres being used as the measure of activity with which to flex the budget).

Flexible budget cost allowance   = £20,000 + (2 × 100,000)
                              = £(20,000 + 200,000)
                              = £220,000

For the purposes of cost control, this flexed cost can be compared with the actual cost and the resulting variance investigated if necessary.

46   PARMOD PLC

> **Tutorial note**. Task (b) was quite tricky. You had to realise that, because production volume would be greater than sales volume, there would be closing stocks of computers and so you had to calculate a unit cost for stock valuation purposes. What is more, you had to remember to value finished stocks on the basis of 80% activity.

BPP PUBLISHING

(a) *Trygon Ltd*
Flexible budget at 75% activity

	80%	40%	Variable cost per unit	75%
Activity level				
Sales and production (units)	120,000	60,000		112,500
	£	£	£	£
Direct materials	24,000,000	12,000,000	200	22,500,000 (W1)
Direct labour	7,200,000	7,200,000		7,200,000 (W2)
Light, heat and power	4,000,000	2,200,000	30	3,775,000 (W3)
Production management salaries	1,500,000	1,500,000		1,500,000 (W2)
Factory rent, rates and insurance	9,400,000	9,400,000		9,400,000 (W4)
Depreciation of factory machinery	5,500,000	5,500,000		5,500,000 (W4)
National advertising	20,000,000	20,000,000		20,000,000 (W4)
Marketing and administration	2,300,000	2,300,000		2,300,000 (W4)
Delivery costs	2,400,000	1,200,000	20	2,250,000 (W5)
Total costs	76,300,000	61,300,000		74,425,000
Sales revenue	84,000,000	42,000,000		78,750,000 (W6)
Operating profit/(loss)	7,700,000	(19,300,000)		4,325,000

Workings

1   Direct material cost per unit = £24,000,000 ÷ 120,000 = £200

     ∴ Direct material cost at 75% activity level = £200 × 112,500 = £22,500,000

2   Production below 120,000 units pa

     ∴ No overtime and no bonus

3   Variable cost of (120,000 − 60,000) units = £(4,000,000 − 2,200,000)

     ∴ Variable cost per unit = £1,800,000 ÷ 60,000 = £30

     ∴ Variable cost at 75% activity level = £30 × 112,500 = £3,375,000

     ∴ Fixed cost = £4,000,000 − (120,000 × £30) = £400,000

     ∴ Total cost at 75% activity level = £(400,000 + 3,375,000) = £3,775,000

4   Part of factory fixed costs and therefore constant, whatever the actual activity level.

5   Variable cost of (120,000 − 60,000) units = £(2,400,000 − 1,200,000)

     ∴ Variable cost per unit = £20

     ∴ Fixed cost = £(2,400,000 − (120,000 × £20)) = £0

     ∴ Cost at 75% activity level = £20 × 112,500 = £2,250,000

6   Price per unit = £84,000,000 ÷ 120,000 = £700

     ∴ Sales revenue for 112,500 units = £700 × 112,500 = £78,750,000

(b)
REPORT

To: Board of Directors
From: Management Accountant
Date: 1 June 20X6
Subject: **Budgeting at Trygon Ltd**

In accordance with the instructions of the Managing Director, this **report contains**:

(i)   a recalculation of the flexible budget based on production at 95% capacity, assuming fixed overheads in finished stock are based on 80% activity;

(ii) an explanation as to why the revised flexible budget differs from that circulated at the meeting on 23 May;

(iii) answers to issues raised by Alan Williams at the aforementioned meeting;

(iv) a discussion of budget preparation responsibilities.

We will now look at these issues in detail.

(i) *Trygon Ltd*
Flexible budget at 75% sales activity/95% production activity

	£	£
Factory costs		
Direct materials (142,500 × £200)		28,500,000
Direct labour (£7,200,000 + (22,500 × £70))		8,775,000
Light, heat and power (£400,000 + (142,500 × £30))		4,675,000
Production management salaries		
(£1,500,000 + (22,500 × £15))		1,837,500
Factory rent, rates and insurance		9,400,000
Depreciation of factory machinery		5,500,000
		58,687,500
Less: closing stock ((142,500 − 112,500) × £430)		(12,900,000)
(See Appendix 1)		
Factory cost of sales		45,787,500
Non-production expenses		
National advertising	20,000,000	
Marketing and administration	2,300,000	
Delivery costs (112,500 × £20)	2,250,000	
		24,550,000
Cost of sales		70,337,500
Sales (112,500 × £700)		78,750,000
Operating profit		8,412,500

(ii) If sales activity remains at 75% capacity but the production level is increased to 95% capacity, **budgeted profit increases** by £(8,412,500 − 4,325,000) = £4,087,500, despite the additional costs of overtime and bonus payments. This is mainly **due to the treatment of overheads**.

When all the units produced in a period are sold, there are no closing stocks and so all fixed overheads are charged against the profit of the period in which they are incurred. If the number of units produced is greater than the number of units sold, however, the **fixed overhead included in the valuation of closing stock** will not be charged against the current period's profit but will be **carried forward and charged against the profit of a subsequent period**.

In Trygon Ltd's case, if production is greater than sales by 30,000 units, £140 (see Appendix 1 at the end of this report) × 30,000 = £4,200,000 of fixed overhead will be carried forward rather than being charged against profit.

The increase in profit is therefore the net result of the treatment of fixed overheads and the overtime/bonus payments.

(iii) **Fixed and flexible budgets**

The original budget prepared by Mike Barratt at the beginning of the budget period is known as a fixed budget. By the term 'fixed', we do not mean that the budget is kept unchanged. Revisions to a fixed master budget will be made if the situation so demands. The term **'fixed' means the following**.

(1) The budget is prepared on the basis of an estimated volume of production and an estimated volume of sales, but **no plans are made for the event that**

actual volumes of production and sales may differ from budgeted volumes.

(2) When actual volumes of production and sales during a control period (possibly month or four weeks) are achieved, a fixed budget is **not adjusted in retrospect to the new levels of activity**.

Fixed budgets are therefore used as a **starting point** for the on-going budgeting process. They provide a **plan or target** for where an organisation wants to be at the end of a budget period and, by integrating all the subsidiary budgets, a means of coordination which facilitates the identification of bottlenecks and their reduction before production and selling commences.

The budget which has been prepared is a **flexible budget**. Flexible budgets are designed to **change so as to relate to the actual volume of production and sales in a period**, and can be used in one of two ways. Firstly they can be used at the **planning** stage and help to show the likely results if conditions were to change (for example if 112,500 units are sold instead of 120,000). Secondly, they can be used **retrospectively**; the flexible budget identifies what the costs or revenues and profit *should have been* at the actual volume of activity and, by comparing it to the actual results, management can see how good or bad actual performance has been.

Note that **flexible budgets** are constructed around the **assumption** that **fixed costs remain unchanged** when activity levels change whereas **variable costs increase in proportion to increases in volume**.

Budgeting objectives

For a budget to have any value or meaning, the organisation must have a clear, unambiguous objective. If managers are unaware of the organisation's objective or there are a number of conflicting objectives, attempts to achieve the budget will be difficult. If some managers believe the maximisation of sales revenue to be the overall objective and some believe it to be the production of a quality product, it is unlikely that a budget based on the objective of, say, reducing costs will be achieved simply because managers are concentrating their efforts in the wrong places.

The manipulation of budget data

It is clear that we are unlikely to meet the budget target set at the beginning of the year. If Parmod plc is simply concerned with profits, however, we are able to meet the original profit target by manipulating the results. All we need to do is produce more computers. We do not have to actually sell the computers produced. Although variable costs will increase in proportion with the increase in production, fixed costs will remain at the same level and, because there will be more units in closing stocks, a greater proportion of those fixed costs will be carried forward in closing stock to be set against the sales revenue of another period rather than the current period. **By increasing production to an appropriate level, we will appear to have achieved our budgeted profit target.**

(iv) Turning to the issue raised by Anne Darcy, there is an **intuitive feeling** that **participation** by managers in the budgeting process will **improve** their **motivation** and so will **improve** the **quality of their decisions** and their **efforts to achieve their targets**. It would also seem **logical** that **budgets should be developed by lower level managers**, based on their perceptions of what is achievable and the associated necessary resources, rather than being developed by top management, with little or no input from operating personnel. The belief is that morale and motivation will be improved and that acceptance of and commitment to organisational goals and objectives by operational managers will increase. Moreover, it is argued that operating managers are the only ones with sufficiently detailed knowledge to develop a meaningful budget.

Unfortunately, it is **naïve to believe that participative approaches to budgeting are always more effective than more imposed or authoritative styles**. A budget should be drawn up so as to ensure that the goals or objectives of top management and the goals of other employees harmonise with the goals of the organisation as a whole. This is known as **goal congruence**. But because, as I explained in part (c) of this report, organisational objectives are sometimes not clearly defined (and one organisation is likely to have a number of different objectives anyway), different managers will perceive their objectives differently and so could have incompatible budget demands. There are other **disadvantages** to a participative approach to budgeting.

(1) It requires more time.

(2) Coordination of the various subsidiary budgets may be difficult

(3) It may cause managers to introduce budgetary slack.

(4) Managers may be ambivalent about participation or even unqualified to participate and hence the budget may be unachievable.

(5) It can support 'empire building' by subordinates.

(6) Managers may base future plans on past results instead of using the opportunity for formalised planning to look at alternative options and new ideas.

It is therefore unclear whether it is advisable for Anne Darcy to have been responsible for providing the original budget.

Appendix 1

As production volume will be greater than sales volume, there will be closing stocks of computers at 31 December 20X6. We therefore need to calculate a unit cost for stock valuation purposes.

Following the instructions of the Group Finance Director, **finished stocks are to be valued on the basis of 80% activity.**

Unit cost calculation

	£	£
Direct materials		200
Direct labour (£7,200,000 ÷ 120,000)★		60
Light, heat and power (variable element)		30
Fixed factory overheads★:		
Light, heat and power (fixed element)	400,000	
Production management salaries	1,500,000	
Factory rent, rates and insurance	9,400,000	
Depreciation of factory machinery	5,500,000	
	16,800,000	
	÷ 120,000 units	140
		430

★**Labour element and fixed factory overheads element always based on production level of 120,000 units.**

47   CLUB ATLANTIC

> **Tutorial note**. Always take careful note of the format in which your answer is required. In this instance it was a letter but a memo or report may be asked for. Remember to change the degree of formality you use to suit the circumstance of the question.

(a)   *Club Atlantic restaurant performance statement for month ended 31 October 20X8*

	Budget	Flexed Budget	Actual	Variance
Number of guests days	9,600	11,160	11,160	
	£	£	£	£
Food (W1)	20,160	23,436	20,500	2,936 (F)
Cleaning materials (W2)	1,920	2,232	2,232	-
Heat, light and power (W3)	2,400	2,790	2,050	740 (F)
Catering wages (W4)	7,200	8,370	8,400	30 (A)
Rent, rates, insurance and deprecation (W5)	1,800	1,860	1,860	-
	33,480	38,688	35,042	3,646 (F)

Workings

1   $\dfrac{£20,160}{9,600} = £2.10$ per guest day. $11,160 \times £2.10 = £23,436$

2   $\dfrac{£1,920}{9,600} = £0.20$ per guest day. $11,160 \times £0.20 = £2,232$

3   $\dfrac{£2,400}{9,600} = £0.25$ per guest day. $11,160 \times £0.25 = £2,790$

4   $\dfrac{£7,200}{9,600} = £0.75$ per guest day. $11,160 \times £0.75 = £8,370$

5   $\dfrac{£1,800}{30} = £60$ per day. $31 \times £60 = £1,860$

(b)

Hall and Co
Accountants and Registered Auditors
4 The Parade
Crockham Hill
Kent TN42 1LY

The Directors
Club Atlantic
Beach Street
Grovedale BP14 8AW

XX December 20X8

Dear Sirs,

Further to our recent meeting, please find detailed below some comments which I hope that you will find of use.

(i)   **Do budgets motivate managers to achieve objectives?**

Motivation is what makes people behave in the way that they do. If employees are motivated, they will be keen to put in a lot of effort to achieve the goals of the organisation they work for. I believe that the following should be evident.

(1) The managers at Club Atlantic must have a clear idea of the organisation's goals.

(2) The budgets of Club Atlantic need to be attainable and to be in line with the goals of the organisation.

(3) Managers should feel positive about the goals of the organisation, and *want* to achieve them.

(4) Managers must feel that they can exert an influence on whether the goals are achieved or not.

(5) Managers should feel stimulated and challenged by the goals set by the organisation.

(6) Manager should be rewarded if the goals are achieved, for example having a bonus scheme in operation.

(ii) **Do budgets lead to improved performance by managers?**

Improved performance should be achieved by managers who are motivated. However, the abilities of individual managers will have an influence on whether or not performance is improved. Other factors to consider may be the amount of training or the level of management skills that an individual has.

(iii) **Does the current method of reporting motivate managers to be more efficient?**

The current method of reporting compares actual results against a fixed budget. In the Club Atlantic restaurant there are many variable costs, which means that for this division, the current method of reporting would not seem to be appropriate. Brian Hilton's expenses are mainly fixed costs which means that it is quite suitable for him to be comparing the actual costs of the swimming pool and the golf course against the budgeted costs.

Susan Green may find this current method unfair. Brian Hilton enjoys regular bonuses, unlike Susan Green who rarely receives a bonus. This method of reporting may therefore have a de-motivating effect on Susan as she may feel that the monthly comparisons made do not reflect the true position. The **preparation of flexible budgets is more likely to motivate Susan Green**. Brian Hilton on the other hand may not be motivated because all of his targets may be easily achieved. He may therefore not feel the need to improve his performance, if his budgets rarely report adverse variances.

Yours faithfully,

A Technician

48 VIKING SMELTING COMPANY

> **Tutorial note**. We suggest answering in turn the points raised at the management meeting in your report.

Answers

(a) *Viking Smelting Company*
Flexible budget report *for the reclamation division May 20X8*

Production budget

	Fixed budget	Flexible budget	Actual results	Variance
Production (tonnes)	250	200	200	
	£	£	£	£
Costs for which Reclamation Division are responsible				
Wages and social security costs (W1)	45,586	43,936	46,133	2,197 (A)
Fuel (W2)	18,750	15,000	15,500	500 (A)
Consumables (W3)	2,500	2,000	2,100	100 (A)
Power (W4)	1,750	1,500	1,590	90 (A)
	68,586	62,436	65,323	2,887 (A)
Costs for which Reclamation Division are not responsible				
Divisional overheads (W5)	20,000	20,000	21,000	1,000 (A)
Plant maintenance (W5)	5,950	5,950	6,900	950 (A)
Central services (W5)	6,850	6,850	7,300	450 (A)
	101,386	95,236	100,523	5,287 (A)

Workings

1   Number of employees = $4 \times 6 = 24$
     Number of hours worked = $24 \times 42 \times 4 = 4{,}032$ hours
     Wages paid = $4{,}032$ hours $\times £7.50 = £30{,}240$
     Social security and other employment costs = 40% of £30,240 = £12,096
     Total wages = £30,240 + £12,096 = £42,336
     Bonus = 200 tonnes $\times £8$ per tonne = £1,600
     Total wages including bonuses = £42,336 + £1,600 = £43,936

2   Fuel costs = $200 \times £75 = £15{,}000$

3   Consumables = $200 \times £10 = £2{,}000$

4   Power = fixed charge + variable charge = $£500 + (200 \times £5) = £500 + £1{,}000 = £1{,}500$

5   Overheads directly attributable to the division, plant maintenance and central services costs are all fixed costs. These costs are therefore not the direct responsibility of the reclamation division.

(b)   MEMORANDUM

To: The management of the reclamation division
From: D Ross, deputy financial controller, reclamation division
Date: XX June 20X8
Subject: **Revised flexible budget report**

Following my meeting with Sharon Houghton, it has become clear that there is some confusion about the performance reports which you have recently been presented with. Sharon has passed on to me the queries which were raised by the team at the management meeting when the original report was presented. I hope that the following will help to answer your queries.

(i)   The budget figures are based on two-year old data taken from the original proposal. The main reason for this is because the original data provides a plan which shows how we should like the reclamation division to be performing in the future. For this reason we base our budgets on the **two-year old data**, and we are provided with a **target** of where we are aiming to be in the future.

(ii) The **budget data should be based on what we are proposing to do, rather than what we actually did**. As mentioned above in (a), the company should always have a target to aim for. In this case, our proposals show where we are aiming for as these were drawn up at the planning stage. It is important to always keep them in mind when looking at the actual results on a monthly basis.

(iii) The initial performance report that you were presented with for May 20X8 simply compared actual results of 200 tonnes of production with a budget of 250 tonnes of production. In such cases, it is likely that the lower the production, the more favourable the variances will be, since the costs involved with making lower than budgeted production, are likely to be less than budgeted costs. The **revised performance report takes into account the actual level of production**, and the flexible budget is based upon the actual activity level. The revised performance report therefore compares actual costs of 200 tonnes of production with a budget based on 200 tonnes of production (as opposed to 250 tonnes of production).

(iv) **Plant maintenance** is essential in all divisions of a manufacturing company, and in Viking Smelting it is **apportioned to each division on the basis of capital values**. The **reclamation division** was established in April 20X6, at which time there was a large amount of expenditure on **capital equipment**. This equipment has a **higher value** than the equipment in other divisions because it has not yet been depreciated to any great extent. This means that a **greater proportion of the maintenance department's costs** are apportioned to the reclamation division.

The maintenance department is a service department. Almost all of the costs that they incur are due to the work they are doing for other divisions. For this reason, the costs of running the maintenance department should be apportioned to the divisions who use the services of this department.

(v) The comments which explain the variances could, and shall be improved by giving an explanation of why the variance has occurred. When variances are investigated, and satisfactory explanations obtained, these comments should be noted in the performance report. These comments will add value to the reports and management should be able to see at a glance why variances have occurred.

(vi) It is best to investigate all material variances on a performance report, whether they are adverse or favourable. However, it is fairly essential that **all adverse variances can be explained. Favourable variances should not be ignored**, since they may indicate that a manager has contributed to the performance of the division, and managers should be held responsible for favourable variances as well as those which are adverse.

(vii) Showing the costs of central services on the divisional performance report may help to control these costs to some extent since central services, like the maintenance department are a service department. If the divisions within the company are more efficient, then this may have an effect on the costs of the central services department. These costs may therefore be controlled to some extent by the Divisional Managers. This in turn may have a motivational effect on the managers.

The main objective of the revised performance report is to compare the actual costs for May 20X8 with a flexible budget which takes into account the actual production for the month. The flexible budget shows costs which would be expected for 200 tonnes of production, and this is compared with the actual results for 200 tonnes of production to give more meaningful variances than those calculated when comparing with a budget for 250 tonnes of production.

The revised performance report has a number of **advantages** over the original report.

Firstly, it divides the costs into controllable and uncontrollable, thereby showing clearly the variances which have occurred in the areas for which divisional managers are responsible. Secondly, they are less demotivating for divisional managers since actual results are compared against a more meaningful budget. Managers may be not keen to increase production if variances are going to be unfavourable. With flexible budgeting, managers will not be put off increasing production, since the flexible budget will be amended to reflect the increased activity levels.

49 VECSTAR LTD

> **Tutorial note**. Don't forget to include the fixed cost component of the semi-variable costs and to convert your total for a control period into an annual total when calculating the normal annual production volume in (a)(ii).

(a) (i) **FLEXIBLE BUDGET** STATEMENT
4 WEEKS ENDED 29 MAY 20X8

	Actual	Flexible budget	Variances
Units produced	60,000	60,000	-
	£	£	£
Costs			
Material (W1)	18,546	15,600	2,946 (A)
Labour (W2)	7,200	7,200	-
Power (W3)	900	1,300	400 (F)
Maintenance (W4)	1,600	1,800	200 (F)
Supervision (W5)	3,400	3,440	40 (F)
Rent and insurance (W5)	2,050	1,820	230 (A)
Deprecation (W5)	4,000	4,000	-
	37,696	35,160	2,536 (A)

Workings

1   Variable cost per unit = £12,480/48,000 = £0.26
Budget cost for 60,000 units = 60,000 × £0.26 = £15,600

2   Variable cost per unit = £5,760/48,000 = £0.12
Budget cost for 60,000 units = 60,000 × £0.12 = £7,200

3   Budget cost = £(100 + (60,000 × £0.02)) = £1,300

4   Budget cost = £(1,200 + (60,000 × £0.01)) = £1,800

5   These are fixed costs and so do not change as activity levels change.

(ii) **Fixed costs**

	£
Power	100
Maintenance	1,200
Supervision	3,440
Rent and insurance	1,820
Depreciation	4,000
	10,560

Fixed overhead absorption rate = budgeted annual fixed costs ÷ normal annual production

$\therefore £0.20 = (£10,560 \times 13) \div$ normal annual production

$\therefore$ Normal annual production $= £137,280 \div £0.20 = 686,400$ units

(b)

Green & Co
Auditors and Registered Accountants
Main Road, Big Town

James Close
Managing Director
Vecstar Ltd
Side Road
Big Town

Dear Mr Close,

I refer to your recent letter in which you raised a number of queries about the flexible budget prepared for Vecstar Ltd.

(i) The original budget is based on the budgeted level of output of 48,000 units, while the flexible budget is based on the actual level of output of 60,000 units. Because costs change in different ways when activity levels change, some costs are the same in the flexible budget as in the original budget, but others are different.

There are basically three cost **behaviour patterns**.

(1) Over what is known as the **relevant range of output** (the range of output at while the organisation has had experience of operating at in the past and for which cost information is available), **fixed costs** such as rent and insurance remain the **same** irrespective of changes in output and so will be the same in both budgets.

(2) **Variable costs** such as labour **change in proportion to changes in the level of output**. If output increases, there is a proportional increase in variable costs. If output falls, there is a proportional drop in variable costs. Because the actual output for the four weeks to 29 May was greater than the budgeted output, the variable costs in the flexible budget (which is based on the actual output volume) will be greater than the variable costs in the original budget.

(3) **Semi-variable costs** are made up of a **fixed cost element and a variable cost element**. The semi-variable costs in the flexed budget will be greater than those in the original budget because of the increase in the variable cost element, as explained above.

(ii) **ESTIMATED COST OF THE ALPHA PRODUCT**
4 WEEKS ENDING 26 JUNE 20X8

Unit cost	
Material ((W1) of (a)(i))	£0.26
Material ((W2) of (a)(i))	£0.12
Power	£0.02
Maintenance	£0.01
Unit variable cost	£0.41
	× 62,000
Total variable cost of producing 62,000 units	£25,420

BPP PUBLISHING

	£	£
Total **variable cost** of producing 62,000 units		25,420
Fixed costs		
Power	100	
Maintenance	1,200	
Supervision	3,440	
Rent and insurance	1,820	
Depreciation	4,000	
		10,560
Estimated cost of producing 62,000 units		35,980
Estimated indexed cost (£35,980 × 165.12/160.00)		37,131

(iii) Care must be taken when interpreting the estimated cost of £37,131 because the **index used may not be an appropriate one** for Vecstar Ltd.

(1) The production resources upon which the index is based may not reflect the resources used by the organisation to produce the Alpha.

(2) The index provides a measure of the average increases in the costs of production. This average may be totally inappropriate for the resource inputs used in Alpha production. Wages may be negotiated on an annual basis rather than a monthly basis, for example.

(3) The index may not be representative of all the regions within a country. The wages and rent paid by Vecstar may not be comparable with those used to draw up the index.

(iv) In using a **flexible budget** instead of a fixed budget, the **difference between the original budget output volume and the actual output volume is not highlighted**, hence your disappointment at the difference between budgeted and actual output not being shown. This could be **rectified by valuing the difference in terms of cost, margin or over-absorbed overheads**, thereby placing a more meaningful value on the difference than one in terms of units.

50 MAYFIELD SCHOOL

> **Tutorial note**. Don't worry if the format you suggested in (a)(ii) is different to ours - although you should have attempted to produce a format that overcame the criticisms you raised in (a)(i).
>
> Part (b) was very straightforward. No complicated techniques are required although you would have needed to read the data very carefully to make sure that you missed nothing.

(a)

MEMO

To: John Smith, Head Teacher, Mayfield School
From: A Technician, Accountant
Subject: **Format of budget statement**
Date: 23 June 20X8

Following our recent meeting to discuss the format of the budget statement, I set out below the information you requested.

(i) The **existing statement** suffers from a number of **weaknesses** as a management report.

(1) There are no actual or budget figures for the current month and hence no monthly variances.

(2) For many cost categories, the 'budget to date' figure is simply ten twelfths of the total budget for the year. No attempt has been made to ensure the

budget mirrors when costs are likely to be incurred. Some costs, such as heating, are unlikely to be incurred evenly throughout the year, being higher in the winter months than in the summer months.

(3) The figures in the budget are based on cash expenditure rather than on the use of accruals. As they stand, the figures may give misleading information about expenditure to date and available funds.

(4) No attempt has been made to divide the types of expenditure into meaningful groups (such as teaching costs, property costs and so on).

(5) Instead of being shown in the statement as revenue expenditure, purchases of fixed assets should be shown separately as capital expenditure and depreciated over their useful economic lives.

(6) The information shown in the 'under/over-spend column' may be difficult for non-accountants to interpret. What does the figure 2,250 Cr mean?

(7) There is no indication of whether the figures are pounds, hundreds of pounds or thousands of pounds.

(8) Information about expected annual expenditure has not been provided. It could prove useful to compare the annual budget with the total of expenditure to date plus the expected costs to the year end.

(ii) Set out below is a **suggestion for the outline of an alternative statement format** which may help you to manage the school more effectively.

MIDSHIRE COUNTY COUNCIL
MAYFIELD SCHOOL
STATEMENT OF SCHOOL EXPENDITURE AUGUST 20X8

Expense category	Monthly data				Year to date data				Year-end forecast			
	Actual	Budget	Variance (A)	(F)	Actual	Budget	Variance (A)	(F)	Forecast	Budget	Variance (A)	(F)
	£	£	£	£	£	£	£	£	£	£	£	£
Teaching costs												
Teachers - full-time												
Teachers - part-time												
Other employee expenses*												
Resources												
Administration costs												
Administrative staff												
Stationery, postage and phone												
Property costs												
Caretaker and cleaning												
Repairs and maintenance												
Lighting and heating												
Rates												
Other costs												
Miscellaneous expenses												
TOTAL REVENUE EXPENDITURE												
Fixed asset purchases												
TOTAL CAPITAL EXPENDITURE												

* Assuming that these are teacher related

(iii) There are a **number** of **advantages to the format of the statement above**.

(1) Actual and budget figures for the current month are identified, as well as the resulting variances. This means that potential problems are highlighted far more quickly, which allows for remedial action to be taken on a more timely basis.

(2) The division of expenditure into more meaningful groups should provide more useful control information. For example, the statement may make it evident that administration costs in general are out of control and require immediate control action to bring them back in line with budget.

(3) Fixed asset expenditure is now shown separately, thereby providing a useful division between the different types of expenditure.

(4) The use of the term 'variance' and the identification of variances as adverse (A) or favourable (F) rather than the use of 'under/-over spend' and Cr provides information which is more user-friendly and easier to understand.

(5) It is now clear that the figures are in £s.

(6) The inclusion of the forecast annual expenditure provides an estimate of the likely annual expenditure, thereby permitting the use of control action now, if necessary, to bring annual expenditure back in line with budget.

I hope this information has proved useful. If I can be of any further assistance, please do not hesitate to contact me.

(b) (i) **Forecast of pupil numbers 20X8/20X9**

Year	Age range	Number in 20X7/X8	Number in 20X8/X9
1	11-12	300	316 (W1)
2	12-13	350	300 (W2)
3	13-14	325	350 (W2)
4	14-15	360	325 (W2)
5	15-16	380	360 (W2)
6	16-17	240	304 (W3)
7	17-18	220	228 (W4)
		2,175	2,183

Forecast of income 20X8/20X9

Years	Number of pupils	Annual income per pupil £	Total income £
1-5	1,651	1,200	1,981,200
6-7	532	1,500	798,000
			2,779,200

Workings

1 *Calculation of proportion of junior school pupils likely to choose Mayfield School*

Junior school	Number in final year	Proportion choosing Mayfield	Number choosing Mayfield
Ranmoor	60	0.9	54
Hallamshire	120	0.8	96
Broomhill	140	0.9	126
Endcliffe	80	0.5	40
			316

2 **Pupil numbers in year N in 20X7/X8 become pupil numbers in year N + 1 in 20X8/X9.**

3 $380 \times 80\%$

4 $240 \times 95\%$

(ii) **Calculation of budgeted surplus 20X8/X9**

	£
Estimated income (see (i))	2,779,200
Estimated expenditure (£2,581,296 × 105%)	2,710,361
Budgeted surplus	68,839

51   HAPPY HOLIDAYS LTD

> **Tutorial note**. Try to provide examples related to the scenario when answering (b)(iii).

(a) (i)   **y = 640 + 40x**

In 20X9, x = 9 and so y (annual demand) = 640 + (40 × 9) = 1,000

∴ Weekly demand in 20X9 = 1,000 ÷ 25 = 40 holidays

(ii)   **Weaknesses of the least squares regression formula in forecasting weekly demand for holidays**

(1) Use of the formula assumes a linear relationship between annual demand and time. This may not be true.

(2) It ignores any seasonal and cyclical variations which might exist. For example, weeks when children are at school might be more popular and during a recession demand may drop significantly.

(3) Its use assumes that the level of demand can be estimated on the basis of time. In reality, demand may depend on several other variables (such as the weather in the UK, whether the economy is booming or in recession, the relative popularity of short-haul and long-haul holidays, crime or political unrest in other holiday destinations, exchange rates, and/or changing tastes of holiday makers).

(4) It is only valid within the range of data used to determine the equation in the first place.

(5) The data used to determine the equation may no longer be relevant. The holiday market in 20X9 is different to that in 20X1, with increased accessibility to long-haul destinations, the opening of the Channel Tunnel, improvements in facilities for those remaining in the UK for their holidays and so on.

(b)   MEMO

To: Financial Controller
From: Accounting Technician
Date: 17 December 20X8
Subject: **Revisions to cost statement for 10 days ended 27 November 20X8**

Following our recent meeting, I set out below the information you requested.

(i)   **Revised cost statement (prepared using flexible budgeting)** *for 10 days ended 27 November 20X8*

	Original budget £	Flexed budget £	Actual results £	Variances £
Aircraft seats	18,000	18,000 (W1)	18,600	600 (A)
Coach hire	5,000	5,000 (W2)	4,700	300 (F)
Hotel rooms	14,000	14,300 (W3)	14,200	100 (F)
Meals	4,800	4,560 (W4)	4,600	40 (A)
Tour guide	1,800	1,800 (W2)	1,700	100 (F)
Advertising	2,000	2,000 (W2)	1,800	200 (F)
	45,600	45,660	45,600	60 (F)

(F) denotes a favourable variance, (A) an adverse variance.

Workings

1   38 tourists travelled and so two blocks of 20 seats purchased for $2 \times 20 \times £450 = £18,000$

2   These are fixed costs and so do not change when the budget is flexed.

3   (4 single rooms $\times £60 \times 10$ days) + (17 double rooms $\times £70 \times 10$ days) = £14,300

4   $£12 \times 10$ days $\times 38$ tourists = £4,560

Note that the original budget was based on (using the cost of meals) $(£4,800 \div £12)/10$ days = 40 tourists.

(ii)   The revised cost statement is more useful for management control of costs. The original statement compares the actual costs incurred when 38 tourists travelled with the costs that should have been incurred when 40 tourists travelled. It is therefore meaningless to compare the two as one would expect variable costs such as the cost of meals and hotel rooms to vary.

The **flexible budget statement compares like with like,** however. The budget represents what costs should have been for the number of tourists who actually did travel. This is compared to the costs actually incurred. The flexible budget therefore provides a **more meaningful target** for managers to aim at, and **more meaningful variances** (the difference between what costs should have been and what costs were).

(iii) **Factors to take into account in deciding whether or not to investigate individual variances**

(1)   **Materiality**. Because a standard cost is really only an average expected cost, small variations between actual and standard are bound to occur. Such variances should therefore not be investigated.

(2)   **Controllability**. If there is nothing that management can do to control the occurrence of the variance (perhaps there has been a general worldwide increase in aircraft fuel prices), the standard should be changed rather than the variance investigated.

(3)   **Variance trend.** Individual variances should not be looked at in isolation. They should be scrutinised for a number of successive periods because, although small variations in a single period are unlikely to be significant, small variations that occur consistently may need more attention.

(4)   **Interrelationships between variances**. Individual variances should not be looked at in isolation. One variance might be interrelated with another, and much of it might have occurred only because the other variance occurred too. For example, if the actual proportion of total tourists who require a single room is greater than the budgeted proportion, there is likely to be an adverse variance on the cost of hotel rooms. However this will be more than offset by the increase in the cost of single tourists' holidays and the resulting selling price variance.

(5)   **Control limits**. Control limits should be decided and only those variances which exceed such control limits should be investigated. Management might set an absolute control limit, such as £50, and any variance exceeding £50 will be investigated. Alternatively they might establish a rule that any variance should be investigated if it exceeds a certain percentage of standard, say 10%.

52 PROFESSOR PAULINE HEATH

> **Tutorial note**. Hopefully you didn't waste your time in task (a)(i) by including figures. It was clearly set out in the task that you were not required to do so.

(a) (i)   **Rearrangement of account headings**

	Actual this month £	Budget this month £	Variance this month £	Actual to date £	Budget to date £	Variance to date £	Annual budget £	Budget remaining £
Tuition fees								
Higher education grant								
Total revenue								
Full-time academic								
Part-time academic								
Teaching and research fees								
Total teaching costs								
Teaching and learning material								
Total non-teaching course costs								
Clerical and administrative								
Agency staff (clerical and admin)								
Total support costs								
External room hire								
Internal room hire								
Rental light and heat recharge								
Total accommodation costs								
Course advertising (press)								
Postage and telephone recharge								
Total other overheads								
Departmental contribution								
Central services recharge								
Departmental surplus/deficit								

(ii)   **Justification for rearrangement of account headings**

In its **original format**, the monthly management report showed information in the **order of what appears to be financial accounting codes**. It is unlikely that such an order is appropriate for Pauline Heath. Moreover it is possible that the way in which data is classified may be **unsuitable**. For example, the Professor is unlikely to be interested in whether part-time staff are on the payroll or invoice the university for their services. She is probably more interested in the total cost of part-time staff.

Within the constraints of the existing system, **accounts have been brought together by function**. This makes it clear the total expenditure on teaching, on support, on accommodation and so on and hence indicates the areas where costs are being incurred, with the result that they should be more easily controllable. It also highlights how favourable variances on one type of functional expense, such as the saving in staff costs resulting from the vacancies, are balanced by adverse variances on another type of the same functional expense, such as the cost of part-time academic staff.

The revised management report has **introduced monthly data**. In the original format, monthly information could only be derived by comparing the current month's year-to-date figures with those of the previous month. Moreover year-to-date variances offer management very little assistance in control since they hide monthly fluctuations about which it is vital management are aware.

The budget remaining figure has been retained. This represents the difference between the annual budget allowance and actual expenditure to date and hence shows the amount of further authorised expenditure possible under the various account headings.

In the variance column the **direction of the variance has been made clearer**. (A) should denote an adverse variance and (F) a favourable variance.

(b) **Strength of the current system**

The principal strength of the current system is that it identifies the amount of the budget allowance remaining under the various account headings, thereby showing the authorised expenditure remaining for each type of expense.

Weaknesses of the current system

As well as the weaknesses referred to in (a)(ii), the current system does have a number of other disadvantages.

(i) The annual budget has been divided into monthly control periods. It appears that the **monthly budget figure is simply one twelfth of the annual figure**. This does not reflect the way in which expenses are incurred. For example, course advertising is likely to be greatest towards the end of the academic year as courses are marketed for the subsequent year (hence a budget allowance of £25,400 remaining of the total allowance of £26,000). This has produced a favourable variance of £12,400 which does not mean that savings of £12,400 have been made because it is unlikely that any of the expenditure bar the £600 should have yet been incurred. Budget to date should therefore be built up of individual monthly budgets rather than various proportions of an overall budget.

(ii) The report **fails to provide any non-financial data** such as the number of students.

(iii) The **actual figures are not prepared on an accruals basis** and hence do not provide a meaningful figure for control purposes. In particular, the current report fails to accrue for part-time salaries.

Proposals to assist with management of the department

To effectively manage her department, Professor Heath needs to know where the department's income is coming from and where and why expenses are being incurred, information which is not provided by the current system.

At the moment, the university appears to view the department as having one activity whereas there are actually several activities going on in the department in the form of different courses. In the private sector these different courses would probably be called products. Effectively, therefore, the **department produces three products**: two degree courses and a diploma course. It is vital that the Professor knows the **contribution** to the departmental surplus made by each of these products and so the first priority in the improvement of the management accounting report is to **extend the coding and account heading system so as to facilitate the recording of revenue and expenses by course.** Some costs, such as teaching materials, can be directly allocated to individual courses whereas other costs, such as the cost of full-time academics, may have to be apportioned.

Consideration should also be given to the introduction of some form of **flexible budgeting** within the department, although this will be of only limited use because of the high proportion of fixed costs. Nevertheless, it would explain whether changes in revenue were due to an increase or decrease against budgeted student numbers or to a change in fees against those budgeted.

(c)

Course	Revenue £	Number of terms	Number of months	Income to date £
MBA	560,000	3	12	280,000 (W1)
MSc	256,000	3	12	128,000 (W2)
Diploma	120,000	2	8	90,000 (W3)
Total tuition fees				498,000
Government grant				375,000 (W4)
Revenue for 6 months to 28 February				873,000

Workings

1   £560,000 × 6/12 = £280,000

2   £256,000 × 6/12 = £128,000

3   £120,000 × 6/8 = £90,000

4   £750,000 × 6/12 = £375,000

53   COLOUR PLC

Tutorial note. Given the frequency with which flexible budgeting appears in the assessment, you should have had no problem with part (a).

(a) (i)   (1) **Material**

This is obviously a variable cost.

Variable cost per unit = £180,000/18,000 = £10 per unit

(2) **Labour**

We need to use the high-low method because it is not immediately clear whether or not this is a variable cost.

Volume Units	£
18,000	308,000
20,000	340,000
2,000	32,000

Variable cost of 2,000 units = £32,000

Variable cost per unit = £32,000/2,000 = £16 per unit

	£
∴ The variable cost of 20,000 units is 20,000 × £16 =	320,000
Total cost of 20,000 units =	340,000
Fixed cost =	20,000

(3) **Power and maintenance**

Again, we need to use the high-low method.

Volume Units	£
18,000	33,000
20,000	35,000
2,000	2,000

Variable cost of 2,000 units = £2,000

Variable cost per unit = £2,000/2,000 = £1 per unit

	£
∴ The variable cost of 20,000 units is 20,000 × £1 =	20,000
Total cost of 20,000 units =	35,000
Fixed cost =	15,000

(4) **Rent, insurance and depreciation**

This is obviously a fixed cost of £98,000.

(ii) RED LTD
REVISED PERFORMANCE STATEMENT
YEAR TO 30 NOVEMBER 20X8

	Flexed budget	*Actual results*	*Variances*
Volume (units)	19,500	19,500	nil
	£	£	£
Material (W1)	195,000	197,000	2,000 (A)
Labour (W2)	332,000	331,000	1,000 (F)
Power and maintenance (W3)	34,500	35,000	500 (A)
Rent, insurance and depreciation (W4)	98,000	97,500	500 (F)
	659,500	660,500	1,000 (A)

(A) indicates an adverse variance, (F) a favourable variance.

Workings

Cost = (19,500 × variable cost per unit) + fixed cost

1 Material cost = (19,500 × £10) + £nil = £195,000

2 Labour cost = (19,500 × £16) + £20,000 = £332,000

3 Power and maintenance cost = (19,500 × £1) + £15,000 = £34,500

4 Rent, insurance and depreciation cost = (19,500 × £nil) + £98,000

(b)   MEMO

To: Tony Brown, Managing Director, Red Ltd
From: Assistant Management Accountant
Date: 6 December 20X8
Subject: **Performance-related pay**

Following our recent telephone conversation, I set out below the information you requested.

(i) If performance-related pay is to lead to improved performance, the following **conditions** are necessary.

(1) Managers need to know the organisational objectives, and budgets must tie in with these objectives.

(2) Managers must feel that the objectives are achievable (although the objectives should provide a challenge) and they must want to achieve them.

(3) The rewards (both financial and non-financial) should motivate managers.

(4) Managers must be able to achieve the objectives (in other words, they must have the necessary skills).

(ii) The particular performance scheme in question **might not be appropriate** for the senior management of Red Ltd for a number of reasons.

(1) The level of production achieved by Red Ltd is dependent on demand by Green Ltd. This factor is therefore outside senior management's control.

(2) Some cost classifications making up unit cost may not be controllable by senior management, such as rent, insurance and depreciation. The level of these costs may be dictated by Colour plc.

(3) The use of profit as a performance indicator would be inappropriate because Red Ltd's product is sold to Green Ltd at cost.

(iii) There are a number of ways in which the managers of Red Ltd could **misuse** the proposed system by achieving performance-related pay without extra effort on their part.

(1) By using cheaper, poor quality material, they could keep unit costs down.

(2) Likewise they could cut back on preventative maintenance.

(3) If the actual number of products required by Green Ltd is greater than that budgeted, the unit cost will fall because the fixed costs are being spread over a greater volume of output.

(4) Management may have overstated the standard unit costs so that it is relatively easy to beat them.

I hope this information is useful. If I can be of any further assistance please do not hesitate to contact me.

54 RIVERMEDE LTD

> **Tutorial note.** You will need to use the high-low method to analyse the costs in part (a)(i). Since you are repeating the same method three times, working in columns will result in a quicker and neater answer.

(a) (i) **Calculation of fixed costs and variable unit costs**

	Original budget	Revised budget	Difference		Variable cost per unit
Production and sales units	24,000	20,000	4,000		
	£	£	£		£
Variable costs					
Material	216,000	180,000	36,000	(÷ 4,000)	9
Labour	288,000	240,000	48,000	(÷ 4,000)	12
Semi-variable costs					
Heat, light and power	31,000	27,000	4,000	(÷ 4,000)	1

The fixed element of heat, light and power costs can now be determined using figures from the original budget.

	£
Total costs	31,000
Variable cost (24,000 units × £1)	24,000
∴ Fixed costs of heat, light and power	7,000

(ii)   **Flexible budget** *comparison for the year ended 31 May 20X5*

		Flexible budget		Actual results	Varia
Fasta production and sales units		22,000		22,000	
		£		£	£
Variable costs					
Material	22,000 × £9	198,000	(£206,800 + £7,520)	214,320	16,32
Labour	22,000 × £12	264,000		255,200	8,80
Semi-variable costs					
Heat, light and power:	£				
variable 22,000 × £1	22,000				
fixed	7,000				
		29,000	(£33,400 – £7,520)	25,880	3,12
Fixed costs					
Rents, rates and depreciation		40,000		38,000	2,00
		531,000		533,400	2,40

Note. (A) denotes an adverse variance. (F) denotes a favourable variance.

(b)

> **Tutorial note.** Any valid reasons can be suggested for parts (ii) and (iii), as long as they are consistent with a favourable cost variance and increased sales volumes respectively.

MEMORANDUM

To: Steven Jones, managing director
From: Management accountant
Date: 31 August 20X5
Subject: **Flexible budget statement** for the year ended 31 May 20X5

This memorandum deals with your queries regarding the latest flexible budget statement.

(i)   **Why the flexible budgeting variances differ from those in the original statement**

The variances in the original statement were derived from a comparison of the budgeted costs for 20,000 units with the actual costs for 22,000 units. Since variable costs increase when output increases, the actual costs are almost certain to be higher than the budget costs, with consequent adverse variances.

The flexible budget statement compares like with like, by determining the budgeted costs for the actual volume of 22,000 units and comparing these with the actual results.

The resulting mixture of adverse and favourable variances is much more realistic. Your assertion that the large reduction in adverse variances is due to the introduction of participative budgeting is not necessarily true.

(ii) **Two reasons why a favourable cost variance may have arisen**

(1) **Managers may have included unrealistically high costs in the original budget.** This is a problem which can arise with participative budgeting; managers include extra cost allowances to ensure that they achieve their budgets. The submitted budgets therefore need careful checking, although this may be difficult because the managers themselves are the ones with the technical expertise.

(2) **Costs may have been lower than the level expected when the original budget was determined.** For example, an expected rise in rent or rates costs may not have occurred. Such savings are not necessarily the result of management control action.

(iii) **Two reasons why higher sales volume may not be the result of improved motivation**

(1) The **market** for Fastas may have **expanded** and Rivermede could have reaped the benefit of a general increase in the demand for this product. This general market increase is not necessarily the result of improved motivation of sales staff.

(2) The sales staff may have **submitted an unrealistically low sales target** for the budget, to ensure that they achieve the target. Thus the fact that the sales volume is higher than budget *may* be a result of participative budgeting, but it may be due to manipulation of the system rather than improved motivation.

55 BOARD OF MANAGEMENT

Tutorial note. In task (b) you may have felt that the top-down approach to budgeting was more appropriate at the museum. Justify your answer and you will receive marks.

MEMORANDUM

To: John Derbyshire
From: Accounting Technician
Date: 5 October 20X8
Subject: **Behavioural aspects of budgeting**

(a) **Motivational implications of imposing the budget reduction**

When setting budgets, certain managers establish a budgeted figure and then add on a bit extra (when budgeting costs) or take off a bit (when estimating revenue) 'just in case'. This extra, which is known as **budgetary slack**, is included or deducted 'just in case' they haven't estimated accurately, costs turn out to be higher than expected or revenue lower than expected or there is some other unforeseeable event which stops them meeting their budget target.

This slack **needs to be removed** from the budget. Senior management therefore have to make an estimate of the slack and ask for the budget submitted by the lower-level manager to be adjusted accordingly. If the manager has not incorporated slack, this can be very demotivating; the entire budgeting process has to begin again and costs reduced/revenues increased to the level required. Moreover, the manager is likely to feel no sense of ownership of the budget, it having been imposed on him/her, and hence he or she will be less inclined to make efforts to meet the targets.

The size of the reduction/increase will determine the effect on morale; a small change is likely to have less effect than a large change.

Given that the Board of Management appear to have requested the reduction from £35,000 to £29,000 with no reason to believe that you have incorporated budgetary slack (£35,000 being £2,000 less than the estimated deficit for 20X8), it is likely have a negative impact on both your motivation and that of other museum staff.

(b) **Top-down budgeting**

In the top-down or **imposed** approach to budgeting, **top management prepare a budget with little or no input from operating personnel** and it is then imposed upon the employees who have to work to the budgeted figures.

In the **bottom-up** or **participatory** approach to budgeting, **budgets are developed by lower-level managers** who then submit the budgets to their superiors. The budgets are based on lower-level managers' perceptions of what is achievable and the associated necessary resources.

Imposed budgets tend to be effective in newly-formed organisations and/or in very small businesses whereas participatory budgets are most often seen in more mature organisations, of medium to large size.

The imposed style of budgeting uses senior management's awareness of total resource availability, decreases the possibility of input form inexperienced or uninformed lower-level employees and ensures that an organisation's strategic plans are incorporated into planned activities.

On the other hand, the bottom-up approach ensures that information from employees most familiar with each department's needs and constraints is included, knowledge spread among several levels of management is pulled together, morale and motivation is improved and acceptance of and commitment to organisational goals and objectives by operational managers is increased. What's more, they tend to be more realistic.

Given that the museum is well established and in view of the advantages set out above, the **bottom-up approach** would seem to be the **more suitable** of the two approaches for the museum.

56   GOVERNMENT DEPARTMENT

> **Tutorial note**. Don't forget that you will get marks for how you lay out your answer. Always provide it in the format requested by the assessor.
>
> Be careful not to write everything you know about, for example, ZBB. Relate your answer to the scenario in the question.

BRIEFING PAPER
BUDGETING IN OUR ORGANISATION

To: Chief Executive
From: Finance Officer
Date: 17 January 20X8

The **aim** of this briefing paper is to explain:

(a)   the role of the budget in the newly-constituted organisation;

(b)   the management development implications of a move from centrally-held to delegated budget responsibility;

(c)   the value of a zero base budget review to the process of budget development.

We will examine each of these aspects in turn.

The role of the budget

A budget is basically an organisation's **plan** for a forthcoming period, expressed in money terms. Our budget will therefore show, for example, the organisation's salary cost for 20X8.

But budgets are not prepared in isolation and filed away: they are the concrete components of what is known as the budgetary planning and control system.

Such systems compel **planning** by forcing management to look ahead, to set out detailed plans for achieving the targets for each department, operation and (ideally) each manager and to anticipate problems.

A budget is a **yardstick** against which actual performance is measured and assessed. *Control* over actual performance is provided by the comparisons of actual results against the budget plan. Departures from budget can then be investigated.

The budget has **additional roles** above those of planning and control, however.

(a) A budget helps to ensure the achievement of the organisation's objectives; quantified expressions of the objectives are targets to be achieved within the timescale of the budget plan.

(b) A budget provides a means of communication; each person affected by the plans is aware of what he or she is meant to be doing.

(c) A budget ensures that the efforts of each department are fully integrated into a combined plan to achieve the company's objectives.

(d) Budgetary planning and control systems provide a framework for a system of responsibility centres and responsibility accounting.

(e) The identification of controllable reasons for departures from budget with the managers responsible provides an incentive for improving future performance.

As you can see, despite the simple definition of a budget, its preparation and subsequent use provides the base for a system which should have far-reaching implications for our organisation.

Moving from centrally-held to delegated budget responsibility

In the past you have managed and controlled our budgetary planning and control system; you have set the budgets and the managers have attempted to meet those targets.

Delegated budgeting is part of the process of **decentralising decision making**. Instead of top management making decisions, **decisions are taken by managers lower down the organisation.** The aim is to **improve** the decision-making process (and hence organisational performance), both from the point of view of the **quality** of the decision (those taking the decisions will have good knowledge of the relevant product, department and so on and should therefore be able to make more informed judgements) and the **speed** with which it is taken (because decisions can be made on the spot by those familiar with the relevant circumstances).

Delegated budgets are developed by lower-level managers (that is, from the bottom up) and are based on their perceptions of what is achievable and the associated necessary resources, thereby ensuring that managers feel that they have 'ownership' of their budgets. The budgets are then submitted to senior management for approval. Their successful operation requires that management have the **necessary budgeting skills** and hence full training must be provided and support given by finance staff and senior management.

There are a number of **implications** of introducing delegated budgeting, including the following.

(a) Acceptance of and commitment to organisational goals and objectives by lower-level managers is improved,

(b) In general, the budgets are more realistic.

(c) Co-ordination between departments is improved.

(d) Senior management's overview of the organisation is mixed with operational level details.

The **change in organisational culture** required for the successful operation of a system of delegated budgeting ties in well with the change in our organisational status. The organisation has been given new powers of self-direction and management; delegated budgeting will give managers the same powers.

Zero base budget reviews

Because we provide services, it is often **difficult to establish a link between activity levels and budgets** in the same way as a manufacturing organisation is able to draw up functional budgets once a sales target has been established. Budgets are therefore often developed on an **incremental basis** (last year's budget plus an adjustment for inflation). Incremental budgeting **perpetuates past inefficiencies**, however, and it encourages slack and wasteful expenditure to creep into budgets. No attempt is made to justify expenditure; to ascertain whether an activity is necessary or whether it could be done better.

If a **zero base budget** review were carried out every three or four years, however, **existing practices and expenditures would be challenged and searching questions asked**.

(a) Does this activity need to be performed?
(b) What would happen if the activity were not performed?
(c) Are there alternative ways for providing this function?

Activities then receive resources on the basis of the answers to such questions, on the basis of how they can be justified. Inefficient or obsolete operations are identified and removed.

The implementation of such a review process would undoubtedly produce significant benefits for an organisation such as ours.

57 ACCOUNTANCY COLLEGE

> **Tutorial note**. The budgets required in task (a) are not particularly difficult to prepare and so it is likely that you will get credit for presentation. Take some time to plan the layout of your budgets, using clearly headed columns. Do not present the assessor with a mass of scribbled workings.

(a) **Budgets for the first year of operation**

    (i) **Revenue budget**

Level	Number of students	Fee per student £	Total revenue £
Foundation	400	2,000	800,000
Intermediate	300	3,000	900,000
Technician	250	4,000	1,000,000
			2,700,000

(ii) Budgeted number of classes

Level	Number of students	Students in each class	Number of classes
Foundation	400	20	20
Intermediate	300	20	15
Technician	250	10	25
			60

(iii) Tuition costs budget

Level	Number of classes	Hours tuition per week per class	Total hours tuition per week	Hours tuition per annum (×30)	Tuition cost per hour £	Total tuition cost £
Foundation	20	16	320	9,600	20	192,000
Intermediate	15	20	300	9,000	22	198,000
Technician	25	22	550	16,500	24	396,000
						786,000

(iv) Budgeted student hours and tuition cost per student hour

Level	Hours tuition per annum (from (iii))	× Students per class	= Student hours	Total tuition cost £	Tuition cost per student hour £
Foundation	9,600	20	192,000	192,000	1.00
Intermediate	9,000	20	180,000	198,000	1.10
Technician	16,500	10	165,000	396,000	2.40
			537,000		

(b) The principal has operated a system of imposed budgets and has not involved or consulted his staff in the preparation of their budgets. There are two main **advantages** in adopting a more **participative approach**.

(i) The forecasts are likely to be more realistic because the individual managers are closer to the day to day running of courses. Realistic forecasts will improve planning as well as providing better yardsticks for control purposes.

(ii) If the staff have been involved in setting the budgets they are more likely to accept them as realistic targets which they are willing to work towards.

The principal should invite the deputy principal and the two heads of department to join him on a **budget committee**. The committee would act as a co-ordinating body in preparing a budget which is a realistic target and which is acceptable to those who will be expected to achieve it.

Control would be improved if separate **cost centres** were set up with a budget for each. Possible budget centres could include the following.

Budget centre	Responsible manager
Administration department	Deputy principal
Accounting studies	Head of department
Business studies	Head of department

The budget for the year should be divided into **control periods**, detailing the revenue and costs for each period separately so that managers have a better yardstick for comparison purposes as the year progresses.

58 WORLD HISTORY MUSEUM

> **Tutorial note**. A useful check is to ensure that the difference between the total cost allowance at the actual level of activity and the total actual cost equals the total of the variances.

(a) and (b)

Analysis of budgeted costs

	Fixed cost £	Variable cost £	Variable cost per course* £
Speakers' fees	-	3,180	530
Hire of premises	-	1,500	250
Depreciation of equipment	180	-	-
Stationery	-	600	100
Catering	250	1,500	250
Insurance	100	720	120
Administration	1,620	-	-

*Variable cost per course = (Total variable cost)/6

FLEXIBLE BUDGET CONTROL STATEMENT FOR APRIL

Expenditure	Fixed cost allowance £	Variable cost allowance* £	Total cost allowance £	Actual cost £	Variance £
Speakers' fees	-	2,650	2,650	2,500	150 (F)
Hire of premises	-	1,250	1,250	1,500	250 (A)
Dep'n of equipment	180	-	180	200	20 (A)
Stationery	-	500	500	530	30 (A)
Catering	250	1,250	1,500	1,500	-
Insurance	100	600	700	700	-
Administration	1,620	-	1,620	1,650	30 (A)
	2,150	6,250	8,400	8,580	180 (A)

* Variable cost allowance = variable cost per course × 5

Note. (F) denotes a favourable variance, (A) an adverse variance.

(c)   MEMORANDUM

To: Chris Brooks
From: Assistant management accountant
Date: Monday 13 June 20X1
Subject: **Participative budgeting**

As requested I enclose brief explanations of the advantages and disadvantages of participative budgeting.

Advantages

(i)   Managers are likely to be demotivated if budgets are imposed on them without any prior consultation. If they are consulted they are more likely to accept the budgets as realistic targets.

(ii) If managers are consulted then the budgets are more likely to take account of their own aspiration levels. Aspiration levels are personal targets which individuals or departments set for themselves. If budget targets exceed aspiration levels then the budgets can have a negative motivational impact because they will be perceived as unachievable. However, if the targets fall too far below aspiration levels then the performance of the individuals or departments may be lower than might otherwise have been achieved.

(iii)   Managers who are consulted may be motivated by the feeling that their views are valuable to senior management.

(iv)   Managers who are closely involved with the day to day running of operations may be able to give very valuable input to the forecasting and planning process.

Disadvantages

(i)   If too many people are involved in budgetary planning it can make the process very slow and difficult to manage.

(ii)   Senior managers may need to overrule decisions made by local managers. This can be demotivating if it is not dealt with correctly.

(iii)   The participative process may not be genuine. Managers must feel that their participation is really valued by senior management. A false attempt to appear to be interested in their views can be even more demotivating than a system of imposed budgets.

(iv)   Managers may attempt to include excess expenditure in their budgets, due to 'empire building' or a desire to guard against unforeseen circumstances.

59   PRACTICE QUESTION: COST REDUCTION

> **Tutorial note**. Your answer to task (b) might be completely different to ours.

(a)   **Cost control** is the **regulation of the costs of operating a business** and is concerned with **keeping costs within acceptable limits**.

In contrast, **cost reduction** is a **planned and positive approach to reducing expenditure**. It starts with an assumption that current or planned cost levels are too high and looks for ways of reducing them without reducing effectiveness.

Cost control action ought to lead to a reduction in excessive spending (for example when material wastage is higher than budget levels or productivity levels are below agreed standards). However, a cost reduction programme is directed towards reducing expected cost levels below current budgeted or standard levels.

Cost control tends to be carried out on a routine basis whereas cost reduction programmes are often ad hoc exercises.

(b)   Two examples of **cost control techniques** are as follows.

(i)   **Standard costing**

Designed to control unit costs rather than absolute levels of expenditure, the use of standard costing depends on the existence of a measurable output which is produced in standard operations. Control action is taken if the actual unit costs differ from standard unit costs by an excessive amount.

(ii)   **Limits on authority to incur expenditure**

Many organisations restrict the authority for their managers to incur expenditure. For example a budget manager may have an overall budget for overheads in a period, but even within this budget the manager may be required to seek separate authorisation for individual items of expenditure which are above a certain amount.

Two examples of **cost reduction techniques** are as follows.

(i) **Value analysis**

The CIMA defines value analysis as 'a systematic inter-disciplinary examination of factors affecting the cost of a product or service, in order to devise means of achieving the specified purpose most economically at the required standard of quality and reliability.' The aim in a value analysis exercise is to eliminate unnecessary costs without reducing the use value, the esteem value or the exchange value of the item under consideration.

(ii) **Work study**

This is a means of raising the production efficiency of an operating unit by the reorganisation of work. The two main parts to work study are method study and work measurement. Method study is the most significant in the context of cost reduction. It looks at the way in which work is done and attempts to develop easier and more effective methods in order to reduce costs.

60 PRACTICE QUESTION: QUALITY

Tutorial note. TQM impacts on *all* areas of an organisation's operations so do not forget about the quality control procedures that can be used once a product has been sold.

Quality control is concerned with trying to make sure that a product is manufactured (or a service is provided) so as to meet certain design specifications. This involves setting controls for the process of manufacture (or providing a service). It is a **'technique' aimed at preventing the manufacture of defective items (or the provision of defective services)**.

There are a number of **quality control techniques** which can be used at various stages of the production process.

(a) **At the product/service design stage.** Quality should be designed into the product or service (such as the safety criteria built into designs for children's toys). It should not be an afterthought.

(b) **At the production engineering stage**. For example the manufacturing 'tolerance' allowable before an item fails to meet its design specification can be set.

(c) **When goods are received** (ie the quality assurance of goods inwards). The acceptance inspection of input material means that suppliers might be categorised according to quality.

(d) **When output is produced** at various stages of the production process it can be inspected.

(e) **When the goods have been sold** or the service provided. Customer complaints can be monitored.

61 LOCAL ENGINEERING LTD

Tutorial note. What the assessor was looking for in task (a)(iii) were the four types of quality-related costs set out in BS 6143. The world 'activities' in the question therefore refers to the types of activity giving rise to the costs.

(a) BACKGROUND PAPER FOR MEETING ON 7 JULY 20X8

To: Jane Greenwood, Management Accountant
From: Assistant Management Accountant
Subject: **Total quality management and the cost of quality**
Date: 30 June 20X8

(i) **The meaning of Total Quality Management**

Total Quality Management (TQM) is a philosophy that guides every activity within a business. It is concerned with **developing and sustaining a culture of continuous improvement which focuses on meeting customers' expectations**.

One of the basic principles of TQM is therefore a dissatisfaction with the *status quo:* the belief that it is always possible to improve and so the aim should be to **'get it more right next time'**. This involves the development of a commitment to quality by all staff and a programme of continuous learning throughout the entire organisation, possibly by **empowering employees** and making them responsible for the quality of production or by introducing **quality circles**.

The customer-centred approach of TQM hinges upon identifying the 'customers', focusing attention on them and then meeting their needs in terms of price, quality and timing. Organisations must therefore be **customer orientated** rather than, as is traditionally the case, production orientated.

One of the goals of TQM is to get it right first time. By continuously improving towards **zero defects**, the quality of the product delivered to the customer is improved. The quality of output depends on the quality of materials input, however, and so either extensive **quality control procedures** are needed at the point where goods are accepted and inspected or quality assurance schemes, whereby the supplier guarantees the quality of the goods supplied, must be in place.

A small proportion of mistakes are inevitable in any organisation but more often than not those mistakes have been 'designed' into the production process. Because TQM aims to get it right first time, however, quality and not faults must be designed into an organisation's products and operations from the outset. Quality control must therefore happen at the production design and production engineering stages of a product's life, as well as actually during production.

In summary, TQM involves getting it right first time and **improving continuously**.

(ii) **Failure of the current accounting system to highlight the cost of quality**

Traditionally, the costs of scrapped units, wasted materials and reworking have been **subsumed within the costs of production** by assigning the costs of an expected level of loss (a normal loss) to the costs of good production, while accounting for **other costs of poor quality** within **production or marketing overheads**. Such costs are therefore not only considered as **inevitable** but are not **highlighted** for management attention. Moreover, traditional accounting reports tend to **ignore the hidden but real costs of excessive stock levels** (held to enable faulty material to be replaced without hindering production) and the facilities necessary for storing that stock.

(iii)/(iv) **Explicit costs of quality**

There are four recognised categories of cost identifiable within an accounting system which make up the cost of quality.

(1) **Prevention costs** are the costs of any action taken to investigate, prevent or reduce the production of faulty output. Included within this category are the costs of training in quality control and the cost of the design/development and maintenance of quality control and inspection equipment.

(2) **Appraisal costs** are the costs of assessing the actual quality achieved. Examples include the cost of the inspection of goods delivered and the cost of inspecting production during the manufacturing process.

(3) **Internal failure costs** are the costs incurred by the organisation when production fails to meet the level of quality required. Such costs include losses due to lower selling prices for sub-quality goods, the costs of reviewing product specifications after failures and losses arising from the failure of purchased items.

(4) **External failure costs** are the costs which arise outside the organisation (after the customer has received the product) due to failure to achieve the required level of quality. Included within this category are the costs of repairing products returned from customers, the cost of providing replacement items due to sub-standard products or marketing errors and the costs of a customer service department.

(v) **Quality costs not identified by the accounting system**

Quality costs which are not identified by the accounting system tend to be of two forms.

(1) Opportunity costs such as the loss of future sales to a customer dissatisfied with faulty goods.

(2) Costs which tend to be subsumed within other account headings such as those costs which result from the disruption caused by stockouts due to faulty purchases.

(b) (i) **Explicit cost of quality**

	£
Reworking (labour cost)	13,500
Customer support (contractors)	24,300
Store inspection costs	10,000
Cost of returns	4,500
	52,300

(ii) Cost of quality not reported in the accounting records

Opportunity cost (lost contribution from 100 X4s due to faulty circuit board) = £795 (W1) × 100 = £79,500.

Workings

		£
1	Labour (W2)	200
	Printed circuit board (£120,000 ÷ 1,000)	120
	Other material (£121,500 ÷ 900)	135
	Marginal cost	455
	Selling price	(1,250)
	Contribution	795

		£
2	Total labour cost	193,500
	less: cost of reworking	(13,500)
		180,000

∴ Unit cost per good unit = £180,000 ÷ 900 = £200

62 PRACTICE QUESTION: RATIO ANALYSIS

> **Tutorial note**. Since we are given an analysis of fixed and variable cost we have started our answer by restating the accounts in marginal costing format. This should provide additional information. The variable costs are determined by applying the percentages given in the question to the total costs. Fixed costs are the difference between total costs and variable costs.

(a)

Year ended 30 November

	20X8		20X7	
	£'000	£'000	£'000	£'000
Sales		1,380		1,250
Variable costs				
Direct materials	440.0		375.000	
Direct wages	334.8		281.250	
Production overheads	160.8		159.375	
Selling and distribution overheads	70.7		59.150	
Administration overheads	9.0		8.000	
		1,015.3		882.775
Contribution		364.7		367.225
Fixed costs				
Direct wages	37.2		31.250	
Production overheads	40.2		28.125	
Selling and distribution overheads	30.3		31.850	
Administration overheads	81.0		72.000	
		188.7		163.225
Net profit		176.0		204.000

Ratios	*20X8*	*20X7*
Return on capital employed	$\dfrac{176}{2,200} \times 100\% = 8.0\%$	$\dfrac{204}{2,000} \times 100\% = 10.2\%$
Net profit/sales	$\dfrac{176}{1,380} \times 100\% = 12.8\%$	$\dfrac{204}{1,250} \times 100\% = 16.3\%$
Sales/capital employed	$\dfrac{1,380}{2,200} = 0.63$ times	$\dfrac{1,250}{2,000} = 0.63$ times
Net profit per employee	$\dfrac{£176,000}{53} = £3,321$	$\dfrac{£204,000}{52} = £3,923$
Selling cost/selling staff	$\dfrac{£101,000}{8} = £12,625$	$\dfrac{£91,000}{8} = £11,375$

Administration cost/administration staff

	$\dfrac{£90,000}{5} = £18,000$	$\dfrac{£80,000}{5} = £16,000$
Sales per employee	$\dfrac{£1,380,000}{53} = £26,038$	$\dfrac{£1,250,000}{52} = £24,038$
Direct material cost/sales	$\dfrac{440}{1,380} \times 100\% = 31.9\%$	$\dfrac{375}{1,250} \times 100\% = 30.0\%$

20X8 fixed cost/20X7 fixed cost $\dfrac{188.7}{163.225} = 115.6\%$

(b) **Profitability** has declined in 20X8 when measured in terms of return on capital employed (**ROCE**). The sales/capital employed ratio (**asset turnover**) has remained constant which indicates that the deterioration in ROCE has been caused by the fall in the profitability of sales. This has reduced from 16.3% to 12.8% which is a substantial reduction.

Sale value per employee was higher in 20X8 because the sales increase was achieved with only one more employee. However, the increases in **cost per staff member** negated the sales improvement so that net profit per employee was lower in 20X8 than in 20X7.

Fixed costs showed a 15.6% increase in 20X8 because the sales increase was achieved with only one more employee. Management should investigate this increase because it is a major factor leading to the deterioration in profit.

63   PRACTICE QUESTION: PERFORMANCE MEASUREMENT

> **Tutorial note**. The measures of performance which should be used to monitor the performance of managers in a hotel chain should be:
>
> • measures which are within managers' control;
> • measures which are a valid measure of performance;
> • measures for which the data is readily available.

Examples include the following.

(a)   Net profit percentage
(b)   Cost per bed per night
(c)   Contribution per bed per night
(d)   Percentage occupancy of rooms
(e)   Contribution per meal served in restaurant
(f)   Number of days stock held
(g)   Contribution per employee
(h)   Value added per employee
(i)   Staff turnover
(j)   Breakages and losses as a percentage of turnover
(k)   Contribution per conference

64   PRACTICE QUESTION: PERFORMANCE INDICATORS

> **Tutorial note**. Always make it clear the basis of the indicator you have calculated. For example, is it a percentage, a rate (which means it will be, for example, X times) or a time (for example, Y days)?

(a)

	Division A		Division B	
	Year 1	Year 2	Year 1	Year 2
Operating efficiency	$\frac{40}{689} \times 100\%$	$\frac{46.5}{695} \times 100\%$	$\frac{108}{2,000} \times 100\%$	$\frac{105}{2,106} \times 100\%$
	$= \underline{5.8\%}$	$= \underline{6.7\%}$	$= \underline{5.4\%}$	$= \underline{5.0\%}$
Activity efficiency	$\frac{280}{4,000} \times 100\%$	$\frac{336}{4,200} \times 100\%$	$\frac{390}{6,000} \times 100\%$	$\frac{390}{6,500} \times 100\%$
	$= \underline{7.0\%}$	$= \underline{8.0\%}$	$= \underline{6.5\%}$	$= \underline{6.0\%}$
Turnover rate	$\frac{689}{280}$	$\frac{695}{336}$	$\frac{2,000}{390}$	$\frac{2,106}{390}$
	$= \underline{2.5}$ times	$= \underline{2.1}$ times	$= \underline{5.1}$ times	$= \underline{5.4}$ times
Debtors turnover	$\frac{657}{4,000} \times 365$	$\frac{552}{4,200} \times 365$	$\frac{1,068}{6,000} \times 365$	$\frac{1,246}{6,500} \times 365$
	$= \underline{60.0}$ days	$= \underline{48.0}$ days	$= \underline{65.0}$ days	$= \underline{70.0}$ days

(b) Both the **operating efficiency** and the **activity efficiency** of division A have deteriorated. The performance of division A was below that of division B in both years.

The **stock turnover rate** for division A deteriorated in year 2 and is generally much lower than that of division B. This may be because the two divisions are holding different types of stock. If this is the case, then it is not really valid to make this comparison.

The **debtors turnover** of division A improved considerably in year 2. However, this may have had an adverse effect on **sales**, which did not increase as much as those of division B. Division B appears to be **allowing customers more time to pay** and this may have helped to boost the **sales turnover** in year 2.

65   REGENT HOTEL

> **Tutorial note**. Remember that if you are bringing costs 'up to date' you must multiply by
> $$\frac{\text{more 'up to date' index number}}{\text{older index number}}$$

(a) **Wages inflated by increase in index of average weekly earnings**

$$= £195 \times \frac{191.2}{173.4} = £215$$

(b)   MEMORANDUM

To: Manager, Regent Hotel
From: Assistant to the Management Accountant
Date: XX June 20X8
Subject: **Earnings of full-time employees**

Following our recent meeting, I have **investigated the rate of increase in the weekly earnings of full-time employees compared with the industry average** and I set out my findings below.

(i)   If the average weekly earnings of the hotel's full-time employees had increased at the same rate as average earnings in the hotel and catering industry, in 20X7 the employees would be earning £215 per week. The average earnings have, however, increased to only £208 per week and so the average weekly earnings of the hotel's full-time employees have indeed fallen behind the industry average.

(ii)   You should bear in mind, however, that the mix of skills and experience of the Regent Hotel's full-time employees is different to the national average and that the rate of pay in our local area may not have risen at the same rate as the national average, thus limiting the usefulness of a comparison between the hotel's employees' earnings and the average for the hotel and catering industry.

(iii) In the past, pay rises have always been based approximately on the annual increase in the Retail Prices Index (RPI).

The RPI measures the monthly change in the cost of living in the UK. Its principal use is as a measure of inflation. The index measures the changes, month by month, in the average level of prices of 'a representative basket of goods' purchased by the great majority of households in the UK. The items in the basket are weighted to take account of their relative importance and prices are collected from all over the UK. The main groups of the basket are food and catering, alcohol and tobacco, housing and household expenditure, personal expenditure and travel and leisure. Certain items such as mortgage payments and money spent on gambling are not included in the RPI but the items and their weights are continually reviewed to ensure that they remain as representative as possible. The base date of the RPI is January 1987 and the increases in prices are measured as weighted averages since that date.

The RPI was probably used by the previous manager as the basis for wage rate increases because he was trying to ensure that full-time employees' earnings kept pace with the rate of inflation.

I hope this information is useful. If I can be of any further assistance please do not hesitate to contact me.

66 HOMELY LTD

> **Tutorial note**. According to the assessor, task (a) was generally well answered although there was a tendency to use shareholders' funds as the denominator for ROCE even though a thorough reading of the data would have shown this to be inappropriate. Of more concern was the inability of many candidates to interpret the results of their earlier calculations in task (b).

(a) **Key ratios 20X8**

	Stately Hotels plc	Homely Limited
	Target	*Actual*
ROCE	26%	22%
Operating profit percentage	13%	8%
Asset turnover	2 times	2.7 times
Working capital period	20 days	34 days
Percentage room occupancy	85%	90%
Turnover per employee	£30,000	£41,000

Workings

1   ROCE = 66/300 × 100% = 22%
2   Operating profit percentage = 66/820 × 100% = 8%
3   Asset turnover = 820/300 = 2.7 times
4   Working capital period = 70/754 × 365 = 34 days
5   Percentage room occupancy = 5,900/(18 × 365) = 90%
6   Turnover per employee = £820,000/20 = £41,000

(b)   MEMORANDUM

To: Management Accountant, Stately Hotels plc
From: Assistant to the Management Accountant
Date: XX March 20X9
Subject: **Appraisal of performance of Homely Limited**

In accordance with your instructions I have carried out an initial assessment of Homely Limited based on an abbreviated set of their accounts for 20X8. I have calculated key accounting ratios based on the information provided and compared them with our organisation's target ratios. The results of and conclusions from my appraisal are set out below, as well as details of any limitations associated with the use of the various ratios for performance comparison.

Return on capital employed (ROCE)

The ROCE achieved by Homely Limited is below the 26% target which we use for monitoring the performance of groups of hotels and individual hotels in our chain. Management action to either improve profit margins or increase asset turnover or both would result in the necessary increase in the ROCE.

The accuracy of the ROCE relies on the figure used for capital employed: an undervaluation will artificially inflate the ROCE; year-end assets may not be representative of assets employed during the accounting period. This obviously limits the use of ROCE for performance comparison.

Operating profit percentage

Homely Limited has achieved an operating profit percentage of just 8%, which is well below the 13% which we set as a target. An increase in profit can be achieved by either cutting costs or increasing room rates but management may need to concentrate on controlling costs so as to avoid dampening demand in Homely Limited's markets.

The operating profit percentage is a measure of an organisation's overall profitability but it should not be used to excess as it fails to show the effect on profit of increases/decreases in room letting rates. Moreover, it fails to take account of differences in organisations' cost structures. Homely Limited hotels may not have leisure facilities whereas our hotels do. This would reduce the usefulness in comparisons of the operating profit percentage.

Asset turnover

Compared with a turnover rate of 2, which we set as our target, Homely Limited's asset turnover rate is 2.7. Despite lower levels of profitability than the hotels in our organisation, Homely Limited hotels' assets generate sales at a better rate. Perhaps they charge lower room rates which reduce their profitability but mean that they are able to generate a higher turnover with the asset level employed.

Because of the interrelationship between asset turnover and ROCE, they both suffer from the same limitation: the valuation of capital employed can have a considerable effect on the ratio reported.

Working capital period

The working capital period of 34 days is almost double the target which we set for our hotels (20 days). Working capital levels are probably too high and management action will be needed to reduce them. This may involve stringent control of debtors, a reduction in stock levels and a more efficient use of available credit facilities. There are two principal limitations in the use of this ratio. The working capital period is based on the working capital level on one particular day which may not, of course, be representative of working capital levels throughout the entire accounting period. In addition, working capital includes a figure for stocks which, although not likely to be large proportion of working capital, is a subjective valuation.

Percentage room occupancy

Homely Limited hotels achieve a 90% room occupancy rate, 5% above the target which we set for our hotels. This may be because, as mentioned earlier, Homely Limited hotels charge lower room rates.

Turnover per employee

The turnover per employee in Homely Limited hotels is another healthy sign, being over $33\frac{1}{3}$ % higher than the target we set. Management should ensure, however, that customer service and quality are not suffering as a result of low staffing levels, a factor which is not revealed by this ratio.

Conclusions

Homely Limited appears to have both strengths which appear to be linked with turnover, and weaknesses, associated with control of costs and working capital. Management's priorities for action should be exploitation of the company's strengths and improvement of its weaknesses.

67   TRADERS PLC

> **Tutorial note**. Don't forget to illustrate your answer to task (b) part (i) with data from the question.
>
> According to the assessor, candidates had difficulty in task (b). In general, they produced poor answers when identifying the strengths and weaknesses of the company under review, with some stating the obvious while others made unwarranted conclusions. Few identified interrelationships between the ratios and many were unable to calculate a simple index.

(a)   ROCE

$$= \frac{\text{£}2{,}906{,}000}{\text{£}7{,}265{,}000} \times 100\% = 40\%$$

Gross profit margin

$$= \frac{\text{£}7{,}236{,}000}{\text{£}26{,}800{,}000} \times 100\% = 27\%$$

Net margin

$$= \frac{\text{£}2{,}906{,}000}{\text{£}26{,}800{,}000} \times 100\% = 10.84\%$$

Asset turnover

$$= \frac{\text{£}26{,}800{,}000}{\text{£}7{,}265{,}000} = 3.69 \text{ times}$$

Turnover per employee

$$= \frac{\text{£}26{,}800{,}000}{200} = \text{£}134{,}000$$

Average age of working capital

$$= \frac{\text{£}1{,}995{,}000}{\text{£}19{,}564{,}000} \times 365 = 37 \text{ days}$$

Comparative performance ratios - *year ended 30 June 20X8*

	Traders plc	*Sellars plc*
Return on capital employed	33.33%	40%
Gross profit margin	25%	27%
Net margin	8.08%	10.84%
Asset turnover	4.12 times	3.69 times
Turnover per employee	£141,176	£134,000
Average age of working capital	30 days	37 days

(b)

BRIEFING PAPER
PERFORMANCE OF TRADERS PLC
YEAR ENDED 30 JUNE 20X8

This paper explains in outline the meaning and limitations of the performance ratios in Appendix 1 (see Task (a)) and considers the strengths and weaknesses of Traders plc as highlighted by the analysis. It also details the growth in sales volume since last year.

(i)/(ii) **Meaning and limitation of ratios and Traders' strengths and weaknesses**

(1)   The **return on capital employed (ROCE)** is an overall measure which shows how well the managers of the organisation have used the resources under their control to generate profit. Profits alone do not show whether the return made is sufficient for the volume of resources committed but ROCE is a relative measure and takes volume of resources into account.

Sellars plc appears to have the more efficient management since they are able to generate 40p of profit from every £1 of resources. This compares with only 33.33p per £1 by the management of Traders plc.

However, the accuracy of the ROCE relies on the figure used for capital or resources employed. For example, the depreciation policy used by an organisation will affect the valuation of capital employed. Traders plc is depreciating its fixtures and fittings and motor vehicles at 20% and 25% respectively, compared with the 10% and 20% used by Sellars plc. Moreover the year-end value of assets used in the ratio may not be representative of assets employed during the accounting period and hence will affect the accuracy of the ROCE as a measure of performance.

(2) The **gross profit margin** is a measure of the profitability of sales. The absolute gross profit is calculated as sales revenue less the cost of goods sold and hence it focuses on a company's trading and manufacturing activities.

Because the ratio takes account of the cost of goods sold it is affected by the stock valuation method used. Moreover, the ratio fails to take account of differences in organisations' cost structures.

For every pound of sales, Sellars is able to generate 27p of gross profit whereas Traders is only able to generate 25p. If both companies have similar pricing policies and similar ranges of goods, the rates might suggest that Sellars' management are more efficient in negotiating terms with suppliers. On the other hand, it might be that the suppliers' terms are very similar but that Traders' management has set low selling prices as part of its marketing strategy.

(3) The **sales margin (or net margin)** shows the operating profit as a percentage of sales. The operating profit is calculated before interest and tax and is the profit over which operational management can exercise day to day control. It is the amount left after all direct costs and overheads have been deducted from sales revenue. The principal disadvantage of the ratio is that it is affected by different stock valuation and depreciation policies.

The return on capital employed is influenced by two factors: the intensity with which assets have been used (the asset turnover ratio (see (4))) and the margin achieved on sales (sales margin ratio). Either increasing the sales margin (by charging higher prices or reducing costs) or obtaining more sales from the same asset base will improve the overall ROCE. Care needs to be taken when interpreting the two ratios since they may be interdependent; an increase in prices (and hence the sales margin) may lead to a fall in sales volume and hence a reduction in the asset turnover.

Sellars has a higher sales margin than Traders, indicating that it is able to squeeze more profit out of each pound of sales.

(4) The **asset turnover** ratio shows sales per pound of assets and demonstrates how effectively the assets of a business are being used to generate sales. Because of the interrelationship between asset turnover and ROCE, they both suffer from the same limitation: the valuation of capital employed can have a significant effect on the ratio reported. Moreover, as noted earlier, the asset turnover ratio might be interrelated with the sales margin. Traders appears to be able to use its assets more effectively than Sellars.

(5) The **turnover per employee** is a measure of how effectively resources are being used. A particular advantage of this ratio is that it is less influenced by accounting conventions and other distortions than, for example, asset turnover. Traders plc appears to be the more successful of the two companies, achieving turnover of £141,176 per employee compared with £134,000 for Sellars plc. Management of Traders plc should ensure that customer service and quality are not suffering as a result of low staffing levels, however, a factor which is not revealed by this ratio. Moreover, care is required when comparing the ratios of the two companies as they may be

BPP PUBLISHING

operating in different segments of the market, those segments requiring different levels of service.

(6) Working capital control is concerned with minimising funds tied up in net current assets while ensuring that sufficient stock, cash and credit facilities are in place to enable trading to take place. Some insight into working capital control can be gained by calculating the **average age of working capital**, which identifies how long it takes to convert the purchase of stocks into cash from sales. There are a number of limitations in the use of this ratio: it is based on the working capital level on one particular day which may not, of course, be representative of working capital levels throughout the entire accounting period; working capital includes a figure for stocks which is a subjective valuation.

Traders have a significantly lower ratio than Sellars; Traders' management therefore appear to have greater control over its working capital (they control debtors, keep stock levels at an acceptable level and make efficient use of credit facilities).

Care needs to be taken when determining the ideal ratio. Reduce it too low and there may be insufficient stock and other current assets to sustain the volume of trade but taking too much credit from suppliers may jeopardise relationships and/or cause suppliers to increase prices.

If the ratios are compared, consideration must be given to the wider reasons for differences. In our example, Sellars might be deliberately allowing credit to customers in order to generate sales although it is, of course, possible that it is paying creditors early to gain discounts.

(iii) **Percentage growth in Traders' sales volume**

Last year's sales at this year's prices

$$= £23,000,000 \times \frac{237.90}{224.50}$$

$$= £24,372,829$$

This year's sales

$$= £24,000,000$$

Growth in current terms

$$= £(24,000,000 - 24,372,829)$$

$$= £(372,829)$$

Percentage growth

$$= \frac{£(372,829)}{£24,372,829} \times 100\% = -1.53\%$$

(iv) **The accuracy of the sales growth figure**

There are a number of reasons why the estimate of sales growth calculated above might not be accurate.

(1) The calculation assumes that prices have remained constant. Traders could well have lowered prices in order to increase market share. Sales *revenue* may have fallen but sales *volume* may have increased.

(2) The use of the trade association's index assumes that Traders' product range is typical of all organisation's in the industry. If this is not the case the index used may not be entirely appropriate since it may not reflect Traders' circumstances.

(3) The trade association index may be a simple average for the whole year whereas much of Traders' sales might be seasonal.

68   FURNITURE PRODUCTS

> **Tutorial note**. Although you are sometimes told how a ratio is calculated within the information provided in the question, this is not always the case and so you *must* know how to calculate the key ratios set out in the BPP Interactive Text.

(a)   Return on capital employed $= \dfrac{34,380}{191,000} \times 100\% = 18\%$

Gross profit margin $= \dfrac{71,000}{191,000} \times 100\% = 37\%$

Sales margin $= \dfrac{34,380}{191,000} \times 100\% = 18\%$

Asset turnover $= \dfrac{191,000}{191,000} = 1$ time

Average age of debtors $= \dfrac{47,750}{191,000} \times 12 = 3$ months

Average age of stock $= \dfrac{40,000}{120,000} \times 12 = 4$ months

Average age of creditors $= \dfrac{8,750}{105,000} \times 12 = 1$ month

(b)   (i)   **Southern Division's ROCE if asset turnover = 1.6 times**

	£
Turnover would be £191,000 × 1.6 =	305,600
Gross profit = 37% of sales =	113,072
Operating profit = £113,072 – fixed costs of £36,620 =	76,452
Capital employed =	£191,000

$\therefore$ ROCE $= \dfrac{76,452}{191,000} \times 100\% = 40\%$

(ii)   **Southern Division's ROCE if its working capital ratios are the same as those of Northern Division**

	£
NBV of fixed assets =	112,000
Stocks = 3/12 × £120,000 =	30,000
Debtors = 1.5/12 × £191,000 =	23,875
Creditors = 2/12 × £105,000 =	(17,500)
	148,375

Operating profit = £34,380

$\therefore$ ROCE $= \dfrac{34,380}{148,375} \times 100\% = 23\%$

(c)   **Limitations of the above analysis**

(i)   Both divisions appear to be depreciating their assets on a straight-line basis at 10% per annum. The average age of Northern Division's assets is therefore £40,000 ÷ £10,000 = 4 years whereas those of Southern division are £48,000 ÷ £16,000 = 3 years old. Southern Division will therefore have a lower accumulated depreciation and hence a higher capital employed. Given similar levels of operating profit, Southern Division's ROCE is therefore likely to be lower.

(ii)   The Southern Division may be paying its creditors more quickly so as to receive cash discounts.

(iii) The level of finished stocks and hence the average of age of stock may not be a direct consequence of activity during the year in the same way as the average age of debtors and creditors reflect past performance. Southern Division may be building up stocks in anticipation of higher sales next year. The fact that Northern Division has a lower average age of stock does not therefore necessarily indicate that it is able to sell its products more quickly.

69 MIDDLE PLC

> **Tutorial note**. It is always a good idea to set out how a ratio is calculated (for example, ROCE = operating profit ÷ net assets) in case you inadvertently use the incorrect figures.

(a) To: Angela Wade
    From: A Technician
    Date: XX December 20X8
    Subject: **West Ltd and East Ltd - Performance Report**

(i) **Return on capital employed (ROCE)**

The ROCE is a key financial ratio which shows the amount of profit which has been made in relation to the amount of resources invested. It also gives some idea of how efficiently the company has been operating.

$$ROCE = \frac{\text{Operating profit}}{\text{Net assets}}$$

$$ROCE \text{ (West Ltd)} = \frac{3,068}{15,340} = 0.2 \times 100\% = 20\%$$

$$ROCE \text{ (East Ltd)} = \frac{2,795}{6,500} = 0.43 \times 100\% = 43\%$$

(ii) **Asset turnover**

The asset turnover is one of the main balance sheet ratios, and is a measure of how well the assets of a business are being used to generate sales.

$$\text{Asset turnover} = \frac{\text{Net turnover}}{\text{Net assets}}$$

$$\text{Asset turnover (West Ltd)} = \frac{17,910}{15,340} = 1.17 \text{ times}$$

$$\text{Asset turnover (East Ltd)} = \frac{17,424}{6,500} = 2.68 \text{ times}$$

(iii) **Sales margin**

The sales margin ratio is a measure of overall profitability and it provides a measure of performance for management. Unsatisfactory sales margins are investigated by management, and are generally followed by control action. Increasing selling prices and reducing costs will have a direct effect on this ratio.

$$\text{Sales margin} = \frac{\text{Operating profit}}{\text{Net turnover}}$$

$$\text{Sales margin (West Ltd)} = \frac{3,068}{17,910} = 0.171 \times 100\% = 17.1\%$$

$$\text{Sales margin (East Ltd)} = \frac{2,795}{17,424} = 0.16 \times 100\% = 16\%$$

(b) **Measure of customer service : faulty sales**

The percentage of faulty sales as a measure of the level of customer service is calculated as :

$$\frac{\text{Returns}}{\text{Gross sales}}$$

$$\text{West Ltd} = \frac{100}{20,000} = 0.005\% \times 100\% = 0.5\%$$

$$\text{East Ltd} = \frac{220}{22,000} = 0.01\% \times 100\% = 1\%$$

(c) **Further measure of customer service**

Another possible measure of the level of customer service which could be derived from the accounting data is the number of days between order and delivery of goods.

This can be calculated as follows.

$$\textbf{Time between order and delivery} = \frac{\text{Orders received in year} - \text{net sales}}{\text{Net Sales}} \times 365 \text{ days}$$

$$\text{West Ltd} = \frac{20,173 - 19,900}{19,900} \times 365 \text{ days} = 5 \text{ days}$$

$$\text{East Ltd} = \frac{22,854 - 21,780}{21,780} \times 365 \text{ days} = 18 \text{ days}$$

The amount of money which the subsidiaries invest in research and development, and training could also provide a measure of customer service.

(d) **Limitations of financial ratios**

Financial ratios as a measure of performance are **only concerned with the data recorded in the accounts.** For example, East Ltd appears to be a much more efficient company than West Ltd based on its ROCE and asset turnover ratios. However, when calculations are made to measure customer service, West Ltd has far fewer days between order and delivery of goods, and half as many faulty sales (as a percentage of gross sales).

The financial ratios also treat **research and development, and training costs as expenses** which are written off to the profit and loss account. These expenses are likely to have an impact on the future profitability of the company, and are **more of an investment than expense**.

Both West Ltd and East Ltd use plant of similar size and technology. There is however, a large difference in the net book values of the plant, and hence a large **difference in the net assets** of each company.

East Ltd purchased its plant before West Ltd, and has a lower cost, and a higher depreciation to date than West Ltd. These differences arise mainly due to the fact that the accounts are prepared using historical cost accounting. The fact that East Ltd's net assets are so much lower than those of West Ltd, means that the ROCE of East Ltd will be much higher than that of West Ltd.

70   PETER SMITH

> **Tutorial note**. Efficiency can also be measured by, for example, the number of products produced per employee, the number of products produced per hour, the employee cost per product and so on (if relevant to the organisation in question).
>
> In the BPP Interactive Text we consider a number of ways of measuring performance in not-for-profit organisations. These include the use of judgement by experts and comparisons between organisations.

Efficiency and effectiveness in not-for-profit organisations

Efficiency and effectiveness

Efficiency is the relationship between inputs and outputs. Effectiveness is the relationship between the outputs of an organisation and its objectives or targets.

Measuring efficiency in commercial organisations

Commercial organisations tend to equate efficiency with profitability. One major way of measuring efficiency in commercial organisations is to calculate the return on capital employed (ROCE). This ratio identifies the relationship between the outputs (profit) and the inputs (net assets) of the organisation.

ROCE as a measure of efficiency in not-for-profit organisations

Commercial organisations generally aim to maximise profits. It therefore follows that the profitability of the organisation is used as a measure of its efficiency.

Not-for-profit organisations such as charities cannot by definition be judged by their profitability. Since ROCE is essentially a measure of profitability, it would appear to be an inappropriate measure of efficiency in not-for-profit organisations.

Performance measures for not-for-profit organisations

A more suitable measure of performance in not-for-profit organisations would be to measure **outputs in physical terms** rather than in financial terms.

A charity which provides sheltered accommodation for pensioners may measure its performance by calculating the number of pensioners placed into accommodation within a given time period. This measure may in turn be related to the cost of providing sheltered accommodation to pensioners within a given time period.

This measure of performance is limited in that it doesn't measure the value of the output (for example, the satisfaction of the pensioners placed in sheltered accommodation).

It is very difficult to measure the output of scientific research, mainly because scientific breakthroughs don't happen very often. The performance of a scientific research charity could be measured by other scientists reviewing the quality of the work that has been carried out by the charity.

71   CAM CAR COMPANY

> **Tutorial note**. If you are unsure how to calculate an indicator requested, use the information provided on the car division to see how that division's indicators have been determined.

(a)

	Van Division	Car Division
Return on capital employed (ROCE)	40%	2.53%
Asset turnover	1.5 times	0.6 times
Wages per employee	£11,000	£11,500
Production labour cost per unit	£2,200	£1,643
Profit margin	26.67%	4.21%
Profit per employee	£11,200	£4,000
Output per employee	5 vehicles	7 vehicles
Added value per employee	£32,500	£29,167

Workings

1 ROCE $= \dfrac{\text{Profit}}{\text{Net assets}} = \dfrac{112}{280} \times 100\% = 40\%$

2 Asset turnover $= \dfrac{\text{Turnover}}{\text{Net assets}} = \dfrac{420}{280} = 1.5$ times

3 Wages per employee $= \dfrac{\text{Production labour}}{\text{Number of production employees}} = \dfrac{110,000,000}{10,000} =$ 11,000

4 Production cost per unit $= \dfrac{\text{Production labour}}{\text{Vehicles produced}} = \dfrac{110,000,000}{50,000} = £2,200$

5 Profit margin $= \dfrac{\text{Profit}}{\text{Turnover}} = \dfrac{112m}{420m} \times 100\% = 26.67\%$

6 Profit per employee $= \dfrac{\text{Profit}}{\text{Number of production employees}} = \dfrac{112m}{10,000} = £11,200$

7 Output per employee $= \dfrac{\text{Vehicles produced}}{\text{Number of production employees}} = \dfrac{50,000}{10,000} = 5$ vehicles

8 Added value per employee $=$

$\dfrac{\text{Turnover} - \text{Materials and bought-in-components}}{\text{Number of production employees}} = \dfrac{420m - 95m}{10,000} = £32,500$

(b)

MEMORANDUM

To: Peter Ross, Management team
From: Management Accountant, Cam Car Company
Date: XX July 20X8
Subject: **Performance indicators for the car and van divisions**

(i)   (1) **Productivity**

Productivity defines how efficiently resources are being used. In the Cam Car Company, productivity would indicate the number of vans or cars produced in relation to the resources put in (the materials and bought-in-components).

(2) **Added value**

Added value gives an indication of how much value has been added to a product by altering its form, location or availability. In the Cam Car Company, the turnover less the cost of materials and bought-in-components represents the added value, ie the amount by which the value of the bought-in-components and materials have increased by converting them into cars and vans.

(ii)   **The profitability of the van division**

The van division may wish to justify their claims in terms of profitability by looking at the following performance indicators:

(1)   profit margin;

(2)   profit per employee.

The profit margin for the van division is 26.67%, compared to 4.21% for the car division.

The profit per employee is £11,200 for the van division, whereas it is only £4,000 for the car division.

These two performance indicators do certainly indicate that the van division is indeed more profitable than the car division.

(iii)   **The productivity of the van division**

The van division may wish to look at the following performance indicators in order to justify their claims in terms of productivity:

(1)   return on capital employed (ROCE);

(2)   added value per employee;

(3)   asset turnover.

The van division has a ROCE of 40%, compared to 2.53% for the car division.

The van division has an added value per employee of £32,500 which is marginally higher than the £29,167 for the car division.

The asset turnover for the van division is 1.5 times, as compared to 0.6 times for the car division.

In conclusion, the van division appears to have performance indicators which indicate that it is more productive than the car division.

Output per employee

The performance indicator 'output per employee' shows that the car division makes 7 vehicles per employee, whereas the van division only makes 5 vehicles per employee. This performance indicator could be used to counter the claims of higher productivity and profitability in the van division.

The main limitation of this performance indicator is that the van and car divisions make different products, and the different products cannot really be compared with each other (the time that it takes to manufacture one car and one van, and the methods used may be very different). It is also important to note that the number of vehicles produced in the van division is only 50,000 whereas in the car division it is 84,000, and there are 12,000 production employees in the car division whereas there are only 10,000 in the van division.

By looking at the output per employee as a performance indicator, it appears that the car division is more productive/profitable than the van division, and these could most certainly be used to counter the claims of the van division.

(iv)   **Overstatement of performance indicators**

The performance ratios calculated in task (a) may be overstated because the van division has fairly low net assets, and the ratio of materials and bought-in-components to turnover is small when compared to the car division.

The ROCE increases as the net assets decrease (if the profit remains constant). The net assets of the van division are low, probably due to the low value of stocks held at the end of the period, and also because the cash balance is overdrawn. These factors affect the net assets of the company and, in turn could cause the ROCE to be overstated.

The added value per employee could be overstated if the materials and bought-in-components are understated. The figure given in the accounts is very low, especially when compared to the car division. It would be useful to check last year's accounts to see whether the ratio of materials and bought-in-components to turnover is similar.

72 GRAND HOTEL

> **Tutorial note**. If the occupancy rate increases from 70% to 80% then the revised turnover is calculated at 8/7 × turnover.

(a) **Maximum occupancy** = number of days in year × number of bedrooms
= 365 × 80 = 29,200

Occupancy rate = annual total of rooms let per night as percentage of maximum occupancy

Annual total of rooms let per night = *accommodation* turnover ÷ charge per night

$$= \frac{£1,635,200}{£80} = 20,440$$

∴ Occupancy rate $= \frac{20,440}{29,200} \times 100\% = 70\%$

Gross margin: accommodation = contribution from accommodation ÷ accommodation turnover
$= \frac{£327,040}{1,635,200} \times 100\% = 20\%$

Gross margin: restaurant = contribution from restaurant ÷ restaurant turnover
$= \frac{£157,680}{£630,720} \times 100\% = 25\%$

Operating profit: hotel = profit before interest but after all other expenses
= £33,296 + £80,000
= £113,296

Sales margin: hotel = operating profit ÷ total turnover
$= \frac{£113,296}{£2,265,920} \times 100\% = 5\%$

ROCE: hotel = operating profit ÷ net assets
$= \frac{£113,296}{£1,416,200} \times 100\% = 8\%$

Asset turnover: hotel = turnover ÷ net assets
= £2,265,920 ÷ £1,416,200 = 1.6 times

(b)

GREEN AND CO
AUDITORS

Ms C Hill
Manager
Grand Hotel

10 December 20X8

Dear Ms Hill

Thank you for your recent letter setting out your proposals for increasing the hotel's return on capital employed. I have evaluated these proposals and I set out my comments below.

(i) **Operating profit required on existing capital employed to give 20% return**

The operating profit required will be 20% of £1,416,200, which is £283,240.

(ii) **Revised profit if proposals achieved**

	£	£
Increase in occupancy rate		
Revised contribution (80/70 × £327,040)	373,760	
Existing contribution	327,040	
Increase in contribution		46,720
Change in restaurant prices/costs		
Increase in turnover (5% × £630,720)	31,536	
Decreases in costs (5% × £473,040)	23,652	
Increase in contribution		55,188
Total increase in contribution		101,908
Current profit		113,296
Revised operating profit		215,204

(iii) **Revised performance in indicators**

(1) Return on capital employed $= \dfrac{\text{revised operating profit}}{\text{current net assets}} \times 100\%$

$$= \dfrac{£215,204}{£1,416,200} \times 100\%$$

$$= 15.2\%$$

(2) Asset turnover = revised turnover/net assets × 100%

To calculate revised turnover:

	£
from accommodation (8/7 × £1,635,200) =	1,868,800
from restaurant (105% × £630,720) =	662,256
	2,531,056

∴ Asset turnover = £2,531,056/1,416,200 = 1.79 times

(3) Sales margin = revised operating profit/revised turnover × 100%

$$= £215,204/£2,531,056 \times 100\%$$

$$= 8.5\%$$

(iv) **Suggestions**

If both of your proposals are implemented and achieved operating profit will increase to £215,204, thereby almost doubling ROCE to 15.2% and increasing the sales margin from 5% to 8.5% but having very little impact on asset turnover (from 1.6 times to 1.79 times). All three measures are, however, below those of hotels in similar categories and locations.

(1) Of the planned increase in profits of £101,908, 45.8% is due to the increased occupancy rate and hence a more intensive use of assets while 54.2% is due to the restaurant's pricing and costing structure (that is, improved sales margins).

(2) Even before the proposed changes to the restaurant's pricing and costing structure, the restaurant's gross margin was better than the industry average. Once the proposals are implemented it is therefore most unlikely that additional profit can be derived from the restaurant.

The proposed occupancy rate is the same as the industry average and so it may be extremely difficult to increase this further. The gross margin on accommodation is, at 20%, below the industry average and hence some improvement may be possible here. It may be possible to raise prices, which would support the asset turnover and the sales margin, or it may be possible to reduce variable costs. Alternatively there may be scope for reducing the level of fixed costs. Cheaper insurance may be available and it is quite likely that cost savings could be made within the administration function. A reduction in fixed costs would increase profits and improve both the hotel's sales margin and ROCE.

I hope that my comments have been useful. If I can be of any further assistance please do not hesitate to contact me.

Your sincerely

A Technician
Auditing Assistant.

73 STUDENT HOUSING SOCIETY

> **Tutorial note**. The revised cash/bank balance in (b)(ii) is made up of the decrease in debtors, the increase in contribution (the difference between the original operating surplus and the revised operating surplus) and the existing cash balance.

(a) (i) Return on net assets = (operating surplus/net assets) $\times$ 100%
= (£12,000/£600,000) $\times$ 100% = 2%

(ii) Operating surplus as a % of rents receivable
= (£12,000/£192,000) $\times$ 100% = 6.25%

(iii) Occupancy rate = (number of rooms occupied/maximum number of rooms) $\times$ 100%
= ((£192,000/£2,400)/100) $\times$ 100% = 80%

(iv) Average age of rent arrears in months
= (rent arrears/rents receivable) $\times$ 12
= (£48,000/£192,000) $\times$ 12 = 3 months

(v) Number of months expenses could be paid from the cash and bank balance
= (cash available/expenses involving cash) $\times$ 12
= (£4,500/£(180,000 − 14,000)) $\times$ 12 = 0.325 months

(b)

MEMO

To: Helen Brown, General Manager
From: Accounting Technician
Date: 30 June 20X8
Subject: **Meeting and objectives**

Further to our recent discussions, I set out below the information you requested. Workings are in the attached appendix.

(i) If a 95% occupancy rate had been achieved, turnover would have been £228,000 and an operating surplus of £42,000 would have been achieved.

(ii) The increased turnover and a reduction in the average age of rent arrears to one month would have caused debtors to fall to £19,000 and the cash/bank balance to increase to £63,500.

(iii) Given the revisions to the occupancy rate and the average age of rent arrears, performance indicators would have been as follows.

    (1) Return on net assets: 6.67%

    (2) Operating surplus as a % of rents receivable: 18.42%

    (3) Cash available to pay cash-based expenses: 4.4 months

(iv) (1) **Efficiency** is the relationship between an organisation's inputs and its outputs.

    (2) **Effectiveness** is the relationship between an organisation's outputs and its objectives (ie the degree to which the objectives are met).

    (3) Commercial organisations generally have profit maximisation as the objective which guides the process of managing resources economically, efficiently and effectively. **Charities** do not generally have such an objective, however, and so **cannot be satisfactorily judged by return on net assets**, the measure often used to assess profit-making organisations.

    The **objective** of our housing society is to provide for the accommodation needs of students. By following this objective we are unable to follow more profitable objectives, such as using the accommodation as a hotel. The fact that resources are not being used to maximise profit means that return on net assets may not be an adequate measure of the efficiency of the housing society.

Appendix

Workings

(i) **Revised operating surplus if 95% occupancy rate achieved**

Revenue and variable costs will have to increase by a factor of 95%/80% = 0.95/0.8 = 1.1875.

	£	£
Rent receivable (£192,000 × 1.1875)		228,000
Variable expenses		
Cleaning (£16,000 × 1.1875)	19,000	
Lighting and heating (£4,800 × 1.1875)	5,700	
Maintenance (£11,200 × 1.1875)	13,300	
		38,000
Contribution		190,000
Fixed expenses		
Rates payable	76,000	
Amortisation	14,000	
Administration costs	58,000	
		148,000
Revised operating surplus		42,000

(ii) **Revised value of debtors** = (revised rent receivable/12) × revised average age of debtors

= (£228,000/12) × 1 month = £19,000

Revised cash balance

	£
Decrease in debtors (£(48,000 − 19,000))	29,000
Increase in contribution★	30,000
Existing cash balance	4,500
	63,500

★ This is the difference between the original operating surplus (£12,000) and the operating surplus calculated in (i)(£42,000).

(iii) (1) **Revised net assets**

	£
Fixed assets	564,000
Debtors	19,000
Cash	63,500
Creditors★	(16,500)
	630,000

★ Does not change as relates to fixed costs, which are unaffected by the change in occupancy rate.

∴ **Revised return on net assets** = (£42,000/£630,000) × 100%

= 6.67%

(2) **Revised operating surplus as a % of rents receivable**

= (£42,000/£228,000) × 100% = 18.42%

(3) **Number of months expenses could be paid from the revised cash/bank balance**

= (revised cash/bank balance ÷ cash expenses) × 12

= (£63,500/(£(38,000 + 76,000 + 58,000)) × 12 = (£63,500/£172,000) × 12

= 4.4 months

74 ELEXTRIX PLC

> **Tutorial note**. If you have trouble remembering how to calculate asset turnover, just reverse the word order - *turnover* divided by *assets*.

(a) (i) Return on capital employed = (operating profit/net assets) × 100%

= (588/1,960) × 100% = 30%

(ii) Asset turnover = turnover/net assets

= (4,900/1,960) = 2.5 times

(iii) Gross profit margin of Class 1 goods = (gross profit/turnover) × 100%

= (1,296/2,700) × 100% = 48%

(iv) Gross profit margin of Class 2 goods = (gross profit/turnover) × 100%

= (660/2,200) × 100% = 30%

(v) Sales margin = (operating profit/turnover) × 100%

= (588/4,900) × 100% = 12%

(vi) Average age of stocks in months = (stock/cost of sales) × 12

= (368/2,944) × 12 = 1.5 months

(vii) Sales per employee = turnover/number of employees
$$= £4,900,000/30 = £163,333$$

(viii) Sales per square metre = turnover/size of store
$$= £4,900,000/5,000 = £980$$

(b)   REPORT

To: Sarah Barker, Finance Director
From: Accounting Technician
Date: 7 December 20X8
Subject: **Effect of reduced prices on performance of Midtown Store**

(i)   If the price reductions set out in the Government report were introduced, Midtown Store's **profit summary** would be **revised** as follows.

	Class 1 goods	Class 2 goods	Total
	£'000	£'000	£'000
Turnover (W1)	2,376	2,024	4,400
Cost of sales	1,404	1,540	2,944
Gross profit	972	484	1,456
Rates and insurance			700
Wages			327
Commission (W2)			88
Depreciation			152
Administration			91
Operating profit			98

Workings are set out in the **Appendix** to this report.

(ii) **Forecast of performance indicators if price reductions are introduced**

(1) Gross profit margin - Class 1 = $(972/2,376) \times 100\% = 41\%$

(2) Gross profit margin - Class 2 = $(484/2,024) \times 100\% = 24\%$

(3) Return on capital employed = $(98/1,960) \times 100\% = 5\%$

(iii) The analysis in (i) is based on a number of **assumptions**.

(1) The price reductions will apply equally to all goods within each class.

(2) The sales mix of Class 1 and Class 2 goods will not alter.

(3) Cost of sales will remain the same proportion of selling price, no attempt being made to cut costs (perhaps by trying to obtain lower prices from suppliers).

(4) Operating costs will remain unchanged.

(iv) There are a number of **limitations of using financial data to measure business performance.**

(1) The value of money may change over time due to inflation, making comparison more difficult.

(2) Even without inflation the price of goods may change due to technology or pricing policy.

(3) Accounting policies (depreciation, stock value) adopted by different divisions, organisations and so on can distort performance.

Appendix

Workings

1   Class 1 = £2,700,000 × 88% = £2,376,000

Class 2 = £2,200,000 × 92% = £2,024,000

2   £4,400,000 × 2% = £88,000

75   DIAMOND LTD

> **Tutorial note**. When asked to find the average age of something (such as debtors) *in months*, don't forget to multiply by 12!

(a) (i)   Return on capital employed $= \dfrac{\text{operating profit}}{\text{net assets}} \times 100\% = \dfrac{£57,600}{£240,000} \times 100\%$

$= 24\%$

(ii)   Gross profit margin $= \dfrac{\text{gross profit}}{\text{turnover}} \times 100\% = \dfrac{£360,000}{£720,000} \times 100\%$

$= 50\%$

(iii)   Asset turnover $= \dfrac{\text{turnover}}{\text{net assets}} = \dfrac{£720,000}{£240,000}$

$= 3$ times

(iv)   Sales (net profit) margin $= \dfrac{\text{operating profit}}{\text{turnover}} \times 100\% = \dfrac{£57,600}{£720,000} \times 100\%$

$= 8\%$

(v)   Average age of debtors $= \dfrac{\text{debtors}}{\text{turnover}} \times 12 \text{ months} = \dfrac{£96,000}{£720,000} \times 12$

$= 1.6$ months

(vi)   Average age of creditors $= \dfrac{\text{creditors}}{\text{purchases}} \times 12 \text{ months} = \dfrac{£51,000}{340,000} \times 12$

$= 1.8$ months

(vii)   Average age of closing stock $= \dfrac{\text{closing stock}}{\text{cost of sales}} \times 12\text{mths} = \dfrac{£60,000}{£360,000} \times 12 \text{ mths}$

$= 2$ months

(b)   MEMORANDUM

To: Angela Newton
From: Financial Analyst
Date: 19 February 20X8
Subject: **Performance of Branch** 24 - year ended 31 December 20X7

Following your recent meetings with Charles Walden and my calculation of Branch 24's performance indicators for the year ended 31 December 20X7, he has asked me to write to you to detail the level of improvement possible in Branch 24's performance if the branch were able to achieve the performance standards laid down by the company.

(i)   Had Branch 24 been able to achieve the company's asset turnover of 4 times per annum during the year to 31 December 20X while maintaining prices and the existing capital employed, return on capital employed would have increased to 74% (see Appendix 1 for workings), which is well in excess of the company's standard of 40%.

(ii) Likewise, had Branch 24 been able to achieve the company's standards for the average age of debtors (0.5 months), average age of creditors (3 months) and average age of closing stock (1 month) while maintaining its existing sales volume, return on capital employed would have increased to 52% and asset turnover to 6.5 times per annum (see Appendix 2 for workings). Both of these figures are well in excess of the company's standards.

(iii) I understand from Charles Walden that you feel that making profit rather than turning over assets should be a branch's primary objective. You are quite correct to emphasise the need for profitability, but if asset turnover can be improved while maintaining the existing level of net assets, turnover will increase. If this turnover results in a positive contribution, both profits *and* return on capital employed will increase.

You have suggested that Branch 24 may not be performing as well as other branches because it has been in existence for two years less than all the other branches. This may well be true. Longer-established branches are likely to have higher levels of accumulated depreciation, resulting in lower asset net book values and hence lower capital employed. It is also possible that the older fixtures and fittings would have been purchased at a lower price so that the annual depreciation charge is less and hence operating profit is higher. Both of these factors would lead to an increased return on capital employed.

I hope this information has been of assistance. If you have any questions please do not hesitate to contact me.

Appendix 1

				£
Revised turnover	=	£240,000 × 4	=	960,000
Cost of sales	=	50% of turnover (task 2.1 (b))	=	480,000
Gross profit			=	480,000
Fixed costs			=	302,400
Operating profit				177,600

Revised return on capital employed	=	(£177,600/£240,000) × 100%	=	74%

Appendix 2

Revised working capital				£
Revised debtors	=	(0.5 × £720,000)/12	=	30,000
Revised stock	=	(1 × £360,000)/12	=	30,000
Revised creditors	=	(3 × £340,000)/12	=	(85,000)
Revised working capital			=	(25,000)
Add fixed assets			=	135,000
Revised capital employed			=	110,000

Return on capital employed	=	(£57,600/£110,000) × 100%	=	52%
Asset turnover	=	(£720,000/£110,000)	=	6.5

76 MICRO CIRCUITS LTD

> **Tutorial note.** To find the average delay in fulfilling orders in (b)(iii), you need to find the difference between orders and turnover (= unfilled orders) and then you need to calculate the delay on this difference as a proportion of turnover, multiplied by 12.

(a) (i) Return on capital employed = (operating profit ÷ net assets) × 100%
= (£975,000/£4,875,000) × 100% = 20%

(ii) Asset turnover = turnover/net assets = £3,900,000/£4,875,000 = 0.8

(iii) Sales (operating profit) margin = (operating profit/turnover) × 100%

$$= (£975,000/£3,900,000 \times 100\% = 25\%$$

(iv) Average age of debtors (in months) = (debtors/turnover) × 12

$$= (£325,000/£3,900,000) \times 12 = 1 \text{ month}$$

(v) Average age of finished stock (in months) = (finished goods stock/cost of sales) × 12 = (£140,000/£840,000) × 12 = 2 months

(b) **Briefing notes on the usefulness of performance indicators**

Prepared for Angela Frear
Prepared by Financial Analyst
Dated: 14 December 20X8

(i) **Return on capital employed**

The return on capital employed can be misleading.

(1) Profits should be related to average capital employed but we compute the ratio using year-end assets. Using year-end figures can distort trends and comparisons. If a new investment is undertaken near to a year end and financed, for example, by an issue of shares, the capital employed will rise by the finance raised but profits will only have a month or two of the new investment's contribution.

(2) The ROCE would be higher if costs such as marketing, research and development and training were not treated as revenue expenditure but were viewed as investment for the future and were capitalised.

(ii) **Sales (operating profit) margin**

The sales (or operating profit) margin can be manipulated in a number of ways. The following activities would result in short-term improvements in the margin, but probably at the expense of the organisation's long-term viability.

- Reducing expenditure on discretionary cost items such as research and development

- Depreciating assets over a longer period of time, so that the depreciation charge is less

- Choosing an alternative stock valuation method to increase the value of closing stock

(iii) **Average delay in fulfilling orders**

	£
Orders during the year	4,550,000
Turnover during the year	3,900,000
Unfulfilled orders	650,000

Average delay = (£650,000/£3,900,000) × 12 months = 2 months

(iv) **Measures of customer satisfaction**

As well as the delay in fulfilling orders, other measures of customer satisfaction include the following.

- Repeat business ((£3,120,000/£3,900,000) × 100% = 80%)
- Cost of customer support per £ of turnover (£400,000/£3,900,000 = 10p)
- Cost of customer support per customer (information not available)

(v) **Measuring performance from an internal perspective**

A number of indicators may help to measure performance from an internal perspective.

- Training costs as a percentage of production costs ((£140,000/£930,000) × 100% = 15.05%)

- Reworked faulty production as a percentage of total production ((£37,200/ £930,000) × 100% = 4%)

- Returns as a percentage of sales ((£100,000/£4m) × 100% = 2.5%)

  The first indicator should be relatively high, the second and third as low as possible.

(vi) **Measuring the innovation and learning perspective**

The innovation and learning perspective could be measured with one of the following indicators.

- Turnover from new products as a percentage of total turnover ((£1.56m/£3.9m) × 100% = 40%)

- Research and development expenditure as a percentage of cost of production ((£750,000/£930,000) × 100% = 81%)

- Research and development expenditure as a percentage of turnover ((£750,000/£3.9m) × 100% = 19.2%)

77 ALV LTD

> **Tutorial note.** Always show the formulae you are using when calculating performance measures. This makes it clearer for you and the marker, and if you make mistakes in your calculations you will still receive full credit for your workings.

(a) **Performance indicators for ALV (West) Ltd**

(i) **Asset turnover**
= turnover/capital employed
= 2,520/2,100 = 1.2 times

(ii) **Net profit margin**
= (operating profit/sales) × 100%
= (378/2,520) × 100% = 15%

(iii) **Return on capital employed**
= (operating profit/capital employed) × 100%
= (378/2,100) × 100% = 18%

(iv) **Wages per employee**
= production labour cost/number of employees
= £260,000/20 = £13,000

(v) **Production labour cost per unit**
= production labour cost/units produced
= £260,000/30,000 = £8.67

(vi) **Output per employee**
= units produced/number of employees
= 30,000/20 = 1,500 units

(vii) **Added value per employee**
= added value/number of employees
= £(2,520,000 – 1,020,000)/20 = £75,000

(viii) **Profit per employee**
= profit/number of employees
= £378,000/20 = £18,900

(b)

REPORT

To: Jill Morgan, chief executive ALV Ltd
From: Accounting technician
Date: 13 June 20X3
Subject: **The efficiency and productivity of ALV (East) and ALV (West)**

This report deals with issues surrounding the productivity and efficiency of ALV (East) and ALV (West).

(i)   **What is meant by productivity and efficiency**

   (1)   **Productivity** is a measure of the quantity of product produced (output) in relation to the resources put in (input).

   (2)   The measurement of **efficiency** tends to focus on the **financial value** generated by the outputs.

   An organisation can be highly **productive** in terms of producing a high level of output in relation to the measured input of resources. If, however, the output has low value or cannot be sold profitably, profitability is reduced. There may therefore be a more **efficient** way to use these resources.

(ii) **Two performance indicators used to measure efficiency**

   A major measurement of efficiency is **return on capital employed**. In this case, the **value** generated by the output is the profit earned, and this is related to the input used to earn this profit, the capital employed. The ratio is therefore measuring the **efficiency** with which the capital has been used to generate the profit (the **value** of the output).

   A second measurement of efficiency is provided by the **net profit margin**.

	ALV (West)	ALV (East)
	%	%
Return on capital employed	18	42
Net profit margin	15	20

   Both of these performance measures indicate that ALV (East) has the most efficient operations.

(iii) **Two performance indicators to measure productivity**

   Major indicators to measure productivity include **output per employee** and **added value per employee** (or alternatively the **profit per employee**).

   These are both relative measures which relate the outputs generated to the inputs used to generate them.

	ALV (West)	ALV (East)
Output per employee (units)	1,500	556
Added value per employee	£75,000	£27,778

   Both of these performance measures indicate that ALV (West) has the higher productivity.

(iv) **Using net fixed assets to measure productivity**

   The fixed asset turnover ratio may be used to monitor productivity.

	ALV (West)	ALV (East)
Turnover	£2,520,000	£840,000
Net book value of fixed assets	÷ £2,100,000	÷ £360,000
Fixed asset turnover	1.2 times	2.3 times

This performance measure appears to indicate that ALV (East) is making more productive use of fixed assets, in terms of generating sales. The value of the ratio is affected by the age of the fixed assets and their value, however, as discussed below.

(v) **Different rankings given by the performance measures**

One reason why the productivity and efficiency measures might give different rankings is the **differences in the fixed asset base of the two companies.**

ALV (West) has a net book value of plant and machinery of £720,000 compared with £60,000 for ALV (East). Furthermore the average age of ALV (West)'s plant and machinery is much lower, as shown by the following calculation.

Proportion of original cost depreciated:

ALV (West)   (£180,000 ÷ £900,000) = 20%

ALV (East)   (£240,000 ÷ £300,000) = 80%

Both the 'newness' of its fixed assets, combined with its **larger asset base**, are likely to help the employees in ALV (West) achieve higher productivity in terms of the number of units output per employee and the added value per employee.

The value and age of the fixed assets also impacts upon efficiency when it is measured in terms of return on capital employed. A **higher value attached to fixed assets** would tend to **increase capital employed**, and may **decrease profit** as a result of a **higher depreciation charge**. These two factors would combine to reduce ROCE, and so may well have impacted on the calculation of ALV (West)'s ROCE.

TECHNICIAN STAGE

NVQ/SVQ LEVEL 4 IN ACCOUNTING

REVISED STANDARDS
DECEMBER 1999 CENTRAL ASSESSMENT

CONTRIBUTING TO THE MANAGEMENT OF COSTS
AND THE ENHANCEMENT OF VALUE
(UNIT 8)

Time allowed - 3 hours plus 15 minutes' reading time

This central assessment is in TWO sections.

You are reminded that competence must be achieved in EACH section. You should therefore attempt and aim to complete EVERY task in EACH section.

You are advised to spend approximately 2 hours on Section 1 and 1 hour on Section 2.

All essential workings should be included within your answers, where appropriate.

SECTION 1

(Suggested time allowance: 2 hours)

Data

You are the assistant management accountant at the Bare Foot Hotel complex on the tropical island of St Nicolas. The hotel complex is a luxury development. All meals and entertainment are included in the price of the holidays and guests only have to pay for drinks.

The Bare Foot complex aims to create a relaxing atmosphere. Because of this, meals are available throughout the day and guests can eat as many times as they wish.

The draft performance report for the hotel for the seven days ended 27 November 20X1 is reproduced below.

Bare Foot Hotel Complex
Draft performance report for seven days ended 27 November 20X1

	Notes		Budget		Actual
Guests			540		648
		$	$	$	$
Variable costs					
Meal costs	1		34,020		49,896
Catering staff costs	2,3		3,780		5,280
Total variable costs			37,000		55,176
Fixed overhead costs					
Salaries of other staff		5,840		6,000	
Local taxes		4,500		4,200	
Light, heat and power		2,500		2,600	
Depreciation of buildings and equipment		5,000		4,000	
Entertainment		20,500		21,000	
Total fixed overheads			38,340		37,800
Total cost of providing for guests			76,140		92,976

Notes

1 Budgeted cost of meals: number of guests $\times$ 3 meals per day $\times$ 7 days $\times$ \$3 per meal

2 Budged cost of catering staff: each member of the catering staff is to prepare and serve 12 meals per hour. Cost = (number of guests $\times$ 3 meals per day $\times$ 7 days $\div$ 12 meals per hour) $\times$ \$4 per hour.

3 Actual hours worked by catering staff = 1,200 hours

Other notes

The amount of food per meal has been kept under strict portion control. Since preparing the draft performance report, however, it has been discovered that guests have eaten, on average, four meals per day.

BPP
PUBLISHING

Your report to Alive Groves, the general manager of the hotel, who feels that the format of the draft performance report could be improved to provide her with more meaningful management information. She suggests that the budgeted and actual data given in the existing draft performance report is rearranged in the form of a standard costing report.

Task 1.1

a)   Use the budget data, the actual data and the notes to the performance report to calculate the following for the seven days ended 27 November 20X1.

    i)   The actual number of meals served

    ii)   The standard number of meals which should have been served for the actual number of guests

    iii)   The actual hourly rate paid to catering staff

    iv)   The standard hours allowed for catering staff to serve three meals per day for the actual number of guests

    v)   The standard fixed overhead per guest

    vi)   The total standard cost for the actual number of guests

b)   Use the data given in the task and your answers to part (a) to calculate the following variances for the seven days ended 27 November 20X1.

    i)   The material price variance for meals served

    ii)   The material usage variance for meals served

    iii)   The labour rate variance for catering staff

    iv)   The labour efficiency variance for catering staff, based on a standard of three meals served per guest per day

    v)   The fixed overhead expenditure variance

    vi)   The fixed overhead volume variance on the assumption that the fixed overhead absorption rate is based on the budgeted number of guests per seven days

c)   Prepare a statement reconciling the standard cost for the actual number of guests to the actual cost for the actual number of guests for the seven days ended 27 November 20X1.

Data

On receiving your reconciliation statement, Alive Groves asks the following questions.

- How much of the labour efficiency variance is due to guests taking, on average, four meals per day rather than the three provided for in the budget and how much is due to other reasons?

- Would it be feasible to subdivide the fixed overhead volume variance into a capacity and efficiency variance?

Task 1.2

Write a memo to Alive Groves. Your memo should do the following.

a)   Divide the labour efficiency variance into that part due to guests taking more meals than planned and that part due to other efficiency reasons.

b)   Explain the meaning of the fixed overhead capacity and efficiency variances.

c)   *Briefly* discuss whether or not it is feasible to calculate the fixed overhead capacity and efficiency variances for the Bare Foot Hotel complex.

222

SECTION 2

(Suggested time allowance: 1 hour)

Data

You are employed as a financial analyst with Denton Management Consultants and report to James Alexander, a local partner. Denton Management Consultants has recently been awarded the contract to implement accrual accounting in the St Nicolas Police Force and will shortly have to make a presentation to the Head of the Police Force. The presentation is concerned with showing how performance indicators are developed in 'for profit' organisations and how these can be adapted to help 'not for profit' organisations.

James Alexander has asked for your help in preparing a draft of the presentation that Denton Management Consultants will make to the Head of the Police Force. He suggests that a useful framework would be the balanced scorecard and examples of how this is used by private sector organisations.

The balanced scorecard views performance measurement in a 'for profit' organisation from four perspectives.

The financial perspective

This is concerned with satisfying shareholders and measures used include the return on capital employed and the sales margin.

The customer perspective

This attempts to measure how customers view the organisation and how they measure customer satisfaction. Examples include the speed of delivery and customer loyalty.

The internal perspective

This measures the quality of the organisation's output in terms of technical excellence and consumer needs. Examples include unit cost and total quality measurement.

The innovation and learning perspective

This emphasises the need for continual improvement of existing products and the ability to develop new products to meet customers' changing needs. In a 'for profit' organisation, this might be measured by the percentage of turnover attributable to new products.

To help you demonstrate how performance indicators are developed in 'for profit' organisations, he gives you the following financial data relating to a manufacturing client of Denton Management Consultants.

Profit and loss account 12 months ended 30 November 20X1			Extract from Balance sheet at 30 November 20X1				
	£'000	£'000		£'000	£'000	£'000	£'000
Turnover		240.0	**Fixed assets**	*Opening*			*Closing*
Material	18.0			*balance*	*Additions*	*Deletions*	*balance*
Labour	26.0		Cost	200.0	40.0	10.0	230.0
Production overheads	9.0		Depreciation	80.0	8.0	8.0	80.0
Cost of production	53.0		Net book value				150.0
Opening finished stock	12.0						
Closing finished stock	(13.0)		**Net current assets**				
			Stock of finished goods			13.0	
Cost of sales		52.0	Debtors			40.0	
Gross profit		188.0	Cash			6.0	
Research and development	15.9		Creditors			(9.0)	
Training	5.2						50.0
Administration	118.9		**Net assets**				200.0
		140.0					
Net profit		48.0					

Task 2.1

James Alexander asks you to calculate the following performance indicators and, for each indicator, to identify ONE balanced scorecard perspective being measured.

a) The return on capital employed

b) The sales margin (or net profit) percentage

c) The asset turnover

d) Research and development as a percentage of production

e) Training as a percentage of labour costs

f) Average age of finished stock in months

Data

On receiving your calculations, James Alexander tells you that he has recently received details of the current performance measures used by the St Nicolas Police Force. Four indicators are used.

*   The percentage of cash expenditure to allocated funds for the year
*   The average police-hours spent per crime investigated
*   The average police-hours spent per crime solved
*   The clear-up rate (defined as number of crimes solved ÷ number of crimes investigated)

He also provides you with the data for the current year used in developing the current indicators, as follows.

*   Funds allocated for the year — $3,000,000
*   Cash expenditure during the year — $2,910,000
*   Number of reported crimes in the last year — 8,000 crimes
*   Number of crimes investigated in the year — 5,000 crimes
*   Number of crimes solved in the year — 2,000 crimes
*   Number of police-hours spent on investigating and solving crimes — 40,000 hours
*   Number of police hours spent on crime prevention — 500 hours

Task 2.2

James Alexander asks you to prepare short notes for him. Your notes should do the following.

a)   Calculate the four indicators currently used by the St Nicolas Police Force.

b)   Identify ONE limitation in the calculation of the clear-up rate.

c)   Briefly suggest the following.

   i)   ONE reason why the percentage of cash expenditure to allocated funds may be an inadequate measure of the final perspective

   ii)   ONE reason why the clear-up rate might be an inadequate measure of the customer perspective other than because of the limitation identified in part (b)

   iii)   ONE reason why the hours spent per crime investigated might be an inadequate measure of the internal perspective

   iv)   ONE measure which might focus on the innovation and learning perspective

BPP
PUBLISHING

CONTRIBUTING TO THE MANAGEMENT OF COSTS AND THE ENHANCEMENT OF VALUE
(UNIT 8)

DECEMBER 1999 CENTRAL ASSESSMENT
SUGGESTED ANSWERS

SECTION 1

> **Tutorial note**. You will need to think carefully when you calculate the variances because they are being applied in a slightly different situation in this task. For example, when you calculate the 'material usage' variance, you will be deciding 'how many meals 648 guests should have *used*'. The method and the reasoning remain the same, but you need to rethink your unit of measure.

Task 1.1

(a) (i) Actual number of meals served
     = 4 meals × 7 days × 648 guests
     = 18,144 meals

(ii) Standard number of meals for actual number of guests
     = 3 meals × 7 days × 648 guests
     = 13,608 meals

(iii) Actual hourly rate of pay
     = $5,280 ÷ 1,200 hours = $ 4.40 per hour

(iv) Standard hours allowed for actual number of guests
     = (648 guests × 3 meals × 7 days) ÷ 12 meals per hour
     = 1,134 hours

(v) Standard fixed overhead per guest
     = budgeted overheads ÷ budgeted number of guests
     = $38,340 ÷ 540 = $71 per guest

(vi) **Total standard cost for actual number of guests**

	$
Meal costs (13,608 meals × $3 per meal)	40,824
Catering staff costs (1,134 hours × $4 per hour)	4,536
Fixed overhead costs (648 × $71 per guest)	46,008
Total standard cost	91,368

(b) (i)

	$
18,144 meals should cost (× $3)	54,432
but did cost	49,896
Material price variance for meals served	4,536 (F)

(ii)

648 guests should have used ((a)(ii))	13,608	meals
but did use ((a)(i))	18,144	meals
Usage variance in meals	4,536	meals (A)
× standard cost per meal	× $3	
Material usage variance for meals served	$13,608	(A)

(iii)

	$
1,200 hours worked should have cost (× $4 per hour)	4,800
but did cost	5,280
Labour rate variance for catering staff	480 (A)

(iv)

Meals for 648 guests should have taken ((a)(iv))	1,134	hours
but did take	1,200	hours
Labour efficiency variance in hours	66	hours (A)
× standard rate per hour	× $4	
Labour efficiency variance for catering staff	$264	(A)

		$	
(v)	Budgeted fixed overhead expenditure	38,340	
	Actual fixed overhead expenditure	37,800	
	Fixed overhead expenditure variance	540	(F)

		$	
(vi)	Actual number of guests	648	
	Budgeted number of guests	540	
	Volume variance – number of guests	108	(F)
	× standard fixed overhead per guest ((a)(v))	× $71	
	Fixed overhead volume variance	$7,668	(F)

Bare Foot Hotel Complex

Standard cost reconciliation *for seven days ended 27 November 20X1*

Budgeted number of guests	540
Actual number of guests	648

	$		$	
Standard costs for 648 guests ((a)(vi))			91,368	
Cost variances				
Material price variance ((b)(i))	4,536	(F)		
Material usage variance ((b)(ii))	13,608	(A)		
			9,072	(A)
Catering labour rate variance ((b)(iii))	480	(A)		
Catering labour efficiency variance ((b)(iv))	264	(A)		
			744	(A)
Fixed overhead expenditure variance ((b)(v))	540	(F)		
Fixed overhead volume variance ((b)(vi))	7,668	(F)		
			8,208	(F)
Actual cost for 648 guests			92,976	

Note. (A) denotes adverse variance, (F) denotes favourable variance.

Task 1.2

> **Tutorial note.** The assessor remarked that, as usual, the discursive elements in this assessment were less well answered than the computational ones.

MEMORANDUM

To:	Alice Groves, general manager
From:	Assistant management accountant
Date:	8 December 20X1
Subject:	**Performance report** for seven days ended 27 November 20X1

This memorandum deals with a number of issues arising from the standard cost reconciliation statement prepared for the seven days ended 27 November 20X1.

(a) **Subdivision of the catering labour efficiency variance**

The adverse catering labour efficiency variance of $264 can be divided into that part due to guests taking more meals than planned and that part due to other efficiency reasons.

Standard hours allowed for 648 guests taking 3 meals ((a)(iv))	1,134 hours
Standard hours allowed for 648 guests taking 4 meals	
= (648 guests × 4 meals × 7 days) ÷ 12 meals per hour	1,512 hours
Excess hours due to guests taking more meals than planned	378 hours (A)
× standard rate per hour	× $4
Efficiency variance due to guests taking more meals than planned	$1,512 (A)
Standard hours allowed for 648 guests taking 4 meals (from above)	1,512 hours
Actual hours worked	1,200 hours
Efficiency variance due to other reasons (in hours)	312 hours (F)
× standard rate per hour	× $4
Catering labour efficiency variance due to other reasons	$1,248 (F)

(b) **The meaning of the fixed overhead capacity and efficiency variances**

The fixed overhead absorption rate for our hotel is based on the budgeted overhead expenditure for the period, divided by the budgeted number of guests.

$$\text{Fixed overhead absorption rate} = \frac{\text{budgeted fixed overhead}}{\text{budgeted number of guests}}$$

If the actual overhead, or the actual number of guests, or both, are different from budget then over or under absorption of overhead may occur, so that there may be a fixed overhead variance.

A **volume variance** arises when the activity level is different from that budgeted, in our case if the actual number of guests is different from the budgeted number. In some organisations it may be possible to sub-divide the volume variance into two parts: the capacity variance and the efficiency variance.

The **capacity variance** arises when the utilisation of the available capacity is higher or lower than budgeted. It is usually calculated as the difference between budgeted and actual hours worked, multiplied by the fixed overhead absorption rate. Under or over utilisation of capacity can potentially lead to under- or over-absorbed overhead.

The **efficiency variance** arises when employees are working at a more or less efficient rate than standard to produce a given output. Producing output at a faster or slower rate could also potentially lead to under- or over-absorbed overhead.

(c) **Calculating the fixed overhead capacity and efficiency variances for the Bare Foot Hotel complex**

The above descriptions of the fixed overhead capacity and efficiency variances highlight the need to be able to measure hours of work so that the volume variance can be subdivided.

It is not feasible to do this for the Bare Foot Hotel complex. We do have a measure of hours worked within the catering activity, but a large proportion of overheads are incurred on entertainment, for which we have no record of hours worked.

The absence of an activity measure based on hours worked therefore makes it difficult and meaningless to subdivide the fixed overhead volume variance into its capacity and efficiency elements.

SECTION 2

Task 2.1

> **Tutorial note.** You may select different balanced scorecard perspectives for some of the performance indicators. For example, you may decide that the sales margin percentage views performance from an internal perspective, since it is affected by cost control. This would be perfectly valid, but if you are in any doubt, it may be a good idea to include a *brief* justification for your choice, as we have done.

See table below for the balance scorecard perspective being measured by each indicator.

(a) Return on capital employed $= $ (net profit $\div$ capital employed) $\times 100\%$

$= (48 \div 200) \times 100\% = 24\%$

(b) Sales margin percentage $= $ (net profit $\div$ turnover) $\times 100\%$

$= (48 \div 240) \times 100\% = 20\%$

(c) Asset turnover $= $ turnover $\div$ capital employed

$= 240 \div 200 = 1.2$ times

(d) Research and development as a percentage of production

$= $ (R and D cost $\div$ cost of production) $\times 100\%$

$= (15.9 \div 53.0) \times 100\% = 30\%$

(e) Training as a percentage of labour cost

$= $ (training $\div$ labour cost) $\times 100\%$

$= (5.2 \div 26.0) \times 100\% = 20\%$

(f) Average age of finished stock $= $ closing finished stock $\div$ cost of sales per month

$= 13 \div (52 \div 12) = 3$ months

The **balanced scorecard perspective being measured by each indicator** is shown below.

Indicator	Balanced scorecard perspective
(a) Return on capital employed	Financial
(b) Sales margin percentage	Financial
(c) Asset turnover	Internal (intensity of asset use)
(d) R and D as a percentage of production	Innovation and learning
(e) Training as a percentage of labour costs	Innovation and learning
(f) Average age of finished stock	Customer (greater stock means shorter wait for customers)

Task 2.2

> **Tutorial note.** Your answers to parts (b) and (c) may be quite different from ours but could still be equally valid. The key requirement is to explain clearly your identified limitations and so on, and to draw on the information provided as much as possible.

BRIEFING NOTES

To: James Alexander
From: Financial analyst
Date: 17 January 20X2
Subject: **St Nicolas Police Force performance measures**

The following notes address your queries on the performance measures currently used by the St Nicolas Police Force.

(a)   **The indicators currently used**

    (i)   **Percentage of cash expenditure to allocated funds for the year**

$$= \text{(cash expenditure} \div \text{funds allocated)} \times 100\%$$
$$= (2,910,000 \div 3,000,000) \times 100\%$$
$$= 97\%$$

    (ii)   **Average police-hours spent per crime investigated**

$$= \text{police-hours spent investigating} \div \text{number of crimes investigated}$$
$$= 40,000 \div 5,000$$
$$= 8 \text{ police-hours}$$

    (iii)   **Average police-hours spent per crime solved**

$$= \text{police-hours spent investigating} \div \text{number of crimes solved}$$
$$= 40,000 \div 2,000$$
$$= 20 \text{ police-hours}$$

    (iv)   **Clear-up rate**

$$= \text{number of crimes solved/number of crimes investigated}$$
$$= 2,000 \div 5,000$$
$$= 40\%$$

(b)   **Limitations in the calculation of the clear-up rate**

Some types of crimes are easier to solve than others, and some crimes may take a longer period of time to solve. This leads to possible distortion if more 'easier to solve' crimes happen to occur in a particular period, or if a number of 'longer' crimes happen to be solved in a period.

This performance measure could be improved through the use of a separate calculation for each type of crime, with each crime being carefully defined to distinguish it from others.

(c)   **Inadequacies of other measures and the balanced scorecard**

    (i)   The **percentage of cash expenditure to allocated funds** may be an inadequate measure of the financial perspective because it focuses on cost control but gives no indication of value created or capital invested in operations.

    (ii)   The **clear-up rate** might be an inadequate measure of the customer perspective because it focuses on only one area of police activity. Customers may feel that prevention of crime is just as important as, or perhaps more important than, the solving of crimes reported. A single performance measure might be inadequate on its own, given the range of services which customers expect from a police force.

    (iii)   The **hours spent per crime investigated** might be an inadequate measure of the internal perspective because it does not provide a basis for monitoring the efficiency of the investigation activity. A longer time spent may indicate more diligent police work, but it could also indicate inefficiencies in investigations.

(iv) A measure which might focus on the **innovation and learning perspective** could be one which monitors training in new skills such as modern crime prevention methods and criminal psychology. The indicator could be calculated as a percentage for the period as follows:

$$\frac{\text{Hours spent training in new skills}}{\text{Total police-hours for period}} \times 100\%$$

BPP PUBLISHING

TECHNICIAN STAGE

NVQ/SVQ LEVEL 4 IN ACCOUNTING

REVISED STANDARDS
DECEMBER 1999 CENTRAL ASSESSMENT

CONTRIBUTING TO THE PLANNING AND
ALLOCATION OF RESOURCES
(UNIT 9)

Time allowed - 3 hours plus 15 minutes' reading time

This central assessment is in **TWO** sections.

You are reminded that competence must be achieved in **EACH** section. You should therefore attempt and aim to complete **EVERY** task in **EACH** section.

You are advised to spend approximately 1 hour on Section 1 and 2 hours on Section 2.

All essential workings should be included within your answers, where appropriate.

SECTION 1

(Suggested time allowance: 1 hour)

Data

You have recently been promoted to the post of management accountant with Northern Products Ltd, a company formed four years ago. The company has always used budgets to help plan its production of two products, the Exe and the Wye. Both products use the same material and labour but in different proportions.

You have been asked to prepare the budget for quarter 1, the twelve weeks ending 24 March 20X0. In previous budgets, the closing stocks of both raw materials and finished products were the same as opening stocks. You questioned whether or not this was the most efficient policy for the company.

As a result, you have carried out an investigation into the stock levels required to meet the maximum likely sales demand for finished goods and production demand for raw materials. You conclude that closing stocks of finished goods should be expressed in terms of days sales for the next quarter and closing stocks of raw materials in terms of days production for the next quarter.

Your findings are included in the data below, which also shows data provided by the sales and production directors of Northern Products Ltd.

Product data	**Exe**	**Wye**
• Budgeted sales in units, quarter 1	930 units	1,320 units
• Budgeted sales in units, quarter 2	930 units	1,320 units
• Budgeted material per unit (litres)	6 litres	9 litres
• Budgeted labour hours per unit	12 hours	7 hours
• Opening units of finished stock	172 units	257 units
• Closing units of finished stock (days sales next quarter)	8 days	9 days
• Failure rate of finished production*	2%	3%
• Finance and other costs of keeping a unit in stock per quarter	£4.00	£5.00

*Failed products are only discovered on completion of production and have no residual value.

Other accounting data

• Weeks in accounting period	12 weeks
• Days per week for production and sales	5 days
• Hours per week	35 hours
• Number of employees	46 employees
• Budgeted labour rate per hour	£6.00
• Overtime premium for hours worked in excess of 35 hours per week	30%
• Budgeted cost of material per litre	£15.00
• Opening raw material stocks (litres)	1,878 litres
• Closing raw material stocks (days production next quarter)	5 days
• Financing and other costs of keeping a litre of raw material in stock per quarter	£1.00

Task 1.1

a) Calculate the following information for *quarter 1*, the twelve weeks ending 24 March 20X0.

   i)   The number of production days
   ii)   The closing finished stock for Exe and Wye in units
   iii) The labour hours available before overtime has to be paid

b) Prepare the following budgets for quarter 1, the twelve weeks ending 24 March 20X0.

   i)   The production budget in units for Exe and Wye, including any faulty production

   ii)   The material purchases budget in litres and value

   iii) The production labour budget in hours and value, including any overtime payments

c) Calculate the savings arising from the change in the required stock levels for the twelve weeks ending 24 March 20X0.

Data

On completing the budget for quarter 1, the production director of Northern Products Ltd tells you that the company is likely to introduce a third product, the Zed, in the near future. Because of this, he suggests that future budgets should be prepared using a spreadsheet. He explains that the use of spreadsheets to prepare budgets not only saves time but also provides flexibility by allowing the results of changes in the budget to be readily shown. The sales director is not convinced.

The production director suggests you demonstrate the advantages of budgets prepared on spreadsheets by using a template of a spreadsheet and sales data for the planned third product.

He gives you the following sales data he has received from the sales director.

*   Estimated annual volume for Zed is 20,000 units.
*   Planned unit selling price is £90.00.
*   Seasonal variations are as follows.

Quarter	Seasonal variation percentage change
1	+20%
2	+ 30%
3	– 10%
4	– 40%

238

Task 1.2

a)   Calculate the budgeted volume of Zed for each quarter.

b)   Using the information provided by the sales director and a copy of the suggested spreadsheet template reproduced below, express the data provided by the sales director as formulae which would enable revised sales budgets to be calculated with the minimum of effort if sales price and annual volume were to change. (You may amend the template if desired to suit any spreadsheet with which you are familiar.)

A	B	C	D	E	F
1	Unit selling price	£90			
2	Annual volume	20,000			
3	Seasonal variations	20%	30%	– 10%	– 40%
4		Quarter 1	Quarter 2	Quarter 3	Quarter 4
5	Seasonal variations (units)				
6	Quarterly volume				
7	Quarterly turnover				

SECTION 2

(Suggested time allowance: 2 hours)

Data

HFD plc opened a new division on 1 December 20X0. The division, HFD Processes Ltd, produces a special paint finish. Because of the technology, there can never be any work in progress. The original budget was developed on the assumption that there would be a loss in the initial year of operation and that there would be no closing stock of finished goods.

One year later, HFD Processes Ltd prepared its results for its first year of operations. The chief executive of HFD plc was pleased to see that, despite budgeting for an initial loss, the division had actually returned a profit of £74,400. As a result, the directors of HFD Processes were entitled to a substantial bonus. Details of the budget and actual results are reproduced below.

		Budget		Actual
HFD Processes				
Operating results				
Year ended 30 November 20X1				
Volume (units)		20,000		22,000
	£	£	£	£
Turnover		960,000		1,012,000
Direct costs				
Materials	240,000		261,800	
Production labour	260,000		240,240	
Light, heat and power	68,000		65,560	
	568,000		567,600	
Fixed overheads	400,000		370,000	
Cost of sales		968,000		937,600
Operating profit/(loss)		(8,000)		74,400

You are employed as a management accountant in the head office of HFD plc and have been asked to comment on the performance of HFD Processes Ltd. Attached to the budgeted and actual results were the relevant working papers. A summary of the contents of the working papers is reproduced below.

- The budget assumed no closing finished stocks. Actual production was 25,000 units and actual sales 22,000 units.

- Because of the technology involved, production employees are paid per week, irrespective of production levels. The employees assumed in the budget are capable of producing up to 26,000 units.

- The cost of material varies directly with production.

- The cost of light, heat and power includes a fixed standing charge. In the budget this fixed charge was calculated to be £20,000 per year. However, competition resulted in the supplier reducing the actual charge to £12,000 for the year.

- During the year, HFD Processes Ltd produced 25,000 units. The 3,000 units of closing finished stock were valued on the basis of direct cost plus 'normal' fixed overheads.

  The number of units was used to apportion direct costs between the cost of sales and closing finished stock.

240

The budgeted fixed overhead of £20 per unit was used to calculate the fixed overheads in closing finished stocks.

The detailed composition of the cost of sales and closing stocks using these policies was as follows.

	Closing finished stocks	Cost of sales	Cost of production
Units	3,000	22,000	25,000
	£	£	£
Material	35,700	261,800	297,500
Production labour	32,760	240,240	273,000
Light, heat and power	8,940	65,560	74,500
Fixed overheads	60,000	370,000	430,000
	137,400	937,600	1,075,000

Task 2.1

a) Calculate the following.

    i)   The budgeted unit selling price

    ii)   The budgeted material cost per unit

    iii)   The budgeted marginal cost of light, heat and power per unit

    iv)   The actual marginal cost of light, heat and power per unit

b) Prepare a flexible budget statement for the operating results of HFD Processes Ltd using a *marginal costing* approach, identifying fixed costs for the year and showing any variances.

Data

You present your flexible budget statement to the chief executive of HFD plc who is concerned that your findings appear different to those in the original operating results.

Task 2.2

You are asked to write a *brief* memo to the chief executive. In your memo, you should do the following.

a) Give TWO reasons why the flexible budget operating statement shows different results from the original operating results.

b) Give ONE reason why the flexible budget operating statement might be a better measure of management performance than the original operating results.

CONTRIBUTING TO THE PLANNING AND ALLOCATION OF RESOURCES
(UNIT 9)

DECEMBER 1999 CENTRAL ASSESSMENT
SUGGESTED ANSWERS

SECTION 1

> **Tutorial note**. The calculations in part (a) are necessary in order to complete the budgets in part (b). Don't forget to use them where appropriate, rather than wasting time calculating the information a second time!

Task 1.1

(a) (i) Number of production days in quarter $1 = 12$ weeks $\times 5$ days $= 60$ days

(ii) Quarter 1 closing finished goods stock:

Exe $= 8$ days $\times (930 \div 60$ per day$) = 124$ units
Wye $= 9$ days $\times (1,320 \div 60$ per day$) = 198$ units

(iii) Quarter 1 labour hours available before overtime
$= 12$ weeks $\times 35$ hours $\times 46$ employees
$= 19,320$ hours

(b) (i) **Production budget for quarter 1,** *twelve weeks ending 24 March 20X0*

		Exe Units		Wye Units
Budgeted sales		930		1,320
Required closing stock (from (a))		124		198
		1,054		1,518
Less opening stock		(172)		(257)
Good production required		882		1,261
Failed product allowance (W)	($\times$ 2/98)	18	($\times$ 3/97)	39
Total production required		900		1,300

Working

Good production represents $(100 - 2)\%$ of total Exe production.

$\therefore$ 882 units $= 98\%$ of total production

$\therefore$ Total production $= 882/98 \times 100\%$

Alternatively, allowance $= 2/98$ of $882 = 2/98 \times 882$

(ii) **Material purchases budget for quarter 1,** *twelve weeks ending 24 March 20X0*

		Litres
Material required for production:	Exe (900 units $\times$ 6 litres)	5,400
	Wye (1,300 units $\times$ 9 litres)	11,700
		17,100
Required closing stock	(5 days $\times$ (17,100/60) litres per day)	1,425
		18,525
Less opening stock		1,878
Material purchases required		16,647
Value of material purchases required ($\times$ £15)		£249,705

(iii) **Production labour budget for quarter 1,** *twelve weeks ending 24 March 20X0*

		Hours
Labour hours required for production:	Exe (900 units $\times$ 12 hours)	10,800
	Wye (1,300 units $\times$ 7 hours)	9,100
Total hours required		19,900
Labour hours available before overtime (from (a))		19,320
Overtime hours required		580

Cost of budgeted labour hours	£
Basic pay (19,900 hours × £6)	119,400
Overtime premium (580 hours × £1.80)	1,044
Total budgeted labour cost	120,444

(c)

	Opening stock	Closing stock	Stock reduction	Storage cost per quarter £ per unit	Saving £
Product Exe	172 units	124 units	48 units	4	192
Product Wye	257 units	198 units	59 units	5	295
Raw material	1,878 litres	1,425 litres	453 litres	1	453
Savings arising from changes in required stock levels					940

Task 1.2

> **Tutorial note.** You can guard against some arithmetical errors by checking that your total sales budget amounts to 20,000 units, after you have adjusted for seasonal variations.

(a)

	Quarter 1 Units	Quarter 2 Units	Quarter 3 Units	Quarter 4 Units
Quarterly sales before seasonal variations (20,000 ÷ 4)	5,000	5,000	5,000	5,000
Seasonal variations	(+20%) 1,000	(+30%) 1,500	(−10%) (500)	(−40%) (2,000)
Budgeted sales volume of Zed	6,000	6,500	4,500	3,000

(b)

> **Tutorial note.** You will need to think carefully to determine the formulae in the spreadsheet. Effectively you are simply putting into formulae form the reasoning that you have applied in part (a).

A	B	C	D	E	F
1	Unit selling price	£90			
2	Annual volume	20,000			
3	Seasonal variations	20%	30%	− 10%	− 40%
4		Quarter 1	Quarter 2	Quarter 3	Quarter 4
5	Seasonal variations (units)	= (C2/4) ★ C3	= (C2/4) ★ D3	= (C2/4) ★ E3	=(C2/4) ★ F3
6	Quarterly volume	= (C2/4)+C5	= (C2/4)+D5	= (C2/4)+E5	= (C2/4)+F5
7	Quarterly turnover	= C6 ★ C1	= D6 ★ C1	= E6 ★ C1	= F6 ★ C1

SECTION 2

Task 2.1

> **Tutorial note.** You will need a sound understanding of the difference between cost of sales and cost of production. The *actual* cost incurred in the period is the cost of *production*. This is then adjusted for the movement in stocks to determine the cost of sales.

(a)   (i)   Budgeted selling price

                = £960,000 turnover ÷ 20,000 units
                = £48 per unit

     (ii)   Budgeted material cost

                = £240,000 material cost ÷ 20,000 units
                = £12 per unit

     (iii) Total budgeted marginal cost of light, heat and power

                           = £68,000 – fixed cost £20,000
                           = £48,000

         Budgeted marginal cost of light, heat and power per unit

                           = £48,000 ÷ 20,000
                           = £2.40 per unit

     (iv) Actual marginal cost of light, heat and power

                           = £74,500 production cost – fixed costs £12,000
                           = £62,500

         Actual marginal cost of light, heat and power per unit

                           = £62,500 ÷ 25,000 units produced
                           = £2.50 per unit

(b)

> **Tutorial note.** A flexible budget prepared using a marginal costing approach should show a separate analysis of fixed and variable costs. The variable cost of sales is determined by multiplying the *sales volume* by the unit marginal cost. The fixed overheads, however, are not based on units. All of the fixed overhead incurred is written off in the period as a period cost. You therefore need to determine the *production* cost of fixed overhead, and charge this amount against the sales value for the period. The assessor noted that a particular area of weakness was flexible budgeting.

HFD Processes Ltd
Flexible budget statement *for year ended 30 November 20X1*

Sales units	Flexible budget 22,000 units		Actual results 22,000 units		Variance
	£	£	£	£	£
Turnover (22,000 × £48 (from (a)))		1,056,000		1,012,000	44,000 (A)
Variable costs					
Material (22,000 × £12)	264,000		261,800		2,200 (F)
Light, heat and power (22,000 × £2.40)	52,800		55,000*		2,200 (A)
		316,800		316,800	
Contribution		739,200		695,200	
Fixed costs					
Production labour	260,000		273,000		13,000 (A)
Light, heat and power	20,000		12,000		8,000 (F)
Fixed overheads	400,000		430,000		30,000 (A)
		680,000		715,000	
Operating profit/(loss)		59,200		(19,800)	79,000 (A)

Note. (A) denotes an adverse variance; (F) denotes a favourable variance.

*Variable cost of light, heat and power = £2.50 (from (a)) × 22,000 = £55,000

Task 2.2

MEMORANDUM

To: Chief executive of HFD plc
From: Management accountant
Date: 8 December 20X1
Subject: **Flexible budget statement for year ended 30 November 20X1**

This memorandum addresses your concerns regarding the results shown in the flexible budget statement.

(a) **Why the flexible budget operating statement shows different results from the original operating results**

    (i) The flexible budget is prepared on a marginal cost basis whereas the original budget and actual results were prepared on an absorption cost basis. Since production was higher than sales, some fixed overhead was carried forward in stock with absorption costing. With marginal costing, however, all of the fixed overheads are charged as period costs against the sales for the period, resulting in a lower reported profit figure.

    (ii) The flexible budget is a realistic target for costs and revenues for the actual activity level of 22,000 units sold. The 2,000 units sold in excess of the original budgeted amount would be expected to increase both revenue and variable costs. The flexible budget makes allowances for these increases caused by the change in volume.

(b) **Why the flexible budget operating statement might be a better measure of management performance**

The flexible budget statement compares like with like. When the activity level changes, the expected revenue and variable costs also change. It is therefore logical to alter the budget to allow for these changes. The resulting variances will provide a better measure for management performance.

Furthermore the profit shown in the original statement, which was prepared on an absorption costing basis, can be distorted by increases or decreases in stock, as fixed overheads are carried forward in, or 'released from', stock. The use of marginal costing, however, avoids such profit distortions.

ORDER FORM

Any books from our AAT range can be ordered by telephoning 020-8740-2211. Alternatively, send this page to our address below, fax it to us on 020-8740-1184, or email us at **publishing@bpp.com.** Or look us up on our website: www.bpp.com

We aim to deliver to all UK addresses inside 5 working days; a signature will be required. Order to all EU addresses should be delivered within 6 working days. All other orders to overseas addresses should be delivered within 8 working days.

To: BPP Publishing Ltd, Aldine House, Aldine Place, London W12 8AW

Tel: 020-8740 2211   **Fax: 020-8740 1184**   **Email: publishing@bpp.com**

Mr / Ms (full name): _____

Daytime delivery address: _____

_____

Postcode: _____   Daytime Tel: _____

Please send me the following quantities of books.

	5/00 Interactive Text	8/00 DA Kit	8/00 CA Kit
FOUNDATION			
Unit 1 Recording Income and Receipts (7/00 Text)	☐	☐	
Unit 2 Making and Recording Payments (7/00 Text)	☐	☐	
Unit 3 Ledger Balances and Initial Trial Balance (7/00 Text)	☐	☐	
Unit 4 Supplying information for Management Control (6/00 Text)	☐	☐	
Unit 20 Working with Information Technology (8/00 Text)	☐		
Unit 22/23 Achieving Personal Effectiveness (7/00) Text	☐		
INTERMEDIATE			
Unit 5 Financial Records and Accounts	☐		
Unit 6 Cost Information	☐		
Unit 7 Reports and Returns	☐	☐	
Unit 21 Using Information Technology	☐		
Unit 22: see below			
TECHNICIAN			
Unit 8/9 Core Managing Costs and Allocating Resources	☐		☐
Unit 10 Core Managing Accounting Systems	☐	☐	☐
Unit 11 Option Financial Statements (Accounting Practice)	☐		☐
Unit 12 Option Financial Statements (Central Government)	☐		☐
Unit 15 Option Cash Management and Credit Control	☐	☐	
Unit 16 Option Evaluating Activities	☐	☐	
Unit 17 Option Implementing Auditing Procedures	☐	☐	
Unit 18 Option Business Tax FA00(8/00 Text)	☐	☐	
Unit 19 Option Personal Tax FA00(8/00 Text)	☐	☐	
TECHNICIAN 1999			
Unit 17 Option Business Tax Computations FA99 (8/99 Text & Kit)	☐	☐	
Unit 18 Option Personal Tax Computations FA99 (8/99 Text & Kit)	☐	☐	
TOTAL BOOKS	☐ +	☐ + ☐	= ☐

Postage and packaging: ⌐@ £9.95 each = £ _____

UK: £2.00 for each book to maximum of £10

Europe (inc ROI and Channel Islands): £4.00 for first book, £2.00 for each extra ⎤ P & P   £ _____

Rest of the World: £20.00 for first book, £10 for each extra

▶ Unit 22 Maintaining a Healthy Workplace Interactive Text (postage free)   ☐ @ £3.95   £ _____

                                                                    GRAND TOTAL £ _____

I enclose a cheque for £ _____ (cheques to BPP Publishing Ltd) or charge to **Mastercard/Visa/Switch**

Card number | □ | □ | □ | □ | □ | □ | □ | □ | □ | □ | □ | □ | □ | □ | □ | □ |

Start date _____   **Expiry date** _____   **Issue no. (Switch only)**___

Signature _____

REVIEW FORM & FREE PRIZE DRAW

All original review forms from the entire BPP range, completed with genuine comments, will be entered into one of two draws on 31 January 2001 and 31 July 2001. The names on the first four forms picked out on each occasion will be sent a cheque for £50.

Name: _____   Address: _____

_____

_____

How have you used this Central Assessment Kit?
(Tick one box only)
☐ Home study (book only)
☐ On a course: college _____
☐ With 'correspondence' package
☐ Other _____

Why did you decide to purchase this Central Assessment Kit? *(Tick one box only)*
☐ Have used BPP products in the past
☐ Recommendation by friend/colleague
☐ Recommendation by a lecturer at college
☐ Saw advertising
☐ Other _____

During the past six months do you recall seeing/receiving any of the following?
(Tick as many boxes as are relevant)
☐ Our advertisement in *Accounting Technician* magazine
☐ Our advertisement in *Pass*
☐ Our brochure with a letter through the post

Which (if any) aspects of our advertising do you find useful?
(Tick as many boxes as are relevant)
☐ Prices and publication dates of new editions
☐ Information on content of products
☐ Facility to order books off-the-page
☐ None of the above

Have you used the companion Interactive Text for this subject?   ☐ Yes   ☐ No

Your ratings, comments and suggestions would be appreciated on the following areas

	Very useful	Useful	Not useful
Introductory section (How to use this Central Assessment Kit etc)	☐	☐	☐
Practice Questions	☐	☐	☐
Central Assessment Style Questions	☐	☐	☐
December 1999 Central Assessment	☐	☐	☐
Content of Answers	☐	☐	☐
Layout of pages	☐	☐	☐
Structure of book and ease of use	☐	☐	☐

	Excellent	Good	Adequate	Poor
Overall opinion of this Kit	☐	☐	☐	☐

Do you intend to continue using BPP Assessment Kits/Interactive Texts? ☐ Yes ☐ No

Please note any further comments and suggestions/errors on the reverse of this page.
Please return to: Nick Weller, BPP Publishing Ltd, FREEPOST, London, W12 8BR

REVIEW FORM & FREE PRIZE DRAW (continued)

Please note any further comments and suggestions/errors below

FREE PRIZE DRAW RULES

1   Closing date for 31 January 2001 draw is 31 December 2000. Closing date for 31 July 2001 draw is 30 June 2001.

2   Restricted to entries with UK and Eire addresses only. BPP employees, their families and business associates are excluded.

3   No purchase necessary. Entry forms are available upon request from BPP Publishing. No more than one entry per title, per person. Draw restricted to persons aged 16 and over.

4   Winners will be notified by post and receive their cheques not later than 6 weeks after the relevant draw date.

5   The decision of the promoter in all matters is final and binding. No correspondence will be entered into.